UnAddicted to You

Loving Yourself Through The Darkness

by Etel Leit

Published by SignShine™
Text and illustrations Copyright ©2020 by Etel Leit

UnAddicted to You
ISBN: ISBN: 978-0-9885952-6-2

For more information regarding permission contact www.EtelLeit.com

Printed in the United States of America

For the father of my children,
I will forever be thankful.

Table of Contents

Three by Three

The number 3 has a meaningful significance in my life, as in many cultural societies. The number 3 contains the beginning, a middle, and an end. It is a symbol of the unity of body, mind, and spirit. Therefore, I chose to write the book on the theme of the number three.

There are twenty-one chapters in this book. Each chapter is divided into three parts.

In many languages, there is a direct relationship between numbers and letters of the alphabet. The numerological value of twenty-one in the Hebrew language is the number three, 3.

Roots

Each one of the twenty-one chapters is built on three consonants, a triliteral *root*. In the Hebrew language, as in other Semitic languages, most words are based on a root with a combination of three consonants. These words will be headlining each chapter and symbolically express the story and the theme in the chapter.

Combining the three consonants with the addition of various vowels creates distinct words from the same root family. Several words can be created from the same root, sometimes expressing multiple meanings.

שׁ.ר.שׁ.
Shin. Resh. Shin.

This triliteral root: *Shin. Resh. Shin* forms the word:

↘ ↓ ↙
Shoresh
שורש

The meaning of the word **Shoresh**:
Root • Source • Origin • Square Root • Foundation

Chapter 1

Into the Light

Alef. Vav. Resh. א. ו. ר.

Light אור• Enlighten מאיר• Enlightenment הארה

◉

Los Angeles, September 2012

A big thump. One second of falling on the cold bathroom floor in slow motion and like rapidly collapsing dominoes, images captured on the slowest shutter speed mode, at a rate of hundreds of frames per second. One frame at a time. First, my weak legs, then my hips, followed by my boneless torso and arms, and lastly, my head, nearly crashing into the toilet seat rim, missing it by half an inch. I collapse onto the bare tile floor, motionless.

An eternity of loud silence.

I try to open my heavy eyes slowly, but they insist on remaining half-closed. My body is sinking onto the bare bathroom floor as I feel gravity with all its might as the corner of the cold tile floor is staring at me. My eyelashes flutter with the dust specks of a sunray glaring from the window.

My ice-cold body is fossilized on the hard floor.

Time has stopped.

Get up. Move. Talk, I command myself without moving my lips.

My body does not respond. My hands are frozen. My legs are motionless. I feel nothingness.

Now I see. I see it.

Beautiful, glowing, vibrant.

The whitest, brightest, shiniest, and most shimmering Light I have ever seen on the horizon appeared. It is calm. The entity within me craves to reach out to it. Touch it. Feel it. But the Light is too far. I want to soar into its beautiful core, immerse myself in it. I want to become one with the Light.

The Light gets stronger. Brighter.

The essence of the Light calls out to me, *"Come, my little child, come to me."* It is the loudest voice I have ever heard – clear, comforting, powerful, loving – and yet has no voice. I get closer by the second, syncing myself to the Light's speed. My being knows this Light. It is the place of total serenity, of kindness, of unconditional love – this is the place I've been yearning for since I was born. This is the place where I want to return.

I know love now. I know I'm home. I know I can trust.

Bigger. Brighter.

Expanding. Vibrating.

Closer. Warmer.

I keep flying and floating. Up, up, up. Bodiless, boundless, and limitless. Faster than time. The closer I get, the Light lovingly glows all the more brilliant.

Take me.

My voice within me reassures me, *Home. This is Home.* I recognize it from years ago before I came here. I am complete. This is my deepest, unspoken, most intuitive familiarity. I am free of pain. My heart is free – at last.

Bigger.

Brighter.

Whiter.

Shiner.

Calmer.

Consoling. Hugging. Loving.

Take me.

Almost there.

Home.

Chapter 2

Passionate Cycles

Chet. Zain. Resh. ‏ח.ז.ר.‏

Cycle ‏מחזור‏ • Return ‏חזר‏ • Courtship ‏חיזור‏

◉

Jerusalem, the 1970s

My mother's passion – or better yet, her obsession – was long hair. Our hair was her status symbol; the shinier, longer, and healthier her four girls' hair, the more content Mother was. All she seemed to want was thick and soft waves of goodness dancing in her hands like an ocean of silk.

As for my mom, she loved her hair cut shoulder-length in the latest style of Farrah Fawcett. Mother's layered hairstyle highlighted her high cheekbones. Women envied her for this exquisite feature. She looked naturally elegant while the other women exhausted all the beauty parlors in the city, searching for the perfect blush to mirror Mother's elegance. Matching her iridescent pale skin and hazel eyes, she bleached her hair blonde. She refused to reveal the tiniest glimpse of rebellious dark roots – especially before the holidays when Dad would come back home from his long trips.

Strangers secretly glanced at her, but she didn't even notice them. She fixated on one thing: Dad's rare and affectionate compliments.

We, the four girls, olive-skinned like our Dad, were allowed to let our long hair down only on the weekends. Away from the lice, away from the boys.

"Before you part the hair to three sections," Mother instructed, "brush it extremely well."

The thick wool brush was bulky in my little six-year-old hands. I held it tightly in my palm to satisfy Mother's desire. It was time. I was the eldest girl and was about to be crowned as their hair braider.

"*Good girl, Ella,*" my sister's hair became velvety, like mom's heart. "Part the hair here, exactly down the middle." While Sharon sat on the chair in front of me, I focused on her hair, parting the long hair with a fine comb. I drew a perfect line on her scalp, from her forehead to the back of her neck, separating her hair into two equal parts.

Sharon didn't move. I wasn't sure who wanted it to end faster, her or me.

"Make sure the two braids are even," my mother commanded me like a drill sergeant.

"Remember, Ella, the braids must be tight," mother continued pointedly.

After diligently straightening, parting, and braiding for months under my mother's supervision, I finally qualified to be my sisters' "professional" hair braider.

I was born into a family of whispering. I learned early to pretend not to see what everyone else saw. Even if all the adults whisper about it, we, the children, would only face shame if we dared to know. The emperor was naked, but we never say so out loud.

Push-pull was my parents' favorite game: a relationship that lived and died with every season and every new baby. It revived itself with blossoming love and destroyed itself by viciously pruning the roots. We watched our parents' relationship swing wildly from spring to winter, one extreme to the other.

My Dad wanted a combination of a living Aphrodite and a caretaker. Everyone called him charming; he was a handsome man with dark skin and penetrating brown eyes. My Dad, the best lady-listener, the best compliment-giver, and the most macho of men, secretly, had the heart of a child.

He loved his real-life nurse at home. He loved her petite figure, her taste in clothes, her delicious cooking, her phenomenal baking, and her devotion to raising their four daughters and, later, their two sons. He was proud of her. He admired her way of making things happen, how she looked slender while still giving birth almost every year, and he loved her laugh, although he rarely heard it. But he also loved other women. My mom was busy with raising, cooking, baking, dieting, cleaning, organizing, working. He needed someone to pay attention to his soul, to him, to the little boy inside him. So he opened his eyes and found forbidden affection from other young women.

"Too smart," said the kindergarten teacher to my parents, "your daughter will go to first grade."

This statement began my journey of entering the first grade. I had a backpack bigger than me, a deep dimple, and smart eyes. I learned to love school more than my home. I immersed myself in books, homework, and learning. I escaped into worlds of letters, words, and numbers.

"Spell CAKE," mom would instruct me while putting the flour and sugar in a bowl.

I wrote neatly on the draft paper, which I put on the little kitchen table between the egg carton, vanilla extract, and the open flour bag carefully to not stain my paper. I neatly wrote C-A-K-E.

Mom would be so happy.

"Now, MAKE," she continued, adding cocoa powder to the mix. My mother never used any measuring cups or spoons; she had the entire recipe in her head and knew the whole process by heart. I skipped a line and wrote on the blue dotted like "M-A-K-E" while my mom battered the cake for teacher Hannah. I would bring them for her the next day; she loved surprising our teachers with her signature cakes.

"A little treat for the teacher can never harm," she revealed her secret.

As the cake was inside the oven and the dishes piled up, my words for my Friday quiz added up. Spell SNAKE. ACHE. SHAKE.

Every Thursday, mom's delicacy filled our home with smells of Shabbat—a spicy Moroccan fish that she learned from her mom. The aroma also consisted of stuffed grape leaves, which my grandma (my Dad's mom) taught her how to cook. Mother's original recipe was red sauce beef stew. While she was cooking, I sat on the corner of the small square table in the kitchen next to the spices, oil, pots, pans, and spoons.

I watched my mom kneading the dough for two loaves of Shabbat Challa bread. She rolled it back and forth with both hands to erase the seams and smooth out the strand. Then she put it aside to allow the dough to rise. After this process, she braided the Challa from three strands, sometimes four, and brushed it with egg wash to give it its shiny brown color.

Mother quizzed me on my weekly Friday spelling test,

Aromas mixed with synonyms and antonyms; my brain stimulated with my mom's love of cooking.

My mom baked an extra special cake to take to school for my sixth birthday. Hannah, my first-grade teacher, took out the yummy, warm chocolate cake with colorful sprinkles from the foil paper and placed it on her table. It was time to celebrate in class before we went home. I was elated to finally join my classmates, all of whom were already six.

Here in school, I could be happy without seeing Mom cry. She caught him again. Our home was sad again. My Dad didn't live with us. Again. But here, at my school, I was away from their stories, away from the sadness.

Right before all the kids sang happy birthday and the teacher finished putting the candles on the cake, there was a knock on the classroom door.

"Hold on, children!" says Hannah in her high-pitch teacher voice. I stand next to her table, seeing the class from a different angle. The smell of the cake is sweet, comforting. I'm thinking about what wish I should make. Should I pray for Dad to come back home? Or should I pray that he never comes back?

Hannah approaches her table. She smiles, "Someone special came to visit you for your birthday!"

I look at the cake and the kids, somehow confused.

"We will wait, don't worry," Hannah read my mind.

Curious and anxious, I go outside. No one ever came to visit me in school.

"Dad!" He hugs me tight. The tighter his hug is, the more I hold back my tears. He has a wrapped gift.

"It's for you!" he says, choked up. I take a deep big-girl breath.

And then I notice the tall lady standing next to him. She wears a frog-green pants suit with big shiny golden buttons. Her hair is up in a bun, and she has too much blush to mimic high cheeks. Our eyes meet as she smiles and says, "Happy birthday, Ella!"

How does she know my name?

"Here, this is for you! Open it." My Dad looks at me with proud eyes.

Slowly, I unwrap the present.

A book. *Apartment for Lease* by Leah Goldberg.

He knows his gift will make my mom happy.

It wasn't the first time Dad went away. After a few months, Dad would come back home with new renovations. He painted the walls, renovated a room, or built an addition. My parents celebrated every visit by renewing their nest, which they would build together and destroy again after a few months. They were junkies for extremes – addicted to each other and their anxieties

◉

Jerusalem, November 1977

Mom couldn't hide her excitement.

Thursday was always a special day – the day before Shabbat dinner. But this Thursday was predominantly filled with anticipation; Dad is coming back again.

"Lee, take out the laundry from the clotheslines.

"Sharon, dust the shelves."

"Libby, fill the bucket with water and soap."

"Ella, wash the floors."

Her voice filled our home with endless commands while she cooked. This loop continued until the house was spotless, ready to welcome the Shabbat and Dad.

"Who likes vegetables? Who likes candies?" We heard Dad climbing the stairs to our duplex.

Liat, Sharon, Libby, and I ran to the doorway when we heard my Dad climbing on the staircase. He sang funny rhymes, which he always did when he wanted to please mom. He smiled like a strong man perfume. Dad is here. My Dad entered, carrying ten bags in his right hand and a big brown box on his left shoulder filled with anything he could spot to fill our fridge, pantry, and Mom's heart. We jumped on him, "Daddy, daddy!"

My mom rushed out from the bedroom with a new outfit and her hair perfectly blow-dried. She smelled like sweet flowers and was glowing like the sun. He approached to kiss her. Blushing, she allowed my Dad to kiss her, but only on the cheeks, "because of the girls." He hugged her like they never were separated before, and we, the four girls, looked at each other smiling and giggling. It felt like home again.

Mom dug her head in the bags – ten filled bags with groceries, meats, snacks, and a big carton filled with fresh fruit and vegetables. My siblings and I organized each thing in its spot while my Dad took a long shower before dinner. As he always did when he was happy, Dad kept singing his funny songs, warming my mom's heart.

Despite her parents' objections when she was eighteen, my mother married my Dad, who is seven years older than her. Her parents did not like his motorcycle and the fact that he wears cologne. But she rebelled and married him, the love of her life. A month past her twentieth birthday, she became a mom to me. We both grew up together, or maybe I grew up faster than her.

My mom took her new title as a wife and a mother to heart. Her nest home was always sparkly clean, with the best homemade cooked food, and with a treasure of books, encyclopedias, and educational games. Her mission was to prove her parents wrong. She loved her darker-skinned husband, and she loved her role as a mom, a wife, a caregiver. She loved her roles to obsession.

My Dad truly loved my mom, but he also loved other women. My mom was determined to fix him. She believed she would fox my Dad's problem and win back her husband from his lovers.

It was finally a whole good year. We moved to a neighborhood on the other side of town,

It was time to enroll me in the second grade in our new neighborhood. I was excited about my new school. I wondered if the teacher in this new neighborhood would be friendly like Hannah, my first-grade teacher. But my mom had never dared even to visit the local elementary school in our new neighborhood.

From her detailed description, it was one of the worst schools in the country – or in her words, the world. Her precious and smart firstborn, who had said the name "Encyclopedia" when she was only one year old, could never attend a low-performing, awful school. Mother was not only concerned about its reputation and low scores; at the halfway mark between our home and school, there was a shady and mysterious sober-living house. A carpet of cigarette butts decorated the entrance to the house, and every day, between their recovery meetings, the questionable addicts added more butts on the burnt trail.

Addiction, Mother proclaimed, must be hidden well.

My overprotective mother subtly persuaded the City Hall to let me attend the elite elementary school located in my paternal grandmother's upscale neighborhood, half an hour bus drive from our home. Even the mayor could not say no to my mom. She always found a way to make things happen.

It was a year of new beginnings for both of us. I started second grade in a new school, and my mother started the job of her life. With her mom, my grandmother's unique connections at the main hospital in the city, my mother was hired to be a "drop of milk" nurse. Her role was to prepare the pre-calculated formulas for premature babies in the neonatal intensive care unit. Mom started leaving home before sunrise to take care of other parents' babies so they would have a warm bottle when they woke up, and I, the responsible firstborn, was left in charge of my three younger sisters.

Mom was methodical in her child-rearing routines: we were to do homework only at our desks, the family was to have dinner only around the table, dishwashing was to be by hand, and drying with towels. Bedtime was at exactly seven-thirty in the evening and lights-off at precisely eight o'clock. I disliked this the most: I wanted one more chapter, one more page, one more paragraph, one more word.

Thirstily I drank in each word of my books in bed while mother prepared our clothes to wear the next day. She organized the clothes according to how we would put them on, like an onion's layers. Each sister had her clothes waiting for her on her chair next to her desk. The layers were endless during cold Jerusalem winters. First a white camisole, then the undershirt, then the shirt, the wool stockings, long pants, turtleneck sweater. My mother also added a vest when it was freezing. The thick socks were ready, one on each boot, which sat next to each chair's legs. She also prepared four coats and placed them by the door with matching color umbrellas. She loved matching colors, even the colors of our socks.

"Mom, don't worry," I reassured her as she prepared our clothes the night before her first day at her new job. "I promise I will make sure everything will be fine tomorrow."

She trusted me.

I woke up in a parentless home; Mother had handed me her scepter. She was already at the hospital, and Dad was away again. He was a truck driver in faraway cities and came home every few days because of the long drives, or, as Mother always suspected, because of the other cheek-less women.

While my sisters were eating a rushed breakfast and packing Mom's premade lunches, I braided their hair into two beautiful thick braids just as Mom taught me. My sisters hated me for being the braider. I vigorously brushed and pulled and yanked their hair to satisfy my mother's fixation.

Mother could never check if we obeyed her braiding rules. Nevertheless, we never dared to leave our home with a single strand of hair in disarray. We knew that one louse would be dramatic enough to shatter Mother's serenity completely.

Good Girl, Ella.

Then we marched, dropping each one of my three sisters off at their destination—Lee to preschool, Sharon to daycare, and Libby to a home caregiver.

Finally, it is my turn. After I dropped off my sisters, I walked to the bus station, at the end of an unpaved dead-end roundabout, the first stop of the line route – or the last – depends on how you look at it. I rode through half the city to study with rich kids who didn't have their hair braided. They also never wore four layers of clothes under their coat.

I sat behind the bus driver to not miss the bus stop when it's time to get off, just as Mother told me. I saw other children with colorful backpacks walking to the local school in their neighborhood along the bus route from the windows. I looked around me; there were no other kids with me on the bus. I was a rare one.

I left household chores, laundry, braids, and dishes behind in the bus's exhaust. No one asked me to watch over my three sisters or clean. There were no loads of laundry, no dusting bookshelves, and no drying racks of dishes; it was just me, the books from our local library, and the bus driver. I could choose the book and the daydream.

When the school bell rang at the end of the day, the rich kids in my new school walked together to their homes in pairs or groups, passing the new green playground the mayor just built. I rushed to the bus stop. My driver waited for me.

"How was school today, Ella?"

"How was your math quiz?"

"What did you make in arts and crafts class?"

I had several drivers who drove my route. Joni usually worked at lunch shift on the way back home, Ben was obsessed with sixties music, and Mike had green apples for breakfast. I knew each bus driver by name, schedule, favorite shirt, and typical jokes.

"Don't worry. If you are ever late, I will wait for you," Abram, the morning bus driver, promised me. If I was late a few seconds because one of my sisters was slow to walk, Abram patiently waited for me as he brushed his black curls with a special comb.

I grew up among strangers on busses, and I built entire life stories without exchanging a single word with any of them. I paid attention, collecting data like a private investigator.

The older woman with her different hats and the old brown purse in her hands always sat in the front seat. The young, very tall, skinny woman who didn't wear a wedding ring always thanked the bus driver in a soft sweet voice after he punched her card. Her eyelashes would flutter like butterflies. The woman with the thick black glasses was chatting with everyone, even if they didn't listen to her. She even missed her bus stop next to the market a couple of times. That made me chuckle.

Then there was the older man with the white tangled beard. He chose a window seat and used to fall asleep, leaning on it with his head sloping to the side. Once, I even heard him snoring. Maybe he had treasures in his beard; he must have been exhausted from carrying them.

The bus rides made me a writer, a journalist, collecting clues and making strangers' lives come together into a finished puzzle.

The humming engine, the squeaky brakes, the yelling at the driver to stop because of the broken bell cord characterized my mornings and evenings. The old ladies complaining, the bearded man snoring, the women gossiping, the whining babies, and the giggles after the driver's jokes.

"Here, take my seat!" people offered a pregnant woman with her big belly touching the head of another woman sitting. Young teenagers would hop out of the bus to help an older man burdened with bags of produce at the market bus stop. One teenager would bring the bags carrying the aroma of the fresh oranges and herbs into the bus, while the other teenager held his hand and helped him climb on board. The bus driver patiently waited.

Ella, the seven-year-old intelligent agent, grew up on the meandering busses of greater Jerusalem and built treasures of stories in her head. It was my private Instagram, two decades before its invention. Picture after picture, I filled my head with creative captions from second to eighth grade.

There are no victims, only volunteers.

Time. You think you may have control over time. You aspire to make every minute count. Or you might attempt to kill time by doing nothing. But truthfully, time cannot be commanded or controlled. Most of all, no one can stop it.

How do you measure your time? The slow movement of a shadow across a sundial? The increasing pile of sand on the bottom of an hourglass? The constant ticking of a stopwatch? A few checkmarks on a calendar or in a daily planner? It's a trick, an illusion. The passage of time is only in your mind.

You want an anticipated event to start quickly. Now! Time is the burly security guard carefully watching you, waiting for your impatient demands, blocking you. You wait for an occasion, a trip, a birthday, a check, promotion, retirement. Stubbornly, time holds you back. Then the long-anticipated event begins, and you devour each precious moment. Time rushes far too quickly now, and you want it to last, begging for the clocks to stop so you can prolong the happiness. And then – then you get bored. Now you find yourself waiting for the next exciting spectacle.

Admit it. You always fixate on time.

When you want something to be over – an illness, an argument with a loved one, a test, a court hearing – time will slow down. Each second stretches its arms to encompass an eternity. This scenario is what we mean by the relativity of time. As Albert Einstein explained it, "an hour sitting with a pretty girl on a park bench passes like a minute, but a minute sitting on a hot stove seems like an hour."

Time doesn't listen.

Time leaves you with memories that, at first, are crisp and vivid. The greater the impact, the more details you may remember. You believe you can describe each moment correctly, and you can almost relive it. Depending on how your memory works, you may color the past with all five senses. The strong smells and tastes, the soothing sounds, the brilliant visions, the tactile feelings; your body participates in the recollection of every moment of your most essential experiences. It's true of your first kiss or your first car accident.

Slowly, memories get hazy, buried under new experiences you collect. They transform into either what you hoped had happened or what you most dreaded.

Time is selfish. But time heals.

Have you ever gone through surgery? Your pain when you came out was probably unmanageable and acute.

You demand painkillers. You want relief from the sharp agony.

"When is it going to be over?" you plead.

After a week of crying, you start to manage the pain. Slowly, you rebuild your strength, your body heals, and your resolve returns.

Time works its magic. Years later, you notice the scar and recall, *once, once I had surgery.*

Time is the master of illusions.

Chapter 3

You Must Be My Lucky Star

Kaf. Kaf .Vet. כ.כ.ב.
Star כוכב • Asterisk כוכבית • Celebrity כוכב

◉

Jerusalem, 1978

Like a bird covering us with her strong feathery wings, my mother protects her four girls from the chaos of the world. She must save her girls from the wolves out there. Among my mother's unwavering rules was that we were never to watch evening television shows unsupervised. For her, anything, even the slightest bit romantic, is terrifying and off-limits to her impressionable little girls.

"Cover your eyes!" she warns us with a determined voice before any and every passionate kissing scene on the screen. According to my mother, television is a gateway to truancy, drug use, pre-marital sex, and permissiveness.

The black and white television in our living room had only one channel. There was no choice except to turn that one channel on or off, which we can only switch with the buttons on the TV itself. When I was in third grade, the country got a second broadcast channel. The additional option brought twice the temptations to our house. Which channel is less alluring?

I didn't mind. Reading books has always been my first option. My mother's eagle eyes carefully measured my exposure to the evil black box was. My parents always wait to watch TV until we are in bed; it was their private time to choose between the only two available channels. My TV comes in the dark as I lay in bed. I see their shows through my imagination, a blurry combination between the sounds from the box and the parent's and their friends' commentary. I rewrite every scene of the movie or the show in my mind.

The women's chatter begins, "She is so beautiful! Look at her dress." I imagine lush curly hair, a gleaming smile, and a floor-length gown.

The men do not comment about the dress or the makeup; instead, they direct the women with urgent voices, "He is right behind you, lady, go across the street. Quick! Turn the corner. Carefully now…"

Another mysterious scene rushes into my imagination from our living room, "Oh, that's scary!"

Building on these vicarious tidbits, my little mind constructs stories and creates characters, looks, and lives. I become my director, painting the sceneries, knitting together plotlines. I also placed the heroes in my stories into my television dramas and comedies. I have a private selection of cues for laughter and long sighs.

And then came the babysitting.

"We cannot find a babysitter," I hear my mother saying with much disappointment in her voice to her friend on the phone.

Again, there is another wedding. People do not spend their money on luxury restaurants or weekly movies. The chief entertainment is hosting a party or going to weddings and Bar Mitzvahs. These celebrations are always in the middle of the week – Tuesday, Wednesday, or Thursday to not ruin the weekend. If the hosts are very

22

close to our family, the daughters usually come along. Freedom of late-night sleep, plenty of dancing, music, and the great surging tides of food flowing out of busy kitchens on heavy trays carried by muscle-bound waiters characterize these events. There is no formal invitation or required RSVP for these grandiose events – the more, the merrier!

These parties are the highlights of our childhood. Mother loves to dress all four girls in the same outfit. A blue corduroy jumper with white stripes on the sleeves' end with matching shiny slippers is one of the most memorable outfits. We enter the party hallway and stand like four perfect blue human cutouts: four girls, born within just five years. Finally, Mom lets our hair down, but she adds one tiny braid on the right side. She is proud of her Good Jerusalem Girls.

"No, I cannot find a babysitter," my mother repeats on the phone.

I can see the disappointment in her eyes. Her daughters aren't going to this wedding; it isn't a close relative, but her colleague's daughter from work. They only invited the parents. But for Mom, it is a rare chance to go out with my Dad, alone.

It is a Wednesday, the anniversary of the day that I was born, twelve twenty at noon precisely. Mom always tells me that I bring her the sun because God created the sun on Wednesday. But on Wednesdays, another episode of *Love Boat* aired, which I'm never allowed to watch. Every Thursday, my fourth-grade mates excitedly chat and gossip about the previous night's episode's latest happenings. The girls let their hair down, humming the famous song:

"Love boat... Love Boat soon will be making another run. The Love Boat promises something for everyone."

I'm the only one who never has anything to contribute or comment. According to Mother's nightly routine, I'm in bed by seven-thirty in the evening. Every school night, I'm allowed to read for precisely one hour, hiding a flashlight from her so that I can continue reading after lights out. That is the extent of my rebellion at this stage in life.

This Wednesday, I upped the ante. Mom hangs up the phone, and I can see her disappointment that our babysitter is not available. It is my chance. I take the risk.

"Mom, maybe you can go with Dad, and I can babysit?"

My mom looks at me with surprise. I notice her gears meshing with careful consideration. I stand, appearing patient, not adding a single word to my offer, so she won't suspect it is not the good girl in me but the curious preteen. In these long few moments, she is holding my admission to the cool-kids' club at school.

Mother is still thinking, which troubles me. She isn't concerned with leaving me with my sisters. I had proved my responsibility by the first grade, or even before we had the television.

Then came the instructions.

"Don't open the door if someone knocks."

"Call this number if anything happens." It was the neighbor's number. "Don't let your sisters get up from the bed."

And then came the central commandment, "If you watch TV, make sure you look away if there is any kissing!"

I nod solemnly.

My parents leave for the night with a trace of an expensive perfume applied only for such occasions, and suddenly my entire world changes.

24

Eight o'clock.

Love Boat.

The characters I have only heard about during school lunchtime come to full life.

"Love boat...Love Boat soon will be making another run. The Love Boat promises something for everyone."

I get the chance to watch Captain Merrill, Julie, Adam, Isaac, and even Dr. Bricker. They are all dancing on the ship deck, happy, joyous, and Julie's smile hooks me. Their laughter is enlivening and thrilling; they are human, and I love them all! I devour each scene, wishing it will last forever. I long to pass through the glass screen and become part of the crew on the fantasy cruise in the vast ocean visiting magical lands.

The next day, I join the *Love Boat* Club at school. I did not watch a wet kiss, but I did grow up in just thirty minutes of babysitting one evening.

Tel Aviv, 1981

This vicious love-hate cycle repeated like a rehearsed script in an unknown world.

My lioness, loving, hurting mom became sick from trying to figure her marriage out. But she was determined. Long phone conversations with her best friends are telling of how miserable she is when he leaves her, chasing after my Dad, pleading with the other women, screaming in the middle of the night, locking our front door so my Dad couldn't get back into the house after his night trysts, and the dishes flying in the air after he gets in from the balcony. My mom's compulsive cleaning and scrubbing was her medicine, and her four obedient daughters followed and helped, rinsed, and washed so she wouldn't become even more upset.

Every fight and separation, I became more proficient in the emotional gymnastics required to keep my sisters and me safe. In second grade, I created a sophisticated game. The fight would start, the yelling, the screaming, vases in the air, doors slamming, cursing, crying. I gathered my three younger sisters into my room and played board games, making me believe that nothing was happening a room away. We were in a fantasy Neverland.

From one lover to another, my mom became more creative and savvier about trying to fix her beloved husband. One hot summer night, between the third and fourth grade, she came to my room.

"Get ready; we are leaving for Tel Aviv. Put on your Shabbat dress."

Tel Aviv? The big city? Any other time I would be happy, but tonight I knew something else is about to happen despite not telling us.

Our neighbor comes over to watch my younger sisters. A humming diesel taxi is waiting for us outside. I'm curious and puzzled; *Taxis are costly.* My mom sits next to the driver while I sit in the back seat, and she starts telling the taxi driver the story of her life, and that I am gifted, that she has four girls, and that her husband is cheating on her with the worst women. I drift from her words, looking out the window on the valleys leading outside the Holy City. It's dark outside, and I could feel her rising anxiety.

My mom is right: I am smart. I'm ten years old, and I know there is one thing I mustn't do. I mustn't talk. I still do not understand what we are doing, but I know we are not going to a play or a show or a concert in the famous theater in the big city, the one's teacher Hannah told us about with sparkles in her eyes.

After an hour's ride, the taxi stops in one of the narrow streets. We arrive at an old condominium building in Tel Aviv – the Bourgeois City, the City of Sins.

"Turn off the lights," mom tells the driver, who can't decide if he is relieved this drive is over or wants to save this drop-dead-gorgeous woman from the suffering of her life.

My mother, almost shaking, pauses for a brief moment in front of the door. She takes a deep breath. *Ding Dong* – Mom rings the doorbell, covering the little door peephole.

A woman in a long silken robe opens the door.

Another pause before the biggest tornado Tel Aviv has ever seen. Screaming, hitting, yelling mixed with tears of pain and hurt. Hair pulling hair and more yelling. Hurt hurts to hurt. Two enmeshed bodies were crying for help like a wounded baby wolf lost in the wilderness.

I do what I was trained to do. I keep quiet.

I cannot recall how and when we get back home. It was never spoken of again.

Not even in whispering.

◉

Tel Aviv, 1983

Uncle Ron is walking fast a few steps ahead of me. Afraid to be left behind on the modern paved streets of Tel Aviv, I double my little steps, trying to catch up as he raced forward, leaving me behind.

He is quiet, rehearsing the next business meeting in his brain. Through the morning sun, I notice in the elegant and dressy Tel Aviv store's windows my becoming-almost-curvy teen silhouette walk-running after Uncle Ron.

Where do these women wear those fancy clothes?

My uncle keeps his measured and confident march. A clean-cut but casual look, and, as always, he wears denim jeans with a brand-new white T-shirt, thus bringing an uncompromised feeling. I feel safe walking with Uncle Ron – tall, wide built, with a thick salt-and-pepper short haircut. He looks like a handsome marine, ready for any surprise.

Not by blood, not by the leap of view, but by love. He is my metropolitan-wise uncle.

We arrive at the trendy coffee shop at eleven o'clock sharp. Being precisely on time is one of the first leadership rules I learn from him.

One middle-aged man is already waiting at a round glass table. I recognize him from when we visited his art studio the week before. His name is Yosel Bergner. Auntie Emma had whispered in my ear that he is very famous. Even though she told me the worth was in thousands, I didn't like his painting. Each painting had a couple – a man and a woman. But their eyes were always sad, just like Mom's eyes after Dad left again for a few months. But I smiled, mimicking the adults, portraying different amber of life, so they won't think I don't understand or appreciate art.

My uncle shakes Yosel's hand firmly, only saying hello with his blue, sharp-sighted eyes. He grabs an extra chair for me and gives me some change from his pocket to insert in the red gumball machine waiting for me in the coffee shop corner. When I come back with blue bubble gum in my hands, holding it carefully so the dye won't melt in my fingers, another man is sitting with them, but I don't recognize him. I am sitting quietly so as not to interrupt their business conversation. Uncle Ron gets himself fresh-squeezed orange juice and a fresh warm poppy seed roll on a small glass plate for me.

I am still nibbling on my poppy seed roll when Uncle Rob gets up from his seat, letting everyone know the meeting is over. I wipe my mouth carefully with the thin napkin from the tin napkin holder on the table, hoping no little black beads are clinging to my teeth. Uncle Ron and the famous artist shake hands, and I notice their friend is smiling. This is how I know the meeting went well. I quickly stand up next to Uncle Ron, ready for the fast-paced walk back.

Politely, I leave the rest of the roll on the table – if I take it, people would think it is better than my mom's chocolate cake, so, shyly, I smile goodbye to the famous artist and the businessman stay behind.

Uncle Ron never said a lot in those coffee shop meetings. But when he talks, people listen. Carefully. Auntie Emma told me that his raw honesty could sometimes sting you like the jellyfish on the beach if you don't watch out.

Uncle Ron was a businessman, but I didn't understand what that meant. Auntie Emma told me he traveled the world to find new partnerships and new ideas to invest in. He often traveled out of the country and came back every few months. His suitcase was usually small. To be precise, it wasn't a suitcase, but a black Kipling duffle bag.

"A man should not have more than what he needs," he later told me.

When Uncle Ron came back from his trips in Europe or The United States, he stayed in five-star hotels for a couple of months at a time. If I had time off from school, and if Dad was at home to convince

Mother that I was a good girl and I could go, I was put in a taxi to Tel Aviv, the big modern city, to stay with Dad's sister, Auntie Emma. Only a fifty-minute drive away from home, and I remember feeling like I was in a magical foreign country.

She took me to visit Uncle Ron at his fancy high-rise hotel. We arrived in a taxi from her home so as not to sweat in the dripping humidity of Tel Aviv. Unlike the stickiness outside, the entrance to the hotel was chilled like a sweet popsicle and smelled like fresh lilies. I imagined I was a tourist, just like all the people in the lobby of the hotel. Auntie Emma ordered filtered coffee, which came in a fancy five-piece set and a white fabric napkin you put on your lap. I drank in every little detail around me: the different accents, the wide hats, high heels, the men with the suits, the giggling kids who hid from their parents behind the enormous plants.

Auntie Emma devoured each sip. Fifteen years ago, she and Uncle Ron had been madly in love, then married, and, instead of perpetuating any hate, lovingly divorced. In the elevator on the way to the penthouse floor, I felt the rush in my belly. I have never been to such a high floor, not even in the hospital, Mom worked at. The hotel room was facing the paintbrush sand and the blue Mediterranean Sea. I took a deep breath and let the warm breeze tingle my face. I wish I didn't have to let it go.

My summer vacations in Tel Aviv were with adults only; I never met any kids. I used to wake up to the Tel Avivian birds singing and wait for Auntie Emma to come back from organizing the files and the life of the top-notch lawyers in Tel Aviv, Mr. and Mrs. Swartz. I cleaned the rooms, vacuumed the antique rugs, dusted the shelves, folded and put away the laundry. If I had time, I organized the endless bookshelves. I used to do it at home anyway – here; it was quieter.

When Auntie Emma came back to her spotless bohemian apartment, she used to dance with joy literally.

"How did you clean everything? I wish you stayed forever!"

My heart danced, too, and my eyes were diamonds."

This is how I got to know Tel Aviv. When Auntie Emma worked, I spent a few hours with her beloved divorcee, Uncle Ron. He took me to his five-minute business meetings in Tel Aviv coffee shops to meet the famous artists at the best art galleries and out to exquisite lunches at the fanciest restaurants in the northern (and most pretentious) part of the city.

After I was introduced around politely, no one ever talked to the little girl. I didn't mind. I loved being on the sidelines. I carefully watched the adults do their business, playing with words like chess, hiding their face like in a poker game. Like in a tennis court, my eyes moved from one side to another, distinguishing what makes a meeting pleasant and what turns into a signed deal.

My entrepreneurial lessons didn't end when we left the coffee shop.

"When people talk too much, they bullshit you," my uncle summarized the meeting.

My uncle never held back his truth, even if it cost him a friendship or business deal. After every venture, he would give me a short description of the person we'd just met and a synopsis of what had transpired. With just a few words, he gave me the truth, not only about business but about human nature itself.

"No bullshit!" he used to tell Auntie Emma if she started going around with words. Bullshit was his worst pet peeve. He called it *Foyle Shtick*.

And this is how I collected his slogans, like a collection of miniature dolls in my manual for life.

"Everything is mine, just not with me."

"Don't be dependent on anyone. Depend on yourself."

"Don't ever pay for a man on a date."

"Life is like riding a Ferris wheel; sometimes you are up and sometimes you are down, when you are up you are scared to be down again, and when you are down, you never believe you will climb again."

My entrepreneur uncle believed in the power of money, but he refused to give it power over him. Splurging was spoiling, and if you spoil someone, you ruin them because people should work hard and be smart with their money. Uncle Ron didn't shower me with many presents, but every visit, I received one special gift right before it was time for me to go back to my other life in the Holy City.

"What did you bring this time?"

My sisters were curious to burrow in my bag when I came back after my urban city adventures at Auntie Emma's. New cute matching outfits, sparkly modern shoes, and a stylish shorter haircut.

"Why so short?" Mother was upset for days after. "I cannot believe she cut your hair again." Mom never called Auntie Emma by her real name.

I kept my stories to myself, but the haircut I couldn't hide. My sister Lee hated me for my clothes and new shoes. I hated them, too. They were a red mark on my forehead. *I am different.*

It was clear that the memories are bullets "Show us! Show us Uncle Ron's present!" The clothes, the shoes, and the haircut were forgotten. We were all excited about the modern and innovative invention from a faraway land. Uncle Ron's gifts were the one thing everyone anticipated. From the newest colorful Swatch to a Rubik's Cube, a T-shirt with special shiny 3D art on it, and, once, even a pure-bred Labrador puppy. That puppy didn't stay long. Mother did not permit four-legged creatures in our home. The voices, the giggling, "Me, me, my turn! Let me play with him!" And the wows and the woohoos of children eating ice cream for the first time. The sounds of a family coming together.

This time the present was tucked into a small box. I tried to guess what it might be, but my uncle didn't like guessing or lingering like my aunt.

"Get to the point," he often said in those meetings. This is why Uncle Ron had never exchanged more than a couple of sentences with his mother.

When my fourteen-year-old hands gently opened my new gift, I was puzzled. A little black plastic box, five square push down buttons, and a lid with two little spinning wheels inside. It looked like it was made for a music cassette like the ones I had in my room, but this device was tiny compared to my huge boombox in my room—simple headphones, which looked like a headband with round sponge covers on the ends.

Connect the jack into the right hole.

Put the headphones on my ears?

Insert my cassette into the player.

Push play.

Music.

The Walkman.

I could choose the music, choose the song, and the music was for me alone. The Walkman ignited me from within. I could feel the songs in every cell of my body. The music in my ears from the little black box was deeper and more profound than anything I had heard before. I savored every note, every sound, every word. I obsessed over one song, repeatedly pushing 'stop' and 'rewind.' I'd hear the cassette wheels whirling backward, and after a few seconds would hit 'play' again. Almost through muscle memory, I perfected rewinding to exactly the right spot.

While all the familiar strangers on the bus ate their apples or stared out the windows, daydreamed, or read their newspapers, I had a full concert between my ears for two hours every school day. The piano, violins, the drums, the music uplifted me and my body to places I had never been before. I was captivated by the imaginary performance, drawing the stage, the lights, the fog, the speaker towers in my mind.

Curious as a fish in cold water, I researched and read everything about the singer's life. I scrutinized every detail about her upbringing, her persistence, her little apartment in New York City, and her daring sassiness, researching everything about her I could find. It wasn't a simple task. Google was not yet invented, and libraries didn't know who this new starlet was yet. My creative search was limited to magazines, rumors from high school friends, and rare TV clips.

She was the person I daydreamed about. She made me smile, laugh, and cry every morning on my way to school. She drove me there and brought me back home. She listened to my teenage falling in love moments and my heartbreaks. Madonna.

I learned to move my body only by listening. I learned how to dance while sitting on hard bus chairs while Madonna's songs played through Walkman headphones into my ears. I practiced my choreography only in my imagination. While my legs are sprawled from the bench, I visualized myself twirling, dancing while the bus was moving forward, turning every ride into my music video clip. I envisioned myself on the sidewalks, jumping over bus stop benches, dancing over water hoses, and spinning in the air. I twirled and turned; I kicked and paused. I taught myself complicated moves, perfecting my style from one bus ride to another.

Secretly, I longed to take dance classes, but my mom instead enrolled me in private, advanced English group lessons. I learned grammar, syntax, the proper way to count years, and add adverbs. I learned words of manners, politeness, and expressions only good girls use.

The forbidden passionate words of love, lust, and romance were taught to me by my Madonna.

In my Holy City, there were many Madonna's. I met them in the stunning, glorious, ancient churches in The Old City, but none of them were like my Madonna. The ma-*Material girl* became my hero. No posters, no tees, keychains, hats, blankets, or souvenir cups with her bold signature. Thousands of miles away from The United States, in a world where flights were luxuries for very rich people only, I kept dreaming about going to one of her concerts. I was prepared to dance, but only in my mind.

Madonna and Good Girl Jerusalem.

We danced, learned another move, and shrugged off the misery of the adults.

She sang. I danced.

She dared. I dreamed.

Half-bleached hair, wearing a mini skirt and a scissor-cut T-shirt with a bold cross necklace, saying what was forbidden. She expressed herself where I could not.

Daydreaming about my first French kiss, I closed the brown blinds which covered every inch of sunlight from outside and listened to *Like a Virgin* full blast and slipped into my fantasies.

Papa, don't preach!

Music, dancing, and books were my escape, running away from their tumult. This was where I could be free, without being questioned or responsible to anyone, without being dragged to their messy, chaotic pandemonium.

My parents danced, too. Their love-hate dance in a codependent relationship spun faster than a hurricane. Every other year, they broke up, nearly got divorced, and ran away until they either missed each other or got bored without any real drama while they are separated, eventually finding their way back to each other's arms again. This lasted for a few months – until the next time. The comfort prize was usually another sibling and my Dad remodeling another room in our little home.

The year I turned fourteen, a few months before I received my Walkman, they finally got divorced. I was relieved.

But the drama didn't end there. From that moment on, we had another secret to keep. We, the six kids from the ages of three months to fourteen, had to keep it a secret. Their divorce was kept classified information from my mom's Dad, and we had to swear before every visit, not to mention it while visiting my mom's family. My Algerian grandfather did not accept divorce in any family. It was a big sin – a curse on the family. It also set us apart at school. The divorce rate in Israel was very low back in those days, and we were the only divorced family in my grade level.

That year I promised myself I would never get divorced. I will fight for my family. I swore to never put a strain on my family due to what happened.

Press fast forward on the Walkman.

Don't compare your inside to someone else's outside.

Who is your Madonna, if I may ask? Or maybe, you could scream out loud and say, "I never liked Madonna anyway!" but it can be anyone. A singer, an actor, an author, a buddha. A person you don't even know, but whom you admire with all of you might.

Who is your idol, whom you aspire to be like? Who is your statue, the thing you worship blindly?

The real question is, who is that one who pushes you to change, try harder, and find the better you? Who is the person who believed in you no matter what, even if they did not know you? Thank them today. Thank them in your way, not for their sake, but for your own. From your soul, for your next step. You owe it to yourself.

Maybe you found your Madonna on Instagram, Twitter, or Facebook — an influencer, a podcast leader, or a best-selling author with reviving self-help books. You have special relationships with all of them. It's personal in your eyes, and they don't even know you. You read them – the self-help books, poems, novels, posts, stories, videos, quotes, and comments. You watch the movies, and you hear the podcasts, you listen to the songs. They give you profound courage, help, and faith. You want everyone to read them, hear them, and watch them so they can change, too. If they do, your life will be happier, more serene, more peaceful. The answers are there. Formulas, phases you follow passionately. In your mind, those are the best recommendations for anyone you love.

"How to Make Your Life Happier with Your Husband." "Letting Go of Your Power." "Three Easy Tricks to Improve Your Happiness at Home." You repost those articles, hoping the person you want to notice and learn from them will read it, you'd leave a book on your nightstand, hoping they may read it, too. We post, repost, tag, and yell what we want to say through another person.

"Read it, read it now."

Self-improvement and the improvement of your loved ones became your drug. But for anyone in the world, you need to go through rock bottom, through pain, through the darkness to find your brighter path.

No one ever created a profound change in their life if someone yelled at them, "Read this!" Ultimately, it must be their path, and what works for them might not work for someone else. This is your path; what works for others might not work for you.

Remember your teenage years. It doesn't matter that everyone told you that what you were going through is normal. The pain, loneliness, the anger at the adult world, the complexity of loving others. No advice, no matter how well-intended, could get you through this. You have to find your way, your path, on your own.

Loving yourself and knowing you are complete just the way you are will return you to your heart, rather than putting your happiness into other people's hands. This condition never works and will fail you again and again. You are too concerned about how others regard you, and this makes you consistently untruthful to yourself. If you live according to someone else's rule, then soon you will forget YOU.

"Change!" if you can, you plead. "Change for me so I can feel better."

You get addicted to the temporary sense of transformation that comes every time. But it is never deep unless you do the real work. Unless you go through the fear, through the darkness and the pain, you cannot understand the harsh reality of life. Only then will you find the courage and be there for yourself.

You must be your lucky star.

Chapter 4

Good Girl

Tet. Vav. Bet. ט.ו.ב.
Good טוב • Favor טובה • Quality טיב • Well היטב

◉

Jerusalem, 1984

"Your report card is boring!"

Up in the air boring and exactly what they wanted: three numbers, a one followed by two zeroes. One hundred percent. In their eyes, numbers were all that mattered – ignoring the fact that we were a people who had been reduced to numbers tattooed on our arms just a few decades earlier. Something that amazed people in our locality as many hit the way.

My parents were amused by this idea and shared it with our family, neighbors, and sometimes gossipy local grocery store looked like a wolf in sheep's clothing.

"How boring!" They walked like peacocks with their colorful long feathers out. Boring report card! How they loved to say it! They had a smart, first-born girl, thanks to their genes, attention, and upbringing. *How Boring!*

I was their report card. My hundreds were their excellency award.

In Hebrew, they called me *Yalda Tova Yerushalayim*, *"Good Girl Jerusalem."*

By the end of seventh grade, after I'd written countless books about my fellow bus passengers in my mind, my school began to test me for high school placement.

The serious-faced evaluators showed up every day in school and sometimes pulled me from class to be tested. The evaluators did not ask me to braid hair, nor did they time me washing dishes. They did not ask me about my babysitting skills or check the pots after I washed them. They didn't ask me why I don't have many friends or the bus driver's name on Tuesdays. Instead, I was asked to solve logic riddles for over a month, complete sentences, and continue shape sequences. At the end of this month of screening, the school counselor, Mrs. Goldberg, asked to meet my parents in her office.

Both of them.

Together.

Something is wrong, I was sure. *Both of my parents? Together? At my school? At the same time? Was it barking up the wrong tree* That day, I tightened my braids more than ever?

I had no explanation for why Mrs. Goldberg called them. After all, I liked school a lot. Now my parents had to miss work because of me.

In her private office filled with cabinets, shelves, books, files, folders, and a sepia family picture in an old gold frame, the counselor explained to my parents the steps in the screening process and the different testing models. Mom and Dad still had no idea what was so urgent and could worth meeting of this nature.

Mrs. Goldberg took out a blank white paper and carefully drew a bell shape. She started drawing many stick figures in the middle of the bell.

"These are students. The average students," she explained. My father cleared his throat. His truck was waiting like agony in waiting. Then Mrs. Goldberg drew a few stick figures on the left side to show the "below-average students."

My parents listened intensely, still skeptical of why she called them to this art lesson. Then she drew one stick figure, all the way on the right side of the bell. This moment would later be retold to every guest that came to our house.

It was me, alone.

"Your daughter is gifted." Mrs. Goldberg put the pen on the table, removed her big-framed black glasses, and looked straight at my parents. "Your daughter has been scouted and accepted to a school for the highly gifted, the most prestigious high school in the country. Boyar, School of Excellence."

My dad shed a tear. He always cried when he got overly emotional, and he wiped them quietly with his fingers, never adding any words. Mom did all the talking.

"I have always known my daughter is gifted!" She started telling Mrs. Goldberg how I sang "Happy Birthday" to myself when I was just one year old, and how I could say the words "encyclopedia" and "individually" while the other kids just said "mama," and that if they would ask her, her daughter doesn't need testing and drawing, because she always knew that her daughter was gifted. She asked if she could get a certificate or even this drawing. Mother already planned to carry it in her purse so everyone would see how smart her first-born is.

In that one instance, my mom became the mother-of-the-year in our neighborhood. Her braid training had turned out to be a smashing success.

◉

Jerusalem, 1985

The summer I became a teenager was full of changes. My body matured, my clothes style has changed, and I let my hair down. My two baby brothers were born, and now we were six kids. We moved again to a new neighborhood. My parents got divorced.

After fourteen years of being separated and getting back together, renewing their membership in the chaotic couple club, my parents made their separation official. My dad truly loved my mom but had grown tired of my mother's accusations that he was too appreciative of the beauty of other women. When he left home, he left us, my mother said. Like Peter Pan, he ran after a younger woman, a 24-year-old new wife (only eight years older than me), to replace my mom. He left his first wife, his home, four girls, a toddler, and a baby. It was the end of my parents' madness and the beginning of my mom's long misery.

In one summer, everything changed. I was still a beginner at teen life, a ninth-grader at a high school for the gifted. Overnight, I was no longer the eldest sister but a young mother to my five siblings. It was a heavy title for a girl like me, and no one asked me or interviewed me for this position. It was thrust upon me.

Mom was a 34-year-old divorcee with six young kids. Sam, my fifth sibling, was two and a half, and Sasi, my youngest sibling only three months old.

Sam and Sasi. Round baby faces, big brown smart eyes, two deep dimples on each cheek, and innocent smiles that capture any heart at the glare. Their straight hair hugs their faces. Inseparable, together they look like twins, yet, as is so often the case with siblings, they are entirely different. One is calm and relaxed; the other is wild and free-spirited. One loves animals and hides stray dogs, cats, and pigeons in our home. The other loves music and composes tracks for the radio without even knowing notes. One can watch tennis for hours, the other plays soccer until he is exhausted. Sam and Sasi, Sasi and Sam.

"Don't tell Grandpa that Dad is not living with us," Mother prepared us before our infrequent visit to our grandparents'. She taught us how to manipulate the truth at a young age, telling half-truths or outright lies to keep others from judging us.

Mother's divorce was a hush-hush within her family, and we, the kids, had to keep it a secret when visiting my grandfather, our old-fashioned and stern patriarch. The D-word, which is freely thrown in the air today, was not acceptable in his world. A divorced woman had a black stain, and it was usually the woman's fault since she couldn't keep her husband at home.

This is how I learned to lie and how I learned to make lies plausible with still more clever lies. This is how I learned to participate in someone else's drama. This is how I pretended with my mom that she was sick with a horrible strain of the flu when she was depressed in bed for days.

Father turned a blind eye and never paid child support, and mother was left without any financial resources and with buckets of shame. My fragile mother was completely over her head trying to support our home and keep herself from slipping into total despair. Three times a week, I met her at one of the few tall government buildings in our city. We cleaned clerks' offices together so we could bring more money home for food. Floor after floor, office after office, room after room emptying paper trash bins, wiping the dust off of desks, and rearranging framed pictures of happy families rekindling the lost hope.

I fantasized about my future family, my husband, my kids.

I will never get divorced, I promised myself. *I will fight for my family.*

I swore this while turning off the lights in each office I finished until the corridor was completely dark and it was time to go home. At home, there was cleaning, laundry, dinner, and, only after everyone was in bed, homework and studying for upcoming tests.

I will marry a man who will never cheat on me. I will keep my family together. Forever.

I prepared chore charts and made sure they were extra quiet when our mother was crying in bed. Each of the girls found her place to deal with – or suppress – the new reality. Sam and Sasi were our comforts. We dressed them up in girls' clothes, sang with them, bathed them, and read them stories with the characters' funny voices.

I took motherhood fiercely to heart. When they organized their toys, I hugged them. When they brought home an art project from preschool, I stuck it on the fridge with pride and showed it off to the family. I taught them how to read their first word, brush their teeth every night, and tie their shoelaces. I told them every day they were the best. I showered them with love, confidence, and courage. I saw the beauty, strength, and uniqueness of each of them and watered their self-esteem every day.

I will never leave you. I whispered in my heart when I tucked them into bed at night.

The depression hits our home like a heavy grey cloud. Thirty-four years old, and the love of her life left for another woman. Six kids and a sad, very sad, Mother, grieving the loss of the love of her life, a tragedy ongoing since she was eighteen. The tragedy just changes face. After burying herself in bed for weeks, telling us it is a terrible flu, my mom finds a reason to get up: she will remodel the kitchen. Breaking walls, changing old cabinets, installing new countertops, demolishing the memories from the past so nothing from the family dinners with "him" will remain.

Erasing the illusions of a family as it existed for fifteen years, replacing them with a new path, new doors, and drawers that contain the unknown.

Caleb, my maternal grandmother's neighbor, is my mom's right-hand man in this transformational operation. Caleb has known my grandma and our family for years now, and he generously gives my divorcée mom a special rate and promises her the kitchen of her dreams.

Every day, Caleb arrives with his workers, toolboxes, big hammers, and heavy black boots. He stands in the kitchen and gives clear instructions to his workers for the day.

"She needs the kitchen soon!"

"Make sure it is the dream kitchen!"

Caleb rushes his workmen, filling them with a sense of urgency. He leaves and comes back in the afternoon to check their work and make more comments.

Caleb has dark brown eyes, dark skin, a strong body, and a full mane of hair. I think he is in his forties, or so. His wife is in her sixth month of pregnancy, and he is going to be a dad for the first time in just a few months. Any extra work is a godsend that will help with the purchase of a new crib, stroller, bed, clothes, diapers, and toys for his first-born baby.

Caleb promises my mom they will finish soon. Mother is elated, soon busying herself with planning, adding details to the tile pattern, considering another faucet, resizing the special shelf for the cookies and the triangle cabinet designated for her famous baking. She is occupied with recreating her life – the new life after "he" destroyed the family. Caleb wears a superhero's cape, and my mother is grateful for warm black coffee and pastries she saves for whenever he arrives. She gives him advice on how to raise his child, as she is an expert with six of her own. Her eldest is gifted, and she raves; she is the special one. Nothing can replace my mom's thrill about the grand opening of her new kitchen.

My still-young mom, thirty-four years old, can't carry the entire burden of six kids without child support assistance. The government assigned a social worker who comes to evaluate the sadness in our home every month. They write a report and recommend sending two of my sisters away to find joy in faraway beds at boarding school. We are left with fewer meals, fewer books, less attention to divide, and more space.

My mom and I are a team. Endless laundry, the two babies, market, meals, divide our chores and manage our home. Every Thursday, I deep clean the house while she cooks for Shabbat, especially every other Shabbat when the sisters visit for the weekend. She goes to the market, and I put everything away. We are four hands working together. She takes my brother to daycare in the morning, and I bring him back as she arrives late from her second or third job cleaning government offices. If I don't have loads of homework at school, I join her there.

It is two o'clock in the afternoon, and I am happy to have a new weekly schedule at my high school. Some days are longer, and some days are shorter. But every day is filled with assignments and tests. After all, it is a school for the gifted, and we have a reputation to uphold. I arrive home and start my project before Lee, my younger sister, returns and before I have to bring my two baby brothers, Sam and Sasi, home from daycare.

I love this special quiet time in the early afternoons – sacred alone for me and my books. I am by myself at home – a moment as rare as the white peacock you can spot only in Australia.

After taking the two long busses home, I climb the one-hundred-and-one stairs of our building to the third floor. The front door is unlocked, and I presume the workers went to bring something. Tools and dust are everywhere. I make noises stepping on long brown paper, and make a path to the girls' bedroom.

I sit at my desk and bury myself in the new English project. Shmuel, our American English teacher, is giving us creative writing assignments to write stories from our imaginations. I write about a beautiful, stunning, shy girl in a village whom the handsome, smart prince falls in love with. He is coming to save her. I write it in English and, although it is not my native language, my words swim easily on the paper. I drift with the princess and her imaginary new castle. He whisks her away from her low-income family, and they live happily ever.

"Hi." Caleb is standing at the entrance to my room, "how was school today?" he asks.

He doesn't wait for an answer and enters the room. He stands behind me.

"What are you doing?" he is hovering over me, much too close.

"English," I whisper. If he cannot hear my words, perhaps he will leave.

"Let me see." Caleb's sweaty smell is disgusting. I feel his rough dirty hand on my shoulder. He puts his hand through my school shirt, and he touches my breast. I am frozen.

"Good girl," he says as he continues to feel me.

My heart pounds. I am numb. I hear his heavy breathing. He reeks of cigarettes and sweat. He moves his hand around and around my breast. It is only a few moments, but it seems to last forever.

When he leaves, I sit, glued to my chair for a long time. I cannot bring myself to move.

Fear.

Shame.

Embarrassment.

My mom arrives home in the afternoon, happy about the demolition. I haven't heard mom laughing like this for a long time. She makes Caleb sugary black coffee, takes out sweet, fresh almond cookies. He loudly sips from the tiny coffee cup, and with each bite, he boasts about how she is the best baker in the city and what he accomplished today. Their laughs stab at my skin.

When he leaves, I do what my mother taught me best: I keep it quiet. Her kitchen is her glimpse of light, and there is no room for darkness.

The next day, Caleb comes to my room again after sending the workers home a little earlier. When he comes in, I know what to expect. I keep my eyes on my books. I don't even dare to look anywhere. I try to numb both my thoughts and my body before he even touches me. I think about the princess-to-be in my story. She is dancing with her prince, and he might save her.

"Good girl," he leaves the room. I don't cry. Good girls don't cry. *I will forget everything that happened here until the kitchen is done._*

The bus ride home the following day is not so smooth. I dread going home. I am afraid, but I know my mom's kitchen is more important, and I cannot disappoint anyone. *It is soon going to be over.*

From one bus station to another, all I can smell is Caleb's salty, revolting scent. Sitting next to the window, I look up to the sky and whisper a little prayer. Maybe someone up there will help. Maybe a man with a white bird can see me here. But I am such a tiny little speck in this vast world.

I think about practical solutions. Maybe I can wear two shirts today so it will be more difficult for him. No, that will just make him try harder. It will go on even longer. Then, I see a sign written in red. HOTLINE! It is an ad for one of the bus stops.

"Teenagers, call us if you need help! Anonymously."

I recite the number, horrified to write it down so no one will see that I might be that teenager—a bad, bad girl.

Caleb enters my room again that afternoon. I try to recite dates from a history test in my head to make it go faster.

Later that evening, after Caleb and his workers leave, and my mom is busy chatting with our next-door neighbor raving about her upcoming kitchen empire, I take the long-tangled corded phone into my room, making sure no one hears me, and I quietly close the door.

I dial the memorized number. Two rings.

A sweet, loving, confident voice answers the other line.

"Will it stay anonymous?" I ask twice after she asks my age.

"Yes," the sweet woman reassured me, "I am here to help you. I am here for you."

I timidly tell her what happened. I don't linger or tell her details about his thick fingers and how they scratched my skin.

"Next time he shows up at the entrance of your room," says the angel on the other line, "look at him directly in his eyes and say, 'Leave this room now and never, never come in again.'"

She asks me to repeat it with her. I whisper so softly, slowly, swallowing the words.

The angel asks if she can call me the next day, but I am afraid to give her the number.

"You can call me any time," she promises. "I am here for you."

"You can do it," she says when I tell her I need to go. "You are a strong, brave girl."

The next day, I hear Caleb's heavy steps on the brown construction paper on the floor, making their way to my bedroom. I'm sure he can hear my heart pounding, my pulse racing faster and faster the closer he gets.

Just as he gets to the door of my room, I turn and look at him with piercing eyes.

I summon all of my courage and bravery – with my angel from the hotline holding my hand – and say, "Leave this room and never, never come in."

Caleb looks at me, confused. He stalls next to the doorway.

"Now!" I hear my voice and am surprised by its strength.

He turns and leaves.

I take a deep breath of air and release it slowly. I close my eyes and thank the angel. Caleb neither enters my room nor tries to touch me ever again.

This is how I learned to guard my body.

This is how I learned to protect my skin.

This is how I learned to trust only myself.

This is how I learned never to be afraid of anyone.

This is how I learned to fight for myself.

I don't tell my mom the secret. Even when the kitchen is ready. Even three months later, when we all go to Caleb's first son's circumcision.

We are crazy as our secrets.

There are only two prayers. I will explain only two significant players, and they can be worded in many ways: One is *Thank you.* The other is *Help!*

Find that voice in you that can call for HELP without any expectations. That is the true deep calling for help. It kicks, it screams, it is loud without needing to use any other words. That is the magic in calling for help. Its power lies in its unconditional need.

"Help" can be asked only from a place of true surrender – that deep moment when you are powerless, weak, lost, defeated. It's then that you call for assistance, ready to accept it in almost any shape and form.

The help will come, and that's when you have a choice to make. Instead of feeling sorry for yourself, how stuck you are, and how victimized you feel, find trust. Getting help is the first stage, and it's vital – but it isn't the last one. You can't stay stuck in feeling powerless. That's the easy way when we feel pain. You hold tightly to the problem like a shield because this is the only way you know how to live. Letting go and releasing your projections and assumptions might be the most straightforward yet most difficult activities you can take. It's the hardest because no one else can do it for you.

Ask for help from an invisible power beyond your five senses, beyond what your logic can explain. Ask to move beyond the story you've told yourself for years. Ask to break out of the cycle. Unclench the white-knuckled fist holding onto the problem. Call for help with an authentic, pure call. Isn't this the reason you sometimes fall so far to learn what an honest, sincere release and trust is?

The answers will come when you stop putting conditions on the relief you seek. They may not come on your timetable. They almost certainly won't. The peace you crave will come on your Higher Power's timetable, and, though it may seem impossible to imagine, it will be a better solution than what you had planned.

Needing help is a lot like true love. You know it is true love when there is no need for an explanation as to <u>why</u> you love. It just is.

Try it! If you need help, yell, beg, plead, scream, shout, ask, and pray for it! It might be humiliating, it might seem ridiculous, but I promise you that it is also empowering and liberating. It's the best way, maybe the only way, to get what you need most.

Chapter 5

Breaking Golden Cages

Pei. Resh. Tzadi. פ.ר.צ.

Erupt פרץ • Break out לפרוץ • Burst into Tears פרץ בבכי • Crack פרץ

◉

Israel, January 18, 1991

The green neon wall clock shows one a.m. I lie on my very narrow bed, the wool blanket underneath me to keep me from the winter cold. I am still wearing my black boots. I am waiting: one hour, then two. I can hear my heart beating. I can almost hear everyone else's hearts throbbing in the nearby dorms.

All at once, the loud, long, echoing siren reverberates. The wail of the siren warns us to take cover. 'Get into The Sealed rooms! Get into The Sealed rooms!' From top to bottom of our small country, the sirens alert every breathing creature in the country to hide. Missiles are coming, and they might be seconds away. They might be conventional missiles or maybe chemical warheads. Maybe even nuclear. The unknown will be revealed in minutes, but now we have to run. Run to the sealed room.

What is now called the First Gulf War has begun. The United States and its allies have launched an attack against Iraq; Saddam Hussein has refused to abide by UN demands to withdraw from Kuwait. With the start of hostilities, the Iraqi president has promised to launch deadly missiles on Israel to wipe us off the map. Maybe he's bluffing. Maybe he's not.

It is a night. The new moon started only three days ago, and the only light was shining from my pocket flashlight. I quickly get up from the hard mattress. As I have practiced with my fellow soldiers for days now, I hear them in the next dorm, getting up from their beds. Following, they also lay down with their boots on, without a wink of sleep. One by one, everyone steps out of their rooms. Within thirty seconds, everyone is out, lining up in predetermined order. Gas masks are strapped to our belts, and EpiPen syringes are in our pockets.

My eighteen-year-old soldiers count off, whispering, "Eighteen. Nineteen. Twenty." I have twenty soldiers in my unit, and I am only one year older.

We are all here. We hurriedly walk, moving down the path that leads to the shelter in the center of the base. It is quiet. All we hear is the hushing and shushing of rapid footsteps of our boots hitting the pathway.

A whisper, "Ella!"

One of my soldiers, who was dealing with a high school heartbreak just a few weeks ago, huffs from the back of the line.

"Ella, Vivi has fainted!"

I raise my hand. Stop!

I flash my light to the back of the line. I can just make out the pale faces of my girls. I want to pinch my cheeks, so they won't see that I am probably as white as they are—no time for overthinking now. I am afraid to admit it: I am scared. I am frightened, like a three-year-old child who was kidnapped in a busy subway. I snap out of it. I walk to the back of the line and see Vivi leaning on a tree. She is shaking violently and cannot move. Vivi cannot say a word in shock, yet the bombs haven't even started to drop.

Vivi is my co-commander. Twenty girls stare at me for the next order, and the sirens continue.

Now? You faint now? I want to slap her, make her stand, and run with us. I want to murder her. But I can't. We are at war now; we might die, all of us, anyway. There is no point in killing her now.

I am alone, in direct charge of my troops. No commanders above me. Just me, the girls, and my semi-conscious co-commander. The sirens are resounding. The heavy night sneaks into our hearts.

No time to be afraid now, Ella. Fight, flight, or freeze. I fight.

Instinctively, I call the guard, quickly. I inform Bob through the old bulky black walkie-talkie about Vivi, and, before I finish my sentence, Bob runs towards us. Immediately, he follows the procedures and checks Vivi's pulse, then lifts Vivi into his arms and joins us as we rush toward the sealed room.

It seems like hours, but I look at my watch. Only a few minutes have passed. We surge as quietly and quickly as we can, yet we still sound like elephants running on dry leaves.

My family. My baby brothers. Worry over them flashes in my mind. Sam and Sasi are only six and eight years old.

What are they going through? What is happening there at home? Will Saddam spare Jerusalem? I want to hug my baby boys and protect them instead of Vivi. I want to engulf them and reassure them, *"I am here, it is ok, we will win!"* But they are far and deep down. I am not sure of victory myself. This is not a toy soldier game for children.

I don't have time to worry. I push away the intrusive thoughts. We continue into the unknown while the siren warns of the chemical attack. This is not a scene from a big-budget Hollywood movie. This is real, and it is happening now.

The siren becomes more frequent, and the unknown freezes every bone in our bodies. I shake from the inside. I have twenty girls who look up to me for answers, and I don't have any. I hold my breath and pretend I do.

Don't feel, Ella. Don't feel. Fear, get out!

Within a few minutes, we are in the sealed room. It is not a bunker but rather a big hallway turned into a place that might save us during a chemical attack. The windows are taped crisscross and heavy-duty tape along the sides – a precaution if the windows break and shatter. A bucket of water with baking soda is waiting next to the entryway. The soldier on duty dips towels in the simple baking soda solution and pastes them over the doorway's lower crack. In case of a chemical attack, we were promised that a wet rug and baking soda might save our lives.

We are not the only ones who run to shelters. The sealed rooms have been prepared in every home and on every military base across Israel. The war's preparation began a few months previously, as war with Iraq grew more and more likely. The infomercials flooded every TV station: where to get your gas mask according to the number on your identity card, what the best baking soda and tape to use is, and which room in the house is the best to turn into a sealed room. Within three days, nothing was left on the shelves. The resale market was saturated with high-priced baking soda and tape. Some vendors wrapped their baking soda in faux-Gucci packages and claimed it to be an exclusive life-saving powder. The price matched.

In the shelter, we sit on the floor, away from the windows. We don the full-face gas masks, snap the rubber straps tight, and check for any leaks. I can feel the bulky mask and its heavy filter below my chin. My vision is limited beneath the visor of the mask.

I breathe in and out, listening to the breathing of every girl in the room.

The siren stops.

Quiet.

Waiting.

Breathe in.

Breathe out.

Breathe in.

Breathe out.

My heart beats like the fastest train in the world, wild and reckless. There is no way to stop it.

The missiles are launched. The rockets fly above us in the air.

The silence is terrifying. We shiver in the cold.

Is it a gas attack?

A nation waits for the radio to announce the latest news. Millions of my fellow citizens. My family. My three sisters. My two baby brothers. Ten seconds. Twenty seconds. Thirty seconds.

Dead air.

Israeli intelligence puts every broadcast on thirty-second delays. This is a lifetime in military time.

Sitting on the floor, the thoughts about my two little brothers, whom I left at home, push their way through every square inch of my adrenalized heart. Infants cannot possibly put on gas masks, so each baby in the country has a tiny, crib-like mesh cube with a filter. Sam and Sasi are not babies, yet they're not big kids either.

How did they put on their masks? Are they safe? What did they do wrong to be born into such chaos? Maybe living in the Holy City will shield them?

I celebrated my nineteenth birthday only two months ago, and now I am here, on the floor, away from my family, away from my home, away from my bedroom and friends, waiting for the unknown.

This is all I know after graduating from high school, not yet eighteen years old. After much physical and cognitive testing, I was selected to serve in the Israeli Intelligence. No, I never jumped from a helicopter, I never spied on a famous ambassador, I never killed anyone. I was in a special unit comprised of carefully chosen soldiers every year: just twenty girls and two commanders. The first ten months of my service was spent studying, reviewing, and memorizing from six o'clock in the morning until ten o'clock at night, and sometimes until midnight. Our brains worked hard. Examinations, drills, and tests. Inserting more information into our little tiny cortex, engraving the data so it will be embedded for a lifetime. Twice a week, high prestige professors from an elite university joined the forces to drill more information, numbers, and facts than we could even perceive.

Four thirty-minute breaks, three for indulging, fattening meals, and one for quick rest time.

Twenty chosen female soldiers. Second-year into my service in the Israeli Intelligence. I wasn't stationed to do what I was trained for. With the completion of the course and receiving the honoree certificate, two soldiers were chosen to be the next year's course commander. One of them is me. Another stripe on my rank, and I am an eighteen-year-old commander. Here we go. I am doing the course all over again, but this time from a different angle. For two years, my home, the core center where we study, eat, and sleep is stunning from the outside. It is located on the shore of the Mediterranean Sea. Romantic views, wide blue sea, and a fresh breeze – if you look at it from the outside, you would want to run inside. But we wanted to run away. We were not allowed to walk close to the water or ever dip in the sea. Sleep-deprived and overloaded with information, we visited home once every other weekend.

We called it the Golden Cage.

I look around the room from the periphery of my visor and feel as if we are in an action or horror movie, but it is not. It is real, and it is happening right now.

I am holding back my tears. If I burst, then no one will be here to lead my twenty girls. Each one of them is staring at me, but I have no words for them. My worry oscillates between my girls and my boys.

◉

Tel Aviv, November 10, 1992

It's my twenty-first birthday—finally, no more boring, outdated green khaki outfits every single day. Now I can wake up in the morning and stare aimlessly at my tiny, almost empty closet, trying to figure out what to wear. I had missed those moments of trying every outfit in my wardrobe – piling shirts, pants, and dresses on the bed, indecisive of how I want to look. Three years of uniforms, a button-down shirt, high-waisted long trousers, and the rare option had taken a toll. The skirt rule was never to expose the knee, but we, the want-to-be mischievous soldier girls, cut it a bit above the knee to tease the military police officers in the central bus stations every other Friday we took the three buses home.

At the beginning of November, change has settled, and things have started to slow down. Yellow-orange auburn colors are everywhere, decorating every street. There's a sense that we're in-between seasons and in-between decisions. Even elections happen in November – enduring tradition, enduring transition. It's the season of packing away summer clothes and pulling out those long sleeve shirts from the top shelves. A thick duvet replaces a thin blanket. I am changing too.

In Israel, November is devoid of holidays. It is the only month without celebrations, except in my family. In November, we have three birthdays: my birthday and two sisters, Sharon and Libby. Libby's birthday is ten days before mine, and Sharon's ten days after mine. Every year, three times that month, we savored a multi-layered, personally decorated cake baked by Mom, blew out candles, and made wishes. We each got our cake – Scorpio girls wouldn't have it any other way. Three Scorpio sisters._

Most twenty-one-year-olds in the land of opportunity hit that epic birthday night in one of the local bars with childish heavy drinking, proving they can stay upright through yet another vodka shot without puking on the sidewalk. Why? Because their driver's license declares it must be so. Waking up late to stumble to a college class after a blackout in a dive bar is the celebrated rite-of-passage. The success of the celebration lies with the hangover. The more painful the hangover, the more they forgot about the night, the more they remember how impressive and glorious their twenty-first birthday was. But I was born in a different place where your special birthday comes three years earlier. Where I come from, eighteen changes everything.

By law, you are trained to hold what can kill you or another human being at eighteen. You get your license to carry a rifle. Dark khaki green becomes your wardrobe for two or three years, and sleep becomes a luxury. Your thick canvas army belt is marked with little squares colored-in with blue ink, counting down the months left in your service: twenty-four for women, thirty-six for men. Count it forwards, backward mark your wall calendar with every weekend you visit home. Savor those thirty-six hours you are at home – finally home – back in your childhood bed, clean and comfortable. Homemade food and family dinners, a Saturday to sleep in until noon, if your family will let you (they get so little time with you as it is). Your mom will cook up food that can feed an entire brigade. She believes you are a camel and can store the food in your body. You give two or three years of your life to your country. A time of complaining, of feeling miserable. Paradoxically, it is also the best time of your life. One day in the future, you realize that your time in service molded your personality and transformed your life forever.

"How many years did you serve?"

This is the first question curious people ask me. I could count the seconds in every conversation up to this question. Young men have to serve three years, and young women serve two. Everyone joins the military unless you get special permission because you are too religious, psychotic, or, for girls only, you are too committed as a wife. Then you are simply released, set free to live your life. You will miss one of the best and worst experiences on earth, one that will alter your life in the most profound and deep ways you could ever imagine.

I am now the boss of my own time. I was waking up when I want, working wherever I want (almost), eating what I want, and going to the bathroom without asking for permission. It's my life, my new life. Kindergarten, elementary school, high school, army: I've always gone to sleep and woken up on someone else's schedule. Who's in charge of my alarm clock now?

After three years of giving every day of my life to the Israeli Intelligence Service, I am free.

I am like a kid in a candy store who is allowed to get anything she wants but who leaves the store with only one little, yet familiar, candy in her hand. I am afraid to reach out for the unfamiliar candies on the top shelf. I was just released from Israeli Intelligence, and the choices are overwhelming. I soon miss my narrow, uncomfortable bed and the strict, daily routine. I miss Jenna, Petra, and Hannah, my best friends. I ate, slept next to, and cried for three years. I miss everything in my life, and all that doesn't exist anymore. Poof, just like that, in one day, it's over.

My first birthday without obligations. At least, in theory, I am completely uninhibited.

But my twenty-first birthday is much different. I have been a civilian for four months, and I am dating a man named Tony. We have both returned to civilian life in Israel. He returned after five years of living in New York, and I returned from three years of army service. Let's begin to live!

Four months ago, before celebrating my twenty-first birthday, two months before I was released from the service, I had met charming Tony. We met at one of the busy cafeterias. He stood out among the green patch of uniforms, clad in his chic civilian outfit. He made my cappuccino behind the counter with much attention, slowly frothing the milk, making sure it was fluffy and foamy. He snuck another cheeky stare at me with his ocean-blue eyes and know-it-all smile. I blushed.

"My coffee is the best! I'd like to prepare another one for you one day."

Macho Tony hands me a blank piece of white paper from the receipt roll and a pen which was next to the cash register. "Write down your phone number here."

Mumbling and embarrassed from his oh-so-direct-and-ballsy approach, I answer softly, "I don't give my phone number out, but, if you'd like, you can give me yours."

Uncle Ron taught me, "Be the one who has all the control." His dating principles were among the few things that I inherited from him, along with the Tiffany lamp.

While my friends waved me over and called me from the table, he finally handed me a coffee cup with a little note.

"You're hard to get. If you don't want to give out your phone number, here's mine. Call me, or I will chase you down."

A few months later, on my pivotal birthday, it hits me: *I've never rebelled.*

This thought seeps into my heart as I look for ways to celebrate this momentous birthday. Tony, my new cheerleader for all matters of rebellion, is sitting in front of me. He has a brilliant idea of how we can celebrate my twenty-first birthday. With his five additional laps around the sun over me, he gains my full attention.

The plan is a tattoo.

I've been Good Girl Jerusalem for twenty-one years, and it might be the time to break some rules finally.

My wannabe-rebellious-self decides, with the help of wannabe-badass Tony, to satisfy a desire which has been suppressed since my mid-teens.

Not only will my conservative mother be upset, judgmental, and feel ashamed of her failure as a mom, but I have also been legally forbidden from engraving words and pictures onto my body. For three years during my time in khaki uniforms, my body didn't belong to me. It was the property of the army. If one even tries to commit suicide and fails, they are charged with a felony for harming army property. You might survive a suicide attempt, but you will go to prison for a murder attempt.

It is decided. I will get a tattoo. I choose a colorful butterfly tattoo inked onto my left shoulder to replace my rank insignia. It substitutes responsibility with the illusion of freedom.

"Oww! It's painful," I whine like a little girl at the trendy, popular tattoo shop in Tel Aviv. Tony found this talented artist who is the hottest name in the city. They both tease me as I bite my tongue from the persistent and unbearable pain.

"C'mon, Ms. Commander, you can do this!" The buzzing needle goes in and slices through my skin.

Bzzzz.

"This is just a tiny butterfly on your shoulder."

I sink into the reclining chair, ink all over my shoulder. The needle is puncturing my skin like a sewing machine. *Maybe I should get up and run out.* I freeze up. I can vividly see my mom upset, furious, and disappointed that I disrespected my Good Girl Jerusalem, holy body.

"Ella! When you die, you will be buried in the outskirts of the cemetery along with crazy people and the poor ones who took their lives!" My mother lectures me in my head. And I believe her. There is a tradition, not always observed, that those with tattoos cannot be buried in a Jewish cemetery.

The needle keeps buzzing, bringing to life first one wing, then another – bright blue and gleaming pink.

Hey, life, I am bursting forth from my cocoon.

I have the illusion that I have been reborn. I don't feel different today; twenty-one and a day feel exactly like the day before – except for the sharp pain on my shoulder. Tony and I ended the night early, as neither of us felt much like partying.

Early the next morning, I go back to studying for the university's entrance exams. I sit on the sofa, burying my head in the dauntingly thick books and jammed notebooks: math, logic questions, and English. My head spins from trying to remember all the sequences and complex reasoning.

Tony comes home. I am excited about the excuse for a break. I hear his jingling keys on the table. "Ella! I have a surprise for you!"

"Surprise? Is it still my birthday?" Tony knows my weakness for surprises.

But it was yesterday, I think quietly. *If the guy surprises you, just accept it,* I answer back to myself.

Tony comes into the living room and makes his way through the forest of books and binders. He gives me a big soft kiss on the lips, accidentally leaning into me harder than I can handle.

"Ouch! My tattoo," I want my surprise more than the kiss now, "What is it?"

Tony stands up in front of me, looking like nothing so much as a proud young bear. He has the shiny eyes of a child who cannot hide a secret anymore.

"Yeees?" I ask again.

"OK," he says. "Are you ready?"

I roll my eyes upwards, impatiently.

Tony slowly lifts his white t-shirt sleeve. He reveals a three-inch-wide white bandage on his bicep. I am confused. He peels back the tape and reveals a fresh sailor tattoo: a red heart and a ribbon under it, with the words, "Just you, Ella."

I stare at him at first, and then my eyes dart back to his arm. I re-read the tattoo: "Just you..." and then... "Ella."

Tony is smiling from ear to ear, waiting for me to jump on him with admiration and gratitude for this heroic gesture. I say nothing. My heart sinks to the floor, and all I want to say is, "you're crazy!" but my words don't come out. Even my butterfly wants to go back into its cocoon.

It's too much. Tony, the books, the exam papers, the tattoo, my name on someone else's body.

He didn't even ask me. I stare.

That's my name on him! I blink.

How many Ellas do I even know? Not many.

I belong to me, not to anyone else. I stand stiff. My thoughts race.

I am not a supermarket barcode. I sigh.

Tony sits in front of me, waiting for my reaction. We live together in this sweet little apartment in Tel Aviv we have subleased from a relative. We moved here a few weeks ago, as another rebellious impulse told me to not return to my Good-Girl-city. It is already furnished with someone else's taste – the bed, the sofas, even the plants. It is not my smell, not my feeling, not me. Three weeks, and I don't feel connected to my new home. I miss the stiff bed in the army. That was my home for three years. The little window, the narrow cabinet, and my nightstand. It was what I knew. What I crave now in this extraordinary, unfamiliar, eerie apartment in Tel Aviv is what I know as familiar – the one color, a simple and predictable life. I look at Tony, his blue eyes begging for validation. I can't find the words to tell him how I am not flattered. I am confused, scared, surprised, and upset. He didn't even ask me.

"Just you, Ella."

Suddenly, I stand up. I put on my flip flops next to the front door and grab the keys. I wish we had a dog to walk, I think to myself. That would be the best excuse to leave this show.

Restless and unable to grasp what had just happened, I take a walk through my upscale neighborhood in Northern Tel Aviv. In Israel, Jerusalem is religious, serious, and conservative; Tel Aviv, an hour's drive away, is progressive, secular, and wild. This is the time for Good Girl Jerusalem to be the last of these before starting studies at Hebrew University in my hometown.

My mind is swimming between the two cities – and the two tattoos—one with wings and one with chains.

It is a November evening in Tel Aviv. In Jerusalem, it is already so cold you cannot take a walk without bundling up, but here I am in a t-shirt and shorts, exposing my body to a city in which you can do anything.

Anything, including engraving your girlfriend's name onto your body, without her permission.

I can smell the Mediterranean. It is not familiar. In Jerusalem, we smell the mountains, the cold earthy breeze. I hear dogs and televisions from various apartments in the old buildings along the streets. Trying to forget what had just happened, I make up stories about other people's lives, and I play the game of deciding whose life I want to lead: the woman on the balcony who hangs the wet laundry on the lines, the cello player on the second floor, the married couple who are fighting over who will take the dogs for a walk, or the single mom who is feeding her son dinner, waiting for a few moments to herself.

I collect sounds and connect them to stories of lives foreign to me in the Holy City.

Ouch. The burning sensation on my shoulder.

Aimlessly, I stop by the local kiosk and buy a cold drink, my favorite black licorice candy, and roasted almonds to numb the pain. I add the daily newspaper, which was next to the cashier, as well. Maybe, I joke grimly to myself, and my tattoo story made it in the news.

I find a bench on my way home. I sit on it, staring into the night. I am not sure if I like this city. I notice that this neighborhood has no kids. Maybe the local kids are sent to the Holy City before they sin. I open the paper and read about the government, about someone in prison, and the weather. I browse the horoscope and try to fill the crossword puzzle in my mind. I turn the pages over and read even more boring stories about people I don't want to be like. The prime minister. A CEO. A renowned scientist. A celebrated lawyer. Page after dull page.

I realize I have missed the front page. I fold over the grey paper, and I see a picture. A soldier. Handsome. Dirty blond hair, sassy eyes, a mischievous smile. I read further, "An IDF soldier was seriously wounded in an ambush by a Fatah cell in the Gaza Strip."

"The Terrorist lurked in the dark and severely wounded a Givati Brigade Soldier. [The Soldier] was sent into The Gaza Strip, on the outskirts of Khan Younis, on a special mission. He volunteered to replace his friend who was sick on that mission. His commanding officer ordered

him to uncover a hidden terrorist tunnel, painted with camouflage colors on his face and a full outfit to hide each inch of his body. Close to the mission's end, a terrorist lurked and shot [the soldier] in the back. One-shot, straight through his body. He is in critical condition. His family is with him. [The soldier] is fighting for his life and being supported by a respirator."

The words stun me. Here I am, on the Mediterranean coast, sitting on a bench, whining about the painful punctures on my skin, "wounds" I had volunteered to receive. While I was complaining about how my new tattoo was burning under the white bandage, trying not to touch the gauze the artist taped down on my birthday, a helicopter was evacuating this soldier to a hospital. He was fighting for every breath. While I was getting happy birthday phone calls, his family was getting the one phone call they dreaded most.

This soldier became a hero in a split millisecond of his life. I wonder to myself, why is it that heroes' names are never mentioned when the mission is successful? Only when they get hurt or killed, do we read their names in the next day's paper. We remember we cry, and we cherish; we hold them in our hearts. They make the headlines, but only until the next hero gets hurt or dies.

I look back at his picture in the newspaper. Under the soldier's picture is his name, Adam, and his home city, Jerusalem.

Quit giving other people the status of your Higher Power.

Time seems to be the same on every watch, clock, or smartphone. The day of the week is the same, so is the month, the year. It might be tomorrow in Bangkok and yesterday in Hawaii, but those are just artificial ways of organizing time. There is something more real than the clock.

Do you have a one-of-a-kind friend from childhood or your teens? The kind whom you might not see for 20 years, and then pick up a conversation as if you'd never left? That's a friendship that transcends time. What you may not realize is your life is a collection of billions of moments. Some we remember and can describe like it just happened, and some are quickly forgotten in the deep mud of illusory time. We demand the painful moments pass more rapidly than they do; we beg that the joyous ones linger. Because we give in to the lie of time, we rarely get either wish granted. Nonetheless, we treat time like Play-Doh, stretching it to the limit before it breaks or rolling it quickly into a thick ball, trying to erase whatever shape it took before.

They say time heals: heals mourning, separation, pain. Separation is like surgery. At first, it hurts.

"Nurse, nurse!" You scream, needing comfort, needing more meds.

You think the pain will never go away; you will never be able to forget and live your life like before. It is too much to handle. The next week you are released from the hospital and, though the pain is not as acute, you can still not move. Days go by, and then a tiny beige bandage replaces the thick white dressings. You feel a bit better. Then years go by, and someone notices your scar. They ask you about it, and it's as if you've forgotten.

Chapter 6

The Illusion of Time

Zain. Mem. Nun. .ז.מ.נ

Time זמן • Order •הזמנה Available זמין •Invite הזמין • Invitation הזמנה
Invitation הזמנה • Long time מזמן • Available זמין

◉

Jerusalem, 1995

I broke my promise to Sasi and Sam.

A few of my favorite clothes, only one of my childhood photo albums, my three favorite books, my credentials, my BA certification, and my working visa to get into the United States, the Land of Opportunity. I had stuffed two suitcases with what would remind me of the best of the first twenty-two years of my life. I packed and unpacked, calculating what I could cram in only fifty pounds. All packed and condensed, waiting to be popped into the new nest in an unknown land.

I was afraid, the day after I land, I will start teaching high schoolers Hebrew. I will be teaching this foreign, sacred language to twenty-five hormonal teens, 8,000 miles away from home. I wonder if it would be the same as teaching Arabic to teens in Israel. My love of languages and my enjoyment of watching how people learn a new way of expressing themselves are saving me from the drama.

I didn't want to live my mom's life anymore.

The checkered pouch and the white ribbed boy's tank top. I remembered two more items.

I made room in the suitcase for two more things that I could never leave behind. I still have them today in my drawers in my bedroom. I take them out from time to time, smell them, touch them, and know that, even though I broke my promise, I can never break this love.

The first is a square, handmade, red and white checkered pouch with green heart embroidery that reads "It's a boy." When I was in fourth grade, the boys in our school went to carpentry class while the girls went to sewing class. The teacher gave us the freedom to create whatever we wanted, as long as we did it all with our hands. After four girls, the anticipation in my family with my mom's pregnancy was immense. Everyone tried to guess the new baby's gender. While I was sewing the special gift during every arts and crafts class, I prayed to have a baby brother. If it were a boy, perhaps my dad would stay with us forever. I stitched two little hearts, on one embroidering the words "Mom and Dad," and on the other, "Baby Boy." I tried to convince the Universe that four girls and the accompanying feminine chaos were enough in my family. My wish came true; my mother was pregnant with Sam.

In another jammed suitcase, I also packed a tiny, white, ribbed boys' tank top. This was Sasi's.

As I was out the door to go to my linguistics class, the landline rang.

Even though I left home to study at the university, my mother still called me when she needed me, especially the boys. When I was in my first year at the university, Sasi was already in the third grade. "Sasi has been suspended from school!" my mom's frantic voice was on the other end.

"Suspended?!" I was perplexed. I need to solve it quickly and hang up.

"Yes, for three days!" My mom continued.

Not quite expelled but suspended. Still, what could an eight-year-old boy possibly do to be suspended from elementary school?

I somehow found my mature, relaxed, responsible voice and asked my mother to explain what happened. I was mostly trying to calm her down.

Mom's voice was rushed, upset, and worried. She told me that the teacher called her at work. I wasn't sure if she was embarrassed or clueless about what to do with Sasi.

"Sasi's teacher called me five minutes ago. Sasi broke her glasses!" My mom was furious.

"Broke her glasses?" I still couldn't believe this nonsense.

The mother continued explaining what happened and what she thought should have happened. She was worried about Sasi. He was her baby, the source of so much anxiety, especially with his ADHD. She would always drop her tone and whisper that diagnosis.

Sasi's diagnosis added to my mom's worries and feelings of victimhood. Her life story got more complicated and compelling with this diagnosis. Unlike today, ADHD was not a common diagnosis. If today having ADHD and ADD, or any other lettered disorder, will make you unique, back then, it was a black mark, a cloud on your record, and a reason for the teacher to send you out of class.

One day, after a long day of classes at the Hebrew University, I came back to my little rented studio apartment in Jerusalem, and I saw the red light blinking on the answering machine. Mother left me a message, "You see, your brother, only trouble! What should I do with him? You have to help me; I cannot deal with him anymore! I am all by myself since your dad left me." That was her mantra when she was upset. She was alone.

Sasi, wearing the label of Attention-Deficit/Hyperactivity Disorder, matched his outrage by stomping dramatically out of the classroom. His third-grade teacher kicked him out of the class because he was misbehaving. I am not sure who was more furious, the teachers or Sasi. Sasi left the class, ADHD style, with an immense desire to be unforgettable; he slammed the door behind him. In this unfortunate moment, the teacher was standing in the doorway, and the results were a teacher with broken glasses, a suspended third grader, and a miserable mom. Mom sent him to me so I would teach him the consequences.

For the next three days, we prepared dinner together, drew fun pictures, and laid down on my patio grass to talk about our dreams. We laughed and sang. We were in the moment, bonded, creating secrets just between us.

Flight to LAX, September 5, 1995

"Are you OK?" the kind, the immaculate flight attendant asks me for the third time.

My mind returns to the long flight.

"Do you need anything?"

She brings me tissues, a cup of water, and offers me another pillow. Nothing helps. I cannot stop the muffled cries. I am choking with tears and sadness. I already miss my country, my home, and especially Sam and Sasi. I cannot put down the two pictures, and they stay in my hands this entire flight. One photo is of Sam, the other of Sasi. I read and reread their sweet notes on the back of the photographs, and I burst into tears each time. Pure childish handwriting that ends with "I already miss you, and I love you, my big sister." More tears gush out. I feel like someone separates me from my kids, and I am not even a mom yet.

The helpless flight attendant comes again.

Eleven hours from TLV to JFK, I sob.

Five hours from JFK to LAX, I cry quietly.

I left them.

I broke my promise. But I found something new. I discovered my life. I broke free from my mom's dependency; I broke free from the chains of someone else's pain. At least just for a short time.

The United States, November 1995

It is the beginning of November. Change has settled, and things have started to slow down... Yellow-orange auburn colors are everywhere, decorating every street. There's a sense that we're in-between seasons and in-between decisions. Even elections happen in November – enduring tradition, enduring transition. It's the season of packing away summer clothes and pulling out those long sleeve shirts from the top shelves. A thick duvet replaces a thin blanket.

After two months in the land of opportunity, I feel isolated. It costs almost four dollars per minute to call back home. Everything, except for my dreams, is in English. After so much disorientation, I am excited to meet two new Israeli friends who had arrived in Los Angeles a few months before I arrived. These new friends have invited me to Shabbat dinner on a Friday night.

"It is Adam's birthday," Ethan told me on the phone. "Come, celebrate with us."

Not only am I excited about meeting two new friends from my hometown, but this coming Friday is my birthday as well. And just like that, I turned my birthday from a lonely Friday night, sadly missing my family and friends, into an exciting surprise. These are my first two friends in America.

I volunteer, "I'll bake the cake."

I bake an airy, sweet, vanilla cake. I cut it into two equal halves and separate the halves with a big plate. Lovingly, I spread whipped cream onto one half and spread it with fresh sliced strawberries. Before I lay down all the strawberries, I carefully drizzle them with brandy. It's my mom's top baking secret. I lay the second half on top of the strawberries, making sure all the edges are matching, and the cake is stable on the white cake plate. I whip the rest of the cream with vanilla pudding and vanilla extract. The aroma is divine. Lastly, I smother the cake's surface with vanilla frosting and decorate it with little flowers I have designed with my pastry bag. I write in fancy handwriting, "Happy Birthday!" and put it in the fridge to cool down.

My hair smells like brandy and vanilla, and my heart is filled with anticipation and excitement. I'm like a young girl going to her first movie.

It's Friday night. I put on the most beautiful dress I have – one I had brought with me from Israel. With a new song in my mind, I drive myself, the birthday cake, and a salad in my old Ford to see my friends.

I knock on the door, and Ethan answers. He invites me into their small bachelor pad.

"Adam is getting ready in the back room," he tells me. It is a sparse apartment. There is hardly any furniture, no carpets or rugs, no pictures on the walls. It looks like they just moved in a few days before. On the other hand, I am excited to see the kitchen is full of life – pots and pans with bubbling delicacies on the stove, cooking spoons dripping with sauces, spices lined on the counter, and bunches of colorful vegetables ready to be washed. It may not look like a home, but it sounds and smells like home.

Ethan makes some space for my ready-to-be-deservedly-complimented cake on his counter. Ethan is fit, slender, clean-cut, handsome, and has a little dimple. We chat with his back towards me. He takes out a dish from the oven, peels back the tin foil, and puts it back again. The aroma tingles my nose and knocks at my heart.

Loud noises were coming from the other room.

"Is the princess here, yet?" Adam, with a dazzling smile, rolls himself out from the other room in his wheelchair.

He stretches to give me a big warm hug from his chair. He wheels towards the kitchen and parks himself in the spot where a chair is missing from around the small square table. I then noticed there are only three chairs around the table. For a second, I feel embarrassed, ashamed, and awkward.

Do I need to feel sorry for him? How do you behave with a handicapped person? I need to watch my words not to say the wrong thing.

Within a few moments, Adam is making us all laugh. He's got sparkling green eyes, a big smile, dirty blond hair – and a dirtier mouth.

"Did you make this cake? May I get the recipe before I eat it, just in case they ask what I ingested if I get food poisoning?"

We all laugh hysterically at his sarcastic jokes. Adam is sharp, direct, straightforward, and hilarious. Immediately, his sass and charisma become the center of our dinner.

I completely forget about the three chairs, the two big wheels, and my one lonely heart.

I feel my heart belongs somewhere again. The food, the conversation, the inside jokes among three ex-pats who miss their Holy City. We talk about high school friends we may all know, gossip about old teachers, and laugh about the endless varieties of bread in the US. We eat Ethan's delicious food. I am astonished at his cooking skills, yet Adam teases him about adding too much pepper. He finds amusement in everything, or maybe this is how he shows his gratitude.

Adam and Ethan explain why they've come to Los Angeles for only six months. They didn't come to Beverly Hills for pleasure, take pictures next to the Hollywood sign, or read names on the Hollywood Walk of Fame. They didn't come for the enjoyment of Disneyland, Big Bear, or Six Flags. They didn't come to The United States to work and save money or start studying in one of the universities. Ethan and Adam have come to America because Adam was shot in his back in that Gaza tunnel.

A world-renowned doctor has offered Adam an experimental treatment so he might be able to walk again. His best friend has come to accompany him on what may be a miraculous journey. In one more month, the experiment, and the budget, will be over. It will be time to return home.

Adam tells me that, for weeks after he was shot, his life hung in the balance. He was sustained by machines, fighting every day to survive. Finally, during Chanukah, he was out of danger. By all accounts, his survival is a miracle.

Adam says he was reborn on the day he was shot, November 10, 1992.

I pause.

Adam. Suddenly, I remember.

The dirty blond soldier on the cover of the newspaper on the brown bench.

I feel goosebumps all over my body. I gently touch my tattoo. I've had it for three years. On the same day, Adam got a hero's medal, and I got my butterfly wings.

Loudly and with great silliness, we sing happy birthday and cut the strawberry-filled vanilla cake. I celebrate my birthday, and Adam celebrates his rebirth. He compounds it into his new English word, *injury-birthday.*

Leaves fall from the trees, and the late autumn of California forces us to wear light sweaters, while in Jerusalem, our families are wrapped in thick coats. Adam, Ethan, and I become a family far from home. For a few weeks, we spend our evenings together. My apartment isn't set up for hosting an army hero in a wheelchair, so we spend most of our time at Adam and Ethan's apartment. We give each other roles. I am the loving mom, Adam is the stern father, and Ethan is our child. I call him my son. Like a close family, we enjoy what life has provided for us. We splurge on pizza delivery. We watch *Dumb and Dumber* and other comedies.

It is December, and nothing is the same. Adam's treatments are coming to an end. My family is leaving, and I desperately want them to stay. I pray for a miracle that might keep us together.

I have been away from everything I had known for three months now. Exotic a cappella carols about the birth of Jesus play endlessly in stores and pharmacies, along with inexplicable songs about talking snowmen and flying reindeer. Cheerful jingle bells announce that this is the merriest time of the year. Fake-bearded men in fat red suits sit in public places, listen to children on the knee, and promise presents for good – with threats of black coal for the naughty. Fir trees, many of which are fake, are stuffed from floor to ceiling into family rooms, wrapped in ribbons, fancy balls, and blinking multicolored lights. Impossibly large presents are stacked all around the tree trunks. Houses in neighborhoods, rich and poor, are decorated with glowing plastic Santas, plastic deer, plastic sleds, plastic elves, and plastic blankets of glistening snow. Dishes are left out, piled with gooey chocolates and sugary treats, and dazzling Hallmark cards are proudly displayed around fireplaces and along the mantles. It's a bewildering welcome to my first American Christmas.

I grew up only a few miles from where Jesus was born, in what we call Bethlehem. His holy legacy seems forgotten through the visual overload of countless infomercials and exciting advertisements. Everything is bright, gaudy, and full of shiny bric-a-brac, as seen in the 99 Cents Store and discarded after the holidays into the bins at Goodwill. This is not how I remember the Christmas celebrations in Jerusalem. Where did the reverence go?

It will be Chanukah soon, and I stop on my way home to purchase a new Hanukkiah from CVS so that Ethan, Adam, and I can light the Hanukkiah before they fly back to Israel.

"Your menorah is twenty-one dollars and twelve cents."
Menorah?

In The United States, people do not know that the Menorah has seven branches for Jerusalem's seven hills. A Hanukkiah is different and has nine candle holders, eight for the eight days of the miracle, and one tall one to light them all.

I park my car in the underground parking lot of my building and take the elevator upstairs, considering whether I should ask for a miracle from either Santa or the Maccabi. I just don't want these boys to leave.

I find Ethan waiting for me next to my door with his motorcycle, helmet in his hand, wearing a white t-shirt and blue jeans. I wonder what he's doing there in the middle of the day.

"Oh, my son, you missed mommy?" I joke with Ethan, taking on my now-familiar role to cover my sadness that my pretend-dad-and-son are leaving soon. I am an expert in protecting my emotions, shoving them down, so no one will notice that my heart is breaking.

He hesitates. "I have a favor to ask of you."

"I would do anything for you, my son."

And this is how Ethan came to live with me for a few weeks.

Adam's treatments are over, he returns to Israel immediately after Chanukah. Ethan stays behind in America for a few weeks, looking for work to make a little money. I share my small apartment with my so-called-son, making him as comfortable as he can be on my blue sofa. Though it is not the same as when we were all together, Ethan and I are quite the duo. We share stories about work, our yearning for love, and our homesickness. I feel so grateful for Ethan and the unexpected joy of our thrilling friendship. I remind myself that great friendships are miracles.

One day, Ethan's fairytale comes to life. A tall, red-haired gorgeous model from New York City comes to visit the City of Angels. After the briefest and most spectacular of romances, she whisks my "son" away to Sin City, and, in Las Vegas, they sell colorful, delicious sweet ice cream, snow cones, and popsicles from their melodious ice cream truck.

Los Angeles, 1996

My mom was right. English classes were what I needed. But I still wanted to dance.

Searching *the L.A. Weekly*, I finally found it! After years of practicing only in my mind, I was finally going to take my first real dance class at twenty-five years old—Hip-hop for adults. For years, my dance moves were kept to Bar Mitzvahs and wedding dance floors or going out with friends dancing in dark, crowded, smoky clubs. This is my first ever formal dance class. I purchased high leggings with a short shirt barely covering my belly. I put on my best tennis shoes and drive to my first class. Like looking at an art piece for the first time, I enter the studio. Dozens of other dancers were chatting, laughing, stretching on the wood floor. I pretend that I know how to stretch, placing my water bottle next to the wall, away from the tall wall mirror.

The teacher comes in with a big smile, "Who's new?" she yells. I don't raise my hand.

The cheery, energetic, peppy instructor instructs the class with hand motions I don't understand. She taps her head once, and everyone starts from the beginning. *Lock. Pop. Knee Drop.* I am clueless. I feel as if someone poured concrete over my feet. I try to follow the instructor and her exact directions and steps, but she is too fast. I'm embarrassed; I know I have it in me, but my body will not obey. It seems as if the other dancers have been dancing since they were little girls, going with their moms to dance recitals in lavender leotards or pink tutus. I had only ever danced in my imagination.

Until the long-awaited concerts.

I saved my pennies to see Madonna every time she came to town. Before every concert, I got ready for what used to be only in my fantasies. The stage, performance, dancers, background, and crowd – the entire experience captured my soul, body, and mind. Expensive jewelry, gold watches, and luxury brand name purses are far down my priority list, well below concert tickets. I collect my tickets in a stub jar. At first, one, then two, then another concert. I soon add another breath-taking artist to my sweet addiction. The jar sits proudly in my living room, collecting the paper stubs like roses. I water them every season with fresh tickets, curating my memories.

I let my body flow. After a few formal hip-hop dance classes, I gave in. I experimented with street salsa, cumbia, samba, house music, and techno moves. I trip and fall and get up and *Get into the Groove* again. This is how I eventually discovered freestyle dancing. There, I could practice the moves I learned on the bus rides without anyone to correct me. I was dancing freely to my music, letting my body *Justify My Love*.

The only thing we have to fear is fear itself.

Everyone has fear in their lives; though well-hidden at times, it can lash out with mighty power. Fear and doubt can beat you to the ground, even when you cannot name your fear. What is your fear? What is the one thing you would like to do most, the thing that lies on the other side of the fence, guarded by the demon of doubt and anxiety?

Trust. Trust Yourself. Follow Your inner voice. Follow its advice. It will lead you somewhere.

When you have nothing to lose, you dare. You wear your shining armor and do precisely what you believe in without the thought of what others will do, act, or say to inhibit you. You refuse to be afraid.

Recall the moment when you dared to do something you rarely did. You entirely and blindly trusted yourself on a subject about which you knew so little. You did not ask for help, advice, or an opinion. You trusted yourself and my universe one hundred percent.

If you cannot trust yourself, you will be led towards chaos, heartbreak, and pain if you ignore that inner voice and disregard its advice.

Even though the road may be downright terrifying at times, the final destination is fulfillment, love, and wholeness.

Chapter 7

Secret Thrills

Samech. Vav. Dalet. .ד.ו.ס

Secret סוד • Secretive סודי • Soda סודה

◉

West Hollywood, 1997

The plain, gray 20-inch Zenith Television is placed perfectly on the living room's glass cabinet as an art exhibit. The remote control next to it, untouched.

My infatuation with <u>Love Boat</u> was short-lived. After I cracked my fourth-grade social connections, it lost any real interest. Even today, at twenty-six years old, I am still not watching much TV, not even my show. I am starring as a news anchor in a weekly Hebrew-language cultural program on the infamous, rarely watched channel 18. It is a project sponsored by an Israeli multi-millionaire to – as I will learn in the future – cover and launder his porn videotaping operations. Taping the weekly news interests me more than actually watching it. Half an hour of sitting still in front of the glass tube seems like a monumental waste of time.

My 700-square-foot, two-bedroom apartment is my center of love, my center of wisdom, peace, and creativity. This is the first place I have all to myself. I'm not sharing it with five younger siblings, or 59 other girls in army training, or another commander in a tent, or roommates, or a boyfriend, or anyone else. It's my party, and I'll paint if I want to!

Every room has a wall painted with a declaration of color, its personality calling from the wood, from the cement. Rolling up my sleeves, I am a secret artist, rushing back and forth to the local paint store to buy brushes and gallon-size buckets of every exciting color I can imagine. The walls are a riotous celebration of Henri Matisse, Pablo Picasso, and Andy Warhol.

Let me guide you into my masterpiece. Close your mind's eye. Hold my hand. Come with me. Enjoy your VIP tour. There are no stairs, only one step. Follow me. Take a deep breath. Open yourself to my vision.

The entrance opens into the living room, also the sitting room and reading area: the main wine-red wall and a wisely neglected TV. Look over here! A large window with its '80s vertical, wide-blade blinds from floor to ceiling to hide the curiosity of anyone who walks in the outside walkway. Peep inside. This is my private space. This is for me and you. An old air-conditioning unit hums its droning song, making the place relaxed and comfortable during the summer months. Books line the walls, expanding my mind as I visit other worlds and times. The scent is fresh, always crisp like clean linen, sweet as vanilla.

Come, see the dining area, my white galley kitchen. This dining table has many stories to tell, stories I'll never quite know. I inherited the only piece of furniture from the previous tenants the day I moved to L.A. two years ago: a brown, dull old table. But it has a history of its own, remembering all the dishes and plates and cups and glasses that it held up so faithfully. It witnessed Thanksgiving dinners and family discussions I will never know. To balance out the table's heavy memories, I painted the wall yellow, always following the sun: warmth, light, love.

Come now, and peek into my office/guest room.

My seven-hundred-dollars rent (a third of my salary) was a splurge that provided me with an extra room. For this room, I declared, "Green!"

I had searched for its shades and tones, but I had a hard time settling on which green I want most. The neighbor's grass, an army uniform, American money, my Green Card? Or the greenery within me, a fresh soul in this world?

I paint it in a light pastel green to remind me of the softness beneath this city's concrete, where the angels sometimes hide, Los Angeles. While I paint this room, a tiny feeling of homesickness seeps in. I kick it with a brush.

"Move along now. This is my home!" I repeated it aloud, fearing that the missing of my family, my Holy City, my country would show on the brush strokes on the walls forever.

My office/guest room has a twin bed and a narrow desk. A monochrome monitor with a DOS personal computer waits for me to create and connect the large gray tower. It takes up the entire desk, giving me access to ICQ chat rooms with their cute green and pink flowers, an online and offline connection to other colorful rooms in the world.

In between the two bedrooms sits my twenties-style bathroom. Charming, elegant, small white tiles. Soft towels, matching bathroom set, and fragrant cleaners. An always-sparkling mirror to look deeply into the soul. Charming, elegant, small white tiles.

This bathtub is used only for showers. The faucets need replacing. The pipes are rusty, and the idea of a relaxing, luxurious bath always ends up as a fleeting thought, too time-consuming to indulge in, like a spa brochure in a pile of bills.

Are you ready to enter my sanctuary? Here is my bedroom.

You are in my real world.

Take off your judgmental shoes, please. And pause.

Blue.

My favorite color in the world. Not the usual blue. Sapphire blue. The blue created in the sky and the deep ocean in the fleeting moments of night changes into day and day into night—that blue when you can still notice the stars.

I didn't just paint my bedroom. I composed it stroke by stroke with brushes, sponges, towels, with many shades of blue. Some I made by mixing colors, and some I purchased. I even dared to slip into my shopping basket one shade of neon blue.

I have a little UV fluorescent light on the floor that illuminates neon blue streaks at night. Every corner of my bedroom becomes a part of this big vast sky-ocean: the wood closets, the ceiling, all the frames, and the moldings. To be here is to dive, to swim, to fly over the deepest ocean with the stars, the moon, and the clouds for witnesses. They are all a part of my creation in a tiny 700-square-foot, two-bedroom castle.

My castle.

This castle sees me through two-and-a-half serious relationships. It sees me falling in love, heartbreaks, and falling in love again.

This castle watches as I sit up late with thick, consuming books and yellow highlighters through sleepless nights of graduate school.

This castle welcomes eclectic friends coming in and out, in high heels, with ties, with Indian baggy pants. They carry flutes and drums, bottles of wine and new CDs. We dance late into the wild nights.

This castle knows all about the diets, the workouts, the periodic attempts to be a vegetarian.

This castle witnessed three years of people coming in and out like a time-lapse scene in strobe lighting.

And, one day, a knock on my door. Ben, my landlord, is younger than me by a few years. His dad purchased him this six-plex, and he lives in one of the apartments. I open the door. Ben, blond, bright-eyed, muscular, clean-cut, always happy young kid. I am trying to remember if it is already the first of the month. I'm never late paying my rent.

Ben has never given me a personal visit before.

"I am selling the building," he tells me, sharing his big secret. I suspect his dad had purchased him a more significant property.

"Do your homework," he adds, "and don't share it with the other neighbours."

I am the oldest tenant here. When Ben and his dad purchased the building, I was the only tenant who stayed.

"Just be prepared; someone will come in the next few months and talk to you about the eviction."

Eviction? That's a little harsh.

Wearing his typical white t-shirt, he explains with his permanent smile, "The structure will need to come down, making room for a newer, more modern building."

I close the door and sit alone with the news. Looking around my castle, my heart aches – I do not want to let anyone stop my party. I feel like I am losing everything I have built up, like a defeated kingdom losing its castle. *Not my home! Not my Castle!*

I quietly go to the spot I feel safest. I lie on my bed, letting my sky-ocean room cuddle with me. I let the clouds, the waves, and the endless blue shelter hold me safe.

No one will end my party, not like this. I fall asleep, promising my walls that I will be there for them, that I will find a way to save them.

The next day, I wake up feeling a bit stronger, like Wonder Woman, with indestructible bracelets and my Lasso of Truth. Determined to find an answer, I drove to the library. I am in graduate school, but this time it is not for homework. I research all the keywords, "eviction," "breaking lease," "rent control West Hollywood," "demolishing the building," even "giving up my castle." I open huge old books with thin paper and small print in language and terms I don't understand. More books, more indices, searching, more searching, hour after hour. I am clueless. I am tired, and my body is exhausted from looking for a solution. The lights in the library start to dim. And there it was, so simple, so clear. I found my answer: Black and white.

If a tenant complains about anything within six months prior to eviction, the landlord must fix the problem before the eviction date.

Bang! I want to jump up and down on every table and dance on the library desks, twirl on the shelves, but then the serious librarian approaches me with a serious look.

"Ma'am, we are closing."

My gloriously rusty pipes, once a thorn in my side, has saved me, saved my walls, saved my castle.

From that library visit onward, without fail, I write firm yet polite messages on every rent check, "The pipes in the bathroom are rusty, please fix." Every first of the month, I made sure my request on the check can be read from any angle.

"The pipes in the bathroom are rusty; please fix."

This is my castle, and no one will demolish my walls!

Two months later, Ben and two families move out. After a few days of moving tracks in our small driveway with boxes, beds, and sofas flying in and away, the long-anticipated moment arrives. The important Broker comes to meet me with a serious speech. He cites rules in real estate language that few can understand. He declares that I have under a month to leave the place and that he will grant me the mind-blowing sum of $1,000, just to "ease the aggravation." The low amount stuns and amuses me at the same time.

The Broker is arrogant and dismissive, repeatedly looking down at his watch, making sure I know that I am rudely wasting his precious time. He loses his patience. He takes out a folder with documents and continues.

"Please sign here," pointing at one of the pages, "so we can hand you the check the day you move out." He doesn't even make eye contact with me.

The mischievous kid inside me becomes excited. I look at him defiantly and say, "Well, the law requires that you pay two thousand dollars."

The Broker clears his throat and replies, "We can talk about it later, but first sign this document. I think we are very generous with you."

It is time to drop the bomb. A very rusty bomb.

"What about the pipes? They are rusty and need to be fixed before I move out." I smile. I know he'll know what this means.

The Broker turns pale. He does not let me finish my sentence.

"You see, ma'am, we are demolishing the building. What difference does it make?" He starts to mutter. I can tell he wants to leave my colorful party. He wants only one thing, my signature.

He's not going to get it.

He walks away empty-handed. There is no check in the works—just rusty pipes in my very colorful castle.

The following weeks are filled with visits from the Broker. The Broker brings his beige folder and promises me a few extra hundred dollars on top of the original thousand every visit.

My answer is always, "Please fix the pipes."

His reaction swings from frustration to anger to embarrassment and back again. He is getting bombarded with impatient memos by the new landlord. I am a tiny and aggravating pebble inside his cheap, tight shoes. My signature might as well be in gold ink.

I am living in this six-plex by my happy lonesome self. All the other tenants are gone, evicted with some tiny, inadequate payment as consolation. The builders start breaking some of the walls in the back of the building and taking out the windows. The building is soon naked. They slowly reveal the innards of the building. It is just me, my bright walls, and my brave fortress, which are now under siege.

Summer turns to fall. Halloween is upon us. Half a million superheroes, zombies, and sexy pirates are about to walk down Santa Monica Boulevard in West Hollywood for the annual carnival, the largest Halloween party in America. Having fun and being crazy is the easy part. But parking? That's a lot trickier.

Michele comes to visit my fortress. She sees the crowds and hears the craziness and the car horns. As she always did, she comes up with a clever, creative, irresistible idea.

"Let's make money!" she says with her little kid's eyes.

"We have what is in high demand for that night: parking. Parking spaces which are bare and empty and neglected by tenants."

We rent the parking spaces of the doomed building within five minutes. We pocket $300. How much candy and pumpkins can we now buy?

The next day, another visit. The Broker sits on the staircase next to my apartment door. The worn-out folder is on his lap. His arrogance and impatience are gone.

He speaks softly, almost whispering, "Tell me, what is the amount you'll be willing to take? I'll cut the check now."

I can tell he is exhausted. He desperately needs my apartment to be empty.

I look at him, half with mercy, half with boredom, and I dare, "$12,000!" I had nothing to lose.

I'm not sure I'm serious. He is. Without batting an eyelash, he pulls out a large binder with business-size checks.

"I'll write you a check right now for $10,000. And please, please," he says, "sign the documents."

I watch him fill out all four zeroes. I look carefully, not believing my eyes. It is happening. Ten. Thousand. Dollars. He hands me the check.

I sign the papers.

With that money, I purchased my first condominium. I am just 29 years old. But unlike my beautiful castle, I will never repaint my walls.

◉

Los Angeles, December 1997

A magical time. I don't consider the future; my head is all about the moment when I embrace the early morning. Look at the sunrise with its majestic colors – light blue, pink, and brushes of white in the wide-open, crispy sky. I can take in the birth of each moment and continue to welcome the next and the minutes that follow, allowing the seconds to tick one at a time, without diminishing into the hands of the clock.

I am away from my family, far away. Away from their constant needs and my desire to please them, satisfy them, and make them proud. Far from performing, excelling, bringing them the trophies they always wanted. They were disciplined, even though they never asked me to be. As a good girl, I never allowed myself to compromise. I refused to accept anything less than an "A" in each class. Twice a year, my heart would sing on the long bus ride home, eager to show my parents the report card with my teacher's perfect handwriting on it. Eagerly, I would present the perfect stock paper card, and I would anticipate hearing beautiful words and compliments. This was going to be my time, if only for an afternoon. But every semester, my parents would tell me the same thing.

It's Christmas break.

"Let's celebrate your green card!"

Michele and I decide Sin City -- Vegas. I am not a gambler nor a drinker, but I am a freedom chaser, enchanted by the lights, the endless possibility, the glamour. We are going to celebrate becoming a legal permanent resident of the United States, which I received through my work. All by myself, just after a couple of years in the land of opportunities.

I am proud! I leave my university instructor hat at home and pack a small suitcase filled with outfits that have been hidden in my closet for years now, the ones I had planned to wear 'one day.' It was finally that day. Sequined mini dress, bell-bottom high-rise pants, a halter shirt, extra makeup, and two pairs of high heels. I am ready.

Heading down the East 10 Freeway, Michele and I turn off the radio, putting an end to the overplayed Christmas playlists. We insert electronic CDs one after another. Tiesto, Digweed, and various Norwegian DJs boosted our excitement and anticipation. We don't speak much, just listen to the music, which releases all our inhibitions into the night. We feel like Thelma and Louise with the unknown ahead of us. Michele drives the car like a fearless Amazonian woman; her hair is pulled up into a ponytail, fully exposing her piercing blue eyes, which pick up every detail on the road. She is quick and sharp. My Louise laughs freely. I notice this love child of hippie parents, a native of Northern California. Her mom and dad didn't check her report card. They didn't search for A's. Uninhibited, wild girl.

Michele teaches me all the secrets they didn't teach me in school. She is teaching me how to live in the moment. She shows me how to love freely, be who you are, and believe in the beauty in life. She showers me with compliments I craved for years.

She loves me.

She loves me for who I am.

She loves me unconditionally. Like a wild Northern Californian allows you to love.

She doesn't need numbers, grades, or my teachers' notes.

And I don't have to prove this forbidden free love to anyone else.

The music is carrying us to a world of goodness.

However, we are soon stuck in holiday traffic. Our cellphones are not-so-smart phones. Hope is our only navigation app. We slow down, mile after mile, and soon, no one can move forward. Drivers are getting out of their cars, looking at the horizon, yelling, asking, talking. Behind us in the west, the winter December sun sets early. There is no sign of traffic relief.

Three hours later, having replayed all our CDs, yawning and desperate for something to eat, I come up with a genius idea.

"Let's forget about Vegas and drive to Palm Springs!" I know enough to know it is close, fun, and presumably less congested.

Michele looks at me with compassion and amusement, as she always does.

"My silly girl," she says softly.

I can tell she is puzzled by my clever idea. I might get a hundred percent on my report cards, but I'm hopeless when it comes to driving. I'm directionally challenged. Noticing Michele's perplexed look, I try to bring some logic into my traffic-escape-plan.

"Wait, but it's not a detour, is it?" I admit it is the only other place I knew that borders Los Angeles to the east.

Michele nods and touches my hair, putting me at ease even if I don't know the right answer. We both sense a new adventure approaching. The unknown is our magnet. We head on the fifteen freeway to Palm Springs.

The roads are free. No traffic. No wait time, just an empty highway. We can breathe, letting go of the tension of inching forward at three miles per hour. We smile. We embrace the moment. It doesn't matter what will happen. We are together, fully present.

Two hours later, we arrive in what seems to be a ghost town. There are only a few cars in the streets; it is Christmas Eve. Families are full of Christmas dinner. Parents are wrapping the last presents and hiding the leftover wrapping papers. Kids are tucked in bed, trying to fall asleep, anticipating that once-a-year glorious moment: Santa's visit.

We have a small December miracle of our own: a great stylish hotel room for half the regular price, an amazing find on Christmas Eve. It is in a new section of the hotel, and, even at night, the view from the room is stunning. We watch the looming San Jacinto mountains, a breathtaking vision for the night, and the approaching sunrise. There is no past nor future. We live in the present tense.

We enter the remodeled room, and, before we put our suitcases down, I quickly remove the bedspread from the bed, which many others shared before us. It is my hotel habit, no matter what sort of hotel I'm in. No matter how luxurious the property, I always remove the bedspread first. The germs, the stories, the history. I want none of it. Freshly laundered bedsheets. Fresh stories of our own.

After a whole day of driving, I am restless. I let myself be what I feel with Michele. She accepts me wholly with my imperfections.

It's already ten o'clock at night.

Where is the promised adventure? I ask myself, watching Michele staring at me.

She can just enjoy the moment. Every little detail of life gets attention like it is eternity. She rarely gets restless smiles. She can read my mind.

I'm looking for something, a clue, an idea for something to do in this one night a year when everything is closed – my eyes find it on the bedside table—a thick copy of the *Yellow Pages*.

"Let's play!" I say enthusiastically to Michele, who is looking at me with her good eyes. "The first bar I find," I say with a big smile and my sassiest voice, "that's the bar we are going to!"

The little girl who was hidden inside me for years loves scavenger hunts. It is a huge phonebook. There are countless bars in this tourist destination, some listings with ads, some with tiny text. I wave my finger in the air, make a "here we go..." announcement, close my eyes, and then drop it onto one entry. My finger falls with a mischievous giggle.

Catch Bar.

Our next adventure.

We are two mischievous girls trapped in a very good oasis of a city. All I want now is to let loose and enjoy every free second. We have no limits, no responsibilities. Maybe we can even take Santa on our fun and wild quest before he places his hat on his head to visit the well-behaved kids in the world and eat a billion cookies left out for him. Santa deserves a surprising rendezvous, too.

While other girls were falling into the "marriage" and "love" trap, Michele and I were living our lives like it's still the Sixties. Joy, freedom, release, loving the moment, and carefree. We breathe. We enjoy. Life is a wild movie. If we find someone interesting, they join our movie for a scene. Or two. Or three. Sometimes they become the main supporting actor, sometimes just an extra.

We travel, love, and dance together—three people in an exhibit of joyous freedom. But there is one condition, one solid rule. The minute someone starts to worry about the next scene, we fire them. Worry is not part of the contract. Worry pushes them out of the plot.

Worry results in our superhero exit, putting on the black spandex outfit, jumping from one building to the next without ropes or a safety net. We are off to the next adventure. We live fully from moment to moment.

We feel the moment; we are the moment.

Catch, the promising bar, is roughly twenty miles away outside of Palm Springs, as if we haven't driven long enough. But we are not deterred; we are playing the game of the yellow page. Without children to pester us with an endless loop of "are we there yet?" the possibilities are truly endless.

A few cars are outside the neon storefront. Curiously, we enter the bar. Its familiar loud music, the smell of liquor, flashing purple, light blue, and yellow lights. I look around, collecting details. They are embedded in my mind. A young bartender is busy tending to two male customers. I look to my left, to the darker half side of the bar, where a series of small round tables with black armchairs lay. The armchairs are facing a little stage featuring a gorgeous, curvy, scantily clothed girl twirling up and down on the shiny pole.

"A strip club?" Michele and I turn to each other, stunned.

I stand agape, staring and giggling, admittedly intrigued. A seductive blonde stripper wearing a shiny pink bikini climbs down the pole. I've never seen anything like it before; it is my first time in a strip club. My blood rushes. I feel the shame, embarrassment, and curiosity all at once. "Butterfly" by Crazy Town plays in the background. I stare at her, touching the pole with sensuality, confidence, with boldness. She moves her body up and down, walking slowly, then fast. Then she stops. The dancer with the bombshell body matches every move to the music, a stripper in full possession of herself. I cannot take my eyes off her. I fly with the pole; I move, dance, climb the metal pole, and flip-down slowly. I gaze at the dancers who follow the first one, their strength, grace, and sensuality mesmerizing me. I want to do it, too! But that's insane – I'm Good Girl Jerusalem!

Michele touches my shoulder as if she's waking me up. She winks and puts a pool stick in my hand, and gestures for me to follow her. Green table, dark corner. The black, red, and blue balls are hitting each other with a click. *Pak! Pak!* Balls zoom from one corner to the next, searching for their escape down the pockets.

As if entering a completely new scene, I see the shadows of two tall, slender guys leaning on the table, playing pool. Talking. Laughing. One of them makes me stand straighter, fix my outfit, and play with my hair. Pak! He's handsome. Tall, with a great body that's been worked out for hours in the gym and needs nothing but a white T-shirt. With an easy grin and a warm handshake, gorgeous introduces himself.

"Hi, I'm Dan." He flexes his biceps. I pretend I don't notice. "And this is Bob," he introduces his even taller friend.

I can see his shyness, the wisdom in his eyes. Something mysterious is captivating me beyond this odd place on Christmas Eve where beautiful strippers gyrate. I'm hooked by mystery and looking at this man; I am thirsty to know his secrets, angels, and demons. Things that might either save me or kill me one day.

Pak! Pak! The pool balls mimic my pounding heart. I say nothing; I get shy when I am interested in a man, and when I am really curious, I hide it even deeper. But not Michele. Michele is about to devour Dan, and I let her. Girlfriend's Code. I know nothing about pool rules, but I'm thoroughly enjoying the matching man game. I make small talk with Bob. His blue eyes and sweet smile cover the tremendous sadness I can sense beneath. I don't remember one single word we exchanged. Small talk has never interested me.

We were on our way to Sin City one way or another, and we let our fingers lead us to the Oasis before sunrise.

California law closes the place at 1:50 a.m. The bartender is cleaning the counters, and we leave the club for the parking lot. Michele inserts the car key and turns on the engine.

"So, did you get his phone number?" I ask her.

She gasped, "No!"

Without any hesitation, I don't wait for an explanation. I open the car door, zoom over to Dan's car, approach his window, and ask with confidence:

"Are you too shy, or you simply don't give out your phone number?"

What's forbidden is desired.

What's unavailable is sought after.

What's hidden is pursued.

What's forbidden is desired.

What's unavailable is sought after.

What's hidden is pursued.

Babies love peekaboo. Teenagers love roller coasters. Women like elaborate proposals. Men love thrilling car rides. And, generally, people love the word *surprise* at birthday parties. We're more excited to unwrap a gift than to accept it unconcealed. There is a split-second neurological effect in which the brain is cognitively creating a moment of curiosity. Your emotions are triggered, some positive like happiness, and some negative like fear or disappointment. And this is the reason you love those unexpected moments. You take the chance that you will love it. Or hate it forever.

It's an illusion. What's meant to be yours will be yours. What is determined to fall into your life story will be revealed in its own time. You may plan – sometimes to excessive detail – how you will meet the person, how you will marry the love of your life, or how you will be promoted at work. And yet, the Universe has its plan for you. When you look back, it will be revealed to you in the most natural, fluid way you can imagine. You might detour, wanting to experience the ups, the downs, the unknowns. You want to get excited when uncovering the gift, but what's meant to be on your path will find you and haunt you, even if it seems like a detour.

Be excited. Be curious. Be the initiator. But know that being powerful comes from the most humbling moments of being powerless over what you want. So, the next time you get a flat tire, pause. Breathe, and let the Universe guide you to open one more layer in your life to what is coming next.

Chapter 8

As Lovers Do

Alef. Hey. Bet. .א.ה.ב

Love אהבה • Lover מאהב • In love מאוהב • Lovable אהוב

◉

Italy, July 2002

At LAX, the Italian flight attendants spot us sitting in the waiting area. I hear Dan's name being called from the counter. Perhaps they sense the butterflies in our stomachs. We giggle like two playful kids.

"Are we in trouble?" I ask Dan with a shy smile.

With a wide smile exposing her beautiful white teeth, the flight attendant apologizes with her Italian accent and tells us the flight is overbooked, but "Not to be worried," she adds, "we upgrade you to business class!"

I am in Rome: the Holy Chick in the land of the Holy Father.

It's been eight months since I met Dan, seven months since our first thunderous date, and three months since we became a couple. He's booked a surprise romantic trip for us to a place I had never been to before. Italy – the land that melds timeless elegance and art is now coupled with fresh love excitement. This is my first trip to the land of colorful melty gelato, cheesy stone oven pizza, and steamy coffee with a heavenly delicious aroma. In many ways, it's my promised land.

Powerful, inspirational words on stones are everywhere. I pictured myself writing *love* on each stone and rock I come across during our stay in Italy, but when we arrive, each stone we touch seems to already be marked with *love, happiness,* and *passion.* These words would be our signature together, leaving an imprint of deep romance in this ancient world.

The old five-star hotel in the center of Rome speaks love to us. It's an ancient building remodeled to be a luxury hotel offering fun splurges to help a new couple indulge. We dive into each other's bodies each morning and night, trying every position we can imagine, making sure we know every little part of each other. I feel utterly complete when we are naked together.

Dan and I map each other's bodies like curious explorers. We have rambunctious sex in caves and grottos, on deserted rocks, and the side of quiet country roads. He splashes me with love, spoils me with gifts, and treats me to endless compliments alongside his marvelous poetry. With all of that intense and passionate attention, I touched the dazzling vault of heaven.

Italian coffee! I jump from my bed to get my fix. I put on my denim shorts and a tank top, zipping my flip cellphone and camera into my blue fanny pack. I am determined to document all that happens on this miraculous trip. I'm ready to go on a big Roman adventure to find those pure beans and the rich aroma of my promised coffee.

I leave the room, tearing myself from Dan's side. Dan is still on the bed, looking blissful.

"I will be back soon," I add, as it is hard for us to depart even for a few moments.

I choose to take the narrow old stairs, and my heart sings in each step downwards. I do not have to look far; there's a coffee bar on the street across from the hotel. I follow the scent. I will forever love Italian coffee. Strong, rich, direct – just like how I like my men.

Rome is bustling. Beautiful brick roads to walk. Everything is painted white. I take a few breaths; the air is crisp, fresh, and clean.

"Don't cry for me, Argentina..."

I hear a man singing in English from the upper floor of the hotel. I look up two open shutters and the wooden frame. Dan stands there with his arms open wide, singing Evita.

My Romeo is serenading me in Italy!

I am the luckiest woman in the world. I pinch myself – no, I am not dreaming. We are just that deeply in love. I take out my little pocket camera and videotape him singing. This video, featuring him in a white robe serenading me through the hotel window on a perfectly beautiful morning in Italy, will be a part of the surprise video clip I will show him on our wedding day exactly one year later.

Los Angeles, November 2009

Lev is already five, and Liam is two years old. But I do think about it. If they were born in Israel, it would be mandatory, but they can decide, as their mom is Israeli.

Lev, ever since she was a baby, listens to every word, not only with her ears. She sees people's feelings beyond their masks; she reads people intuitively with her heart scanning theirs. If you meet her, she immediately asks you intriguing and interesting questions with genuine interest, invariably surprising her older counterparts. Very determined about what she desires, although she can like something to its core in the morning and despise it in the afternoon, yet she will never change her mind about music and dance – they are what makes my bubbly Lev shine. Her name means heart in Hebrew.

Liam was born two and a half years after Lev. His name means my nation, in Hebrew. Since birth, Liam's hair has been his signature. Big, soft blond curls cover his head.

"Your hair is incredible," people say, astonished when they first see him. "Your hair is amazing," they continue. Shyly and politely, hiding behind the huge curls, Liam whispers a shy "thank you" with his heart-capturing smile. This is the extent of his conversations with strangers. He would rather build sophisticated Lego cities, read the entire series of the "Who Was..." books about history and explore famous hockey and soccer players' lives.

When I was pregnant with Liam, I asked my sister Sharon, who had just given birth to her second boy, how am I supposed to divide my love into two now? Sharon is the responsible one of the two. She always has answers to everything, especially about raising children, kitchen delicacies, and how to clean a pot whose stains are stubborn.

She wisely answered, "You don't have to divide your love; your heart doubles by itself."

Lev and Liam still ask, "Mommy, please tell us the story about..." "and about..." and the one they love the most, "the story about your boyfriend in the army."

They giggle and laugh and, with sparkling eyes, look at each other, and then gaze at me, waiting for the story they have heard many times before. They know it by heart, but they want to hear it from me again. When I was their age, I asked Grandma to tell me the same stories repeatedly. I, too, knew them by heart, but I still loved hearing them often. I tell the children the story once more.

Israel, 1989

"When I was in my first month of the army service, I was in training," I start recounting the tale. "It was my first time sleeping away from home. My parents did not allow me many sleepovers. Remember that I was Good Girl Jerusalem! So, there we were, no fewer than sixty eighteen-year-old girls sleeping in the long barracks, huddled in tiny beds made from metal with rough wool blankets. Five o'clock a.m., even before sunrise, we began getting ready for our first drill. Already at four-thirty a.m., the bathroom was pure chaos. Girls are running, dropping items, rushing back and forth from the barracks to the showers. There was water spilling everywhere, girls yelling and

113

borrowing toothpaste, brushes, and soap bars. Yawning, chuckling, chattering. If just one girl is late, all sixty girls are punished. Time is of the essence, and no one wants to be that late girl. Four-fifty-nine a.m., and we are all lined up in time for the morning drill. Our commanders, who were only nineteen years old, were tough and seemingly illogical. What does it matter if the blanket was exactly folded into nine squares? But it matters. It wasn't about the squares, but about following orders. Exact orders. Getting up on time and transitioning from a rebellious teenager to an obedient soldier."

I get to the part the children love most.

"On my second week as a soldier, still just seventeen years old (I joined the force a month before my birthday), I received my special boyfriend: my beloved rifle. Our commanders gave us a very clear order to keep our boyfriends close and never lose them. Especially – and this came with a dire warning – never lose them during our very minimal sleep."

As they listen, my kids sit taller and straighten their backs, their antennas ready to receive the most confidential information they have heard in their lives.

"At night, the commanders came silently into the barracks to snatch the 'boyfriends' from the arms of these sixty sleeping beauties. If you slept too deeply, which usually was the case because of the constant sleep deprivation, you would lose your cherished boyfriend. At morning drill, panic-stricken faces revealed who had lost her boyfriend and who had remained determined and loyal. The consequences of losing your boyfriend were cruel. From cleaning the bathrooms with the tiniest brush, you can imagine standing at attention and guarding the stairs so they won't move for the day, to four dishwashing shifts in a row instead of the normal one. When you are in the army, you leave your logic at home."

This story always made Lev and Liam laugh. They and that I tell it again and again. In their eyes, their mommy is a cool mommy. She had a special boyfriend, whom she never lost. Not even once.

Only Love creates.

I don't believe people have a heart of stone, but there are people with stones in their hearts.

בלב םינבא םע םישנא שי לבא ,ןבא לש בל םע םישנא שיש הנימאמ אל ינא.

I, too, had many stones in my heart. It wasn't easy to dissolve, melt, sort, and see what's mine and what I carried for others. But slowly, I scraped them one by one. It wasn't easy, but worth every step.

If you feel a heavy heart, if you carry the unnecessary burden of others, you don't have to, and you're not alone. But know that Love, unconditional Love, conquer it all. Not only romantic Love, Love to a human being, your pet, to the self, or your Universe.

But the essence is Love.

Love has no opposite, no dilemma, no fear.

Because only Love creates.

Love will most often happen despite us, not because of us.

We may try to guess what Universe, God, Higher Power, Power grated than ourselves, and Source has in mind. We are always looking, searching, questioning, hypervigilant to seek Love. The goal in our life, the precious gem we seek and yearn to find. If we find it, we win the prize. We ponder, obsess, rethink, analyze and put others as a power greater than ourselves, as we are in a long quest for that golden answer.

That is not how it works.

We may believe that if we behave in a certain way we, can convince the future, we can maneuver our luck. We convince ourselves we have to walk on eggshells, saying, behaving, thinking, and feeling the right thing, while forcing ourselves somehow to be in the right place at the right time, to find Love.

But that's not true.

The Universe's will for us is not hidden. We do not have to control, manipulate or force it. We do not have to be vigilant in order to have it happen.

It is right there inside and around us. It is happening right now. We can notice any of it in our simple five senses. Just be aware and be in presence.

We do have a part. We have the responsibility of loving ourselves. Deeply. We are finding our authentic voice through self-love. Without shame, without guilt. We have to take the simple steps every day like watering the garden, watering the flowers which are yet to be seen. But we do not have to control. Love will come for us. All we have to do is be.

We are Love.

Chapter 9

Accidental Heroes

Gimel. Vet. Resh. .ג.ב.ר

Hero גיבור· Man גבר · Manly גברי · Conquer התגבר· Overcome התגבר
Heroism גבורה· Turn it up הגבר

⊙

Israel, 1990's

I have a favorite story, too, and it's my Grandma's story.
Grandma Esther.

Whenever I would visit my Grandma, I could smell it from the
entrance of her house. When she knew I was coming, she made me my
favorite dish, Mejadara. Mejadara is a Lebanese dish, and it was, and
will always be, my grandma's sign of love. My grandma used to make
the Mejadra in a few steps: First, soak the lentils in water, then cook
them. Cook white rice separately and then cook the two together. In the
end, she added caramelized onions and her secret spices. She took each
step of cooking the divine recipe seriously and with patience, like an
artist drawing his masterpiece. I will never eat any other Mejadra, only
my grandmother's Mejadra. She loved watching me eating it while I
am making noises of pure satisfaction devouring each bite.

When I asked her why it was so delicious, she would tell me
with warmth and pride, "I put my fingers in the recipe," showing
me her smooth long soft fingers. I understand what Grandma Esther

said. She meant, "I put my heart into it." My grandma talked in riddles and idioms.

I could feel that love in that simple dish. There were two blue tin bowls on her kitchen table waiting for me. In one bowl was the prepared mejadra, and in the other tin bowl, she had prepared a chopped salad made of tiny cubes of tomatoes, cucumbers, and spiced with olive oil, lemon, and salt, not yet mixed. A cup of low-fat yogurt was kept in the refrigerator, waiting to be mixed in once I arrived to indulge myself. That was Grandma Esther's special meal. Nothing could compare – each lentil carried the seed of love, of caring.

Grandma taught me that when you love someone, you feed them. You feed them, love.

Along with food, each visit was accompanied by a question and a smile, "Grandma, can you tell me the story about how you walked to Israel?" Even though I'd heard the story many times, it was like new each visit.

Grandma, suppressing her pleasure, taking her time by first making for herself 'Grandma Esther Coffee.' It is her exceptional coffee, a legend in our family. 'Grandma Esther Coffee' is a coffee made from ground espresso beans, mixed with three-quarters cup hot water and milk added to the top. You could smell the aroma of the coffee and see the coffee grounds dancing in the milk. It looked like salt and pepper, and she used to stir it slowly with a spoon, careful not to stain the table.

Grandma Esther was obsessed with cleanliness. Her living room, as well as her entire house, was always meticulously well-kempt. Rarely would you find a dirty dish in her kitchen sink or a chair not exactly in its place. Her house always smells clean and fresh. This is one of the gifts I inherited from my legendary grandma.

After she concluded her coffee ceremony, Grandma used to wash the empty coffee glass cup, would sit down on the right side of the sofa, put a tissue into her sleeve, arrange a small wool blanket on her knees, and, with gleaming eyes, start to tell me her remarkable story. My family's great epic.

Beirut, Lebanon, 1936

"In Beirut, it was heaven," Grandma would always begin, half smiling, marshaling these memories from her vast collection. "During the summer, we used to sleep on the roof because of the sweltering heat. Cherry trees of Lebanon popped up all along the horizon. Everyone slept together on mattresses. We used to sing songs until we fell fast asleep. Every day, we woke up with the sun. It was the best childhood," she told me with a gleam in her eyes.

Grandma continued the story of how she walked from Beirut to Jerusalem when she was only ten years old. Her parents had had the opportunity to leave Lebanon and had to leave their daughter behind. My Grandma was only nine years old when they left. The opportunity to be smuggled into what was then the British Mandate was rare in those days, and it was an opportunity you could not dismiss. When my great-great-grandparents got the chance to join the smuggling group, Grandma and her older sister were on a summer visit in one of the villages far from Beirut. They left their luxurious life in Lebanon – with its wealth, peace, and cherry trees – in order to realize a powerful vision. They came home to touch the Promised Land's earth and create a lasting legacy for the family.

Her older sister was smuggled first, and Grandma was the last one to stay behind. "I was ten. For several months, my cousin attempted to cross the border of Lebanon, and we were caught by the British Brigades and were put in jail," my grandma told me, "but I never gave up."

My Grandma never gave up.

No adults, just herself and her twelve-year-old cousin. They did not have hiking boots, sleeping bags, or warm jackets. My brave, fearless grandmother! Most ten-year-olds that I know are too busy with the latest phone technology, hardly willing to get up from their chair to do something you asked unless they are bribed with gifts and toys. And yet she walked, for weeks, to set foot on the Promised Land, Jerusalem, which was just a barren land of sand and bricks in a broiling desert marred by centuries of warfare.

Israel, 1950's

When Grandma Esther entered any room, people notice her. Unlike most women in her generation, Grandma Esther is an exceptionally tall woman, just like her dad, who was born in Russia. Immaculately dressed, her hair was perfectly tied back in a big bun or two long braids. She had long fingers, like a pianist. Despite her hard life, her hands were very soft, even after she turned ninety. Every wrinkle has a story behind it, a story of mastering any hardship or challenge with determination. Failure was not a word in her vocabulary.

Pregnant women used to sneak a conversation with her in the bazaar, standing in line to get water during the blockade, or even at her front doorstep.

"Do you predict a boy or a girl?"

Before ultrasound technology, she always knew the baby's gender by the belly's shape or the aura over the pregnant woman's head. When she was in the mood, she could release you from the evil eye and cleanse your energy with special spices and tiny exploding magnesium balls in a bowl of boiled water. She has the magic. Her wise eyes know everything. She never told me the secrets, but sometimes I think I have the magic in my genes, too.

I inherited none of Grandma's physical traits, but I did inherit her name, Esther. When I was only a week old, Grandma declared my name as hers! It did not matter that my excited parents had already named me with their firstborn child's dream name. They chose a modern, non-biblical, and stylish name, "Joy." But Grandma was the queen, the matriarch. And so it was. Joy was erased, and Baby Esther was crowned. The compromise was to shorten the biblical version, and add a more modern tweak to it, Ella. Grandma knew already. Her name has magic in it. It had secrets that she could never tell me but live through me. And with her name, I was also granted her best quality – being stubborn. Stubborn with everything I desire, even if it means walking 382 miles in sandals. Even if it requires being captured by the British and sit in a jail cell at the young age of ten. Instead of being a victim of her circumstances, she taught me how to fight for what I truly believe in, without hesitation, without caring what other people will say. She is my heroine.

Grandma Esther is a supreme storyteller from one saga to the next. With both laughter and, sometimes, with painful sadness, she colorfully drew her stories with all five senses – where she was, whom she saw, what she felt, what she ate, and the scents. My grandma is a painter of words. From one story to another, I felt like I was immediately next to her during the story's scene, fighting for her beliefs with courage.

Grandma's courageous journey didn't end when she arrived in Jerusalem. Grandma Esther fearlessly joined Irgun, also known as Etzel. Etzel is the acronym of The National Military Organization in the Land of Israel, an underground group of civilian men and women fighting against the British Occupation. Grandma Esther envisioned only one thing – how to combat the British who had conquered the Promised Land. Today, when I read about Etzel on Wikipedia or the internet, I giggle – to think Grandma Esther was a murderer! Yes, a cold-blooded criminal!

"Etzel," cited from Encyclopedia Britannica, "committed acts of terrorism and assassination against the British, whom it regarded as illegal occupiers, and was also violently anti-Arab."

My grandma used to smuggle grenades. Back then, Grandma Esther was a clever and brave twenty-year-old mother to three kids. She already had two toddlers and had just given birth to my dad. Very distinguished and tall, with two black shiny, thick braids, she dared to wander the streets of Jerusalem after the strict curfew, enforced by the British from 1946 on.

"I used to wrap my baby, your father, with heated towels, which I warmed on the primitive gasoline-operated stove. But before

I covered him with the hot towels, I hid grenades and other small artillery rounds with the baby," she used to tell me.

"You weren't afraid?" I asked Grandma, feeling every one of her steps on the empty and dark streets of Jerusalem.

British military police stopped to check her papers as she was bravely wandering after curfew hours. Grandma Esther would beg the British officer who stopped her in the streets to help urgently get to the doctor. "My baby is burning with a high fever!"

While the British checked her papers, she urged them to touch the baby. "He will die if I don't rush him to the doctor now, here, touch him!"

The proper, overly cautious British would refuse to touch the sick baby, fearing for their own lives, and they would let her go and sometimes even accompany her to her destination. Wisely and strategically, Grandma maneuvered her way, smuggling the grenades from one side of the city to the other.

"If you want something, don't be afraid. Look fear in its eyes," she used to teach me. "They were just policemen doing a job, but we had a stronger vision. And a strong vision always wins."

Grandma Esther didn't desert her mission, and she didn't stop after the British left. She continued to volunteer in distributing water throughout Jerusalem during the cruel blockade. Finally, as history shows, after thousands of years of not being a country, Israel was officially established as its independent State in May of 1948.

Three years after Israel's celebration, in November 1951, Grandma Esther gave birth to her fifth child, another baby boy, Samuel. Her special boy, her precious son. She even admitted it in public. He was her favorite child. She was a different mom to this baby boy.

This boy received everything. Anything she didn't have, and everything my dad and the older siblings could not even dream about. By the time Samuel was born, Grandma Esther didn't have to sew old socks and get hand-me-downs from the neighbors. My grandparents were then established economically, and, finally, Grandma had the means to take care and attend to her family without working both day and night shifts. She still worked, but not as hard as she used to. Grandma Esther was very proud of her baby boy. It was almost like she had a baby for the first time. She loved him like no other. When he told her he wanted to play the guitar, she bought him the best one – something rare and valuable during the fifties in the middle of the sands and wars. He was her everything.

My uncle Samuel was easy to love; everyone loved him. He had a special charm, a pure, shy, gentle manner. Smiling eyes, deep dimples, and a gentle, generous demeanor. He had many friends, and everyone who knew him was touched by his allure, jokes, and willingness to help. He was the boy who secretly helped the neighbors, strangers, and whoever was in need. He brought light to any place he entered and brought joy and melody to everyone's hearts.

Grandma may have been the first woman to own a car in Jerusalem. She no longer needed to rely on the old system of delayed buses and trains. Now she could give her time to her boys and baby boy, Uncle Samuel.

126

When Uncle Samuel served in the military, Grandma Esther almost served with him. Uncle Sam served as a paratrooper. Grandma would cook massive pots of her traditional food, load up as much as possible in her car, and travel up north to his base to spoil "her boys." She especially loved each of the soldiers and made sure they were happy and well-fed during her visits. "My sons," she called the young boys.

Driving up to their bases in her light blue Peugeot filled with big tin pots in the backfilled with special meatballs, rice, vegetables, meat soup, and other dishes, all made with her hands prior to her feeding mission. She brought smiles to their faces and happiness to their bellies. From the simple soldier to the commander, everyone loved Grandma Esther.

Golan Heights, October 1973

When Uncle Samuel was released from the army, there was no happier mom than my Grandma. Her baby boy was home again. Joy and music-filled every room. He played the guitar, and her heart sang.

Two months after Uncle Samuel came back home, I was eighteen months old, Yom Kippur blasted, and he was drafted along with many other men.

Three knocks on the front door changed my Grandma's life forever in October 1973. Two officers in formal uniforms with the heavy black message.

Just twenty days before his birthday, she will never celebrate his twenty-second birthday. Her boy had fallen. Forever.

Her baby is gone.

The pots filled with his favorite food waiting on the stove. His room, which she prepared with new pictures on the walls.

Everything stood frozen.

Grandma didn't touch his room for a year. Instead, she grew plants and the flowers on his grave and nourished them devotionally, sometimes daily.

Grandmother Esther's life would never be the same. From then on, she ended her stories with sadness in her eyes, "I am waiting to see you again, my *broni*"

◉

Jerusalem, February 1982

"It's a boy! It's a boy! My wife gave birth to a baby boy!"

My dad replaced the phone handset in the rotary cradle. He was so happy he ran out of our second-floor duplex and announced to the entire neighborhood that, at last, he had a son.

Five years after my third sister's premature birth, Libby, my mom got pregnant again, this time with her fifth child. If you asked my dad how many kids he had, he always answered "two girls, a daughter, and a baby girl," not revealing immediately that he had four girls. Among five females, he was the only man in the house. Ultrasounds were just starting to develop, or luxury to only the rich or those who had special connections in the hospital, and most pregnant couples were forced to wait until the delivery day to know the child's sex.

"Grandma Esther knew it was a boy!" my dad almost lifted me in the air, but I was already eleven, and I made myself heavy.

The phone rang again.

"Please let me talk to Dad," my mom was on the other line, and I didn't understand how she could talk from the delivery room.

"Dad," I summoned my father, as he looked ecstatically for his car keys, eager to rush to see his new boy, "Mom is on the phone."

"Mom?" My dad was puzzled.

My mom hadn't given birth yet. It would not have been a surprise to anyone if she had. Libby was born prematurely at six months. One pound and nine-ounce preemie, tiny like a small beer bottle, being fed from tubes only for a month in the preemie department, but she survived, to grow and be the tallest of the girls. (add more - did she survive? We don't know there is a miracle; what is the miracle?) Miracles often happen in our family.

"I did not give birth yet," she tried to calm my confused dad.

My mom called from the hospital to tell my dad the doctor had used a new technology on her that was called an "ultrasound." As she was a veteran employee of the hospital, she was one of the first to be given the opportunity to try this new technology. That evening, she told us how the doctor put a very cold stick on her big belly and moved it from one side to another like an Atari game, and then he showed her the face and hands of her child. He told her she was having a boy.

The next few weeks of her pregnancy were the biggest honeymoon for my parents. My dad loved my mom for giving him "The Boy." His name was a foregone conclusion.

Sam.

April 11, 1982

The Brit, or Brit Milah, a Jewish circumcision ceremony, is celebrated on an 8-day-old Jewish boy. My baby brother's Brit was bigger than the mayor's daughter's wedding, saying a lot. People from all over the country came to see this little boy who brought so much joy to our family. My parents were so happy - it was almost as if they were just married. My father strutted around like a proud peacock with his colored feathers spread out. Grandma Esther was beaming. It was the first time she had laughed since that fateful day in October of 1973.

"Broni. Broni," she kept mumbling to my baby brother.

Grandma Esther paid extra for the best food at the party, the most popular band, the most renowned rabbi. She showered her longed-for grandson with anything her mind could come up with. She ordered aunts and uncles from The United States to send him the best blankets and the newest bassinet and to sew his sweaters from a warm, yet lightweight and breathable, expensive wool so he would always be comfortable.

Even though he was spoiled rotten, Sam grew to be the humblest boy. With big, deep, empathetic eyes and a dimple full of charm, he melted everyone's heart. He was the boy who helped older women with their heavy bags, brought home wounded birds and took care of them until they could fly again, and always stood up for any kid who was bullied. Humble, quiet, and lovable. You could find him busy with simple tools; Sam could build a wooden airplane from scratch. When mom asked for help, he was the first one to give her a hand. Sam never raised his voice, he rarely argued, and he was always there to make you laugh to the point of tears.

August 9, 2001

4:30 a.m. The landline in my little apartment in West Hollywood rings. My preemie sister, Libby, is on the other end of Israel. It is early in the morning, and my jet lag is still lingering. I've just made it back from my sister Lee's wedding in Israel. I decided to surprise my sister and had asked Limor, my sister's best friend, to pick me up from the airport. She was my secret woman.

"We cannot find Sam!" Libby yells hysterically from the other line. "Sam!"

She explains there had been a terror attack in Jerusalem, in Sbarro, a pizza place. "We cannot find him!"

She is desperate. She cries. She is almost screaming.

After every terror attack (and there are many this season), all of us siblings call each other to make sure we are safe. But, today, Sam's phone is off.

131

"Call me with any news!" I commanded her, sounding strong. "Don't worry; everything is okay. He will call soon. The lines are probably busy."

I hang up the phone, and the walls close in on my body.

"Sam!" I am shaking.

Without thinking about it, I grab the first book I see. It is a prayer book, and this is the first time in my life I've opened it. I quickly, frantically, browse the words.

"Sam!" I repeat his name, falling on the carpet, my head down to the floor. "God, please, please, not my brother!" I scream and beg.

"God! You have to hear me! No! No! Not my brother!" The pain is cutting through my flesh. My heart is aching. "No! Not my brother."

My body shakes, I read the black words on the somewhat yellow pages again and again. I try to read them aloud.

"Baruch Ata..." I forget any meaning of the words. I scan the words on the floor, crying and begging God for mercy.

I crawl to the living room, find the remote control, and turn on CNN. A horror movie is flickering from my Holy City. The main intersection of my hometown, which we used to call the center of the world when we were kids, is now the center of a terror scene. The street is covered with blood and body parts—ambulances with loud sirens wail. Policemen, paramedics, and civilians run from one body to another. Debris and dust everywhere. The entire restaurant is destroyed, and its ceiling had collapsed. In the short footage that plays on a loop, I hear emergency workers and passersby yelling for help in carrying wounded women and children. There are even bodies of babies. Dead bodies are covered with white sheets.

I cry. I cry first out loud, then quietly like a wounded animal. I plead with God.

"Please, please, not my brother. Please not Sam!"

My sister calls again to update me. Sam is alive! He is alive but was injured severely. Libby doesn't know the details yet, only that the emergency services called mom with news. Sam is being transferred to Hadassah hospital, the best in Jerusalem. My prayers grow louder. It is official: they work. But there is more work to do.

My broken, shivering mom took a taxi and rushed to the hospital as fast as she can. The chaos only intensifies when she gets to the hospital. My brother is not there.

"He is on his way," the trauma psychologist at the emergency room explains to my mom in a calm voice, "he's in the ambulance."

My mom's desperation conquers her body, and she starts yelling at the psychologist.

"You are a liar, tell me what happened! It cannot be that I got here in a taxi, and he is still on his way in an ambulance."

She almost shakes the man, screaming, "Tell me the truth! Is he alive?"

As two nurses hold her up, the emergency doors swing open – and in comes a stretcher. It is Sam. He is unconscious, his uniform is torn, and he is connected to an IV drip with a white bandage over his head. He is covered with blood—my mother races to his side.

Sam will spend three days in intensive care before he is out of danger. His life was saved by a wooden pole that stood between him and the suicide bomber. Fifteen people who were right next to him died, seven of whom were children. Nearly an entire family was among the dead: a father, mother, and three of their kids, with two orphaned siblings, left alive. One hundred and forty people were wounded.

The force of the explosion – which hit Sam as he stood outside the pizzeria – threw my brother twenty feet into the air. He landed on his back in the middle of the intersection, breaking all of his ribs. There were dozens of pieces of shrapnel embedded in his back. The terrorist hid the shrapnel in an unassuming guitar case, along with the explosives.

The suicide bomber, Muhammad Al-Masri, became a hero and a martyr in the eyes of Hamas. The woman who assisted him, Alham Tamimi, never showed remorse during her trial and was sentenced to life in prison. She would be released in a prisoners' exchange on October 18, 2011.

Gradually, Sam got stronger. His lungs healed through a long, tedious process of rehabilitation. Some of the shrapnel came out by itself, and eighteen years later, some remain in his back, forever marking the day innocent people were blown up while enjoying a casual lunch of pizza and lemonade with their families. Throughout his long recovery, Sam never complained and never bragged he survived. The silence was and still is, how he deals with it. All he has ever told us about the immediate aftermath of the bombing is that it was a few moments of prolonged stillness. When he was on the ground afterward, he had raised his head to see if he could help any others around him. This movement of lifting his head is how the emergency workers found him, alive, among the dead bodies.

A week after my brother returned home, my mom added to his name the word Chai. Chai is the Hebrew word meaning life. My brother became Sam Chai: Sam, alive.

Six months after the Sbarro pizza bombing, my sister's friend, Limor, was killed in another suicide attack in the Moment Café in Jerusalem. Seconds before the explosion, my sister's other friend present at the cafe had excused herself to go to the restroom. She survived; ten others, besides Limor, died. During what the press now calls the Second Intifada between 2000 and 2005, nearly a thousand innocent lives were violently taken. Unnecessary deaths.

What's hysterical is historical.

Heroes are generally not the boisterous ones who forcefully conquer. They are not the ones who win wars by reveling in blood and chaos and then marching with fanfare in victory parades down Main Street. Real heroes are more often the quiet ones, the ones who act as if there is no fear at all, combating the obstacles of life with the quiet certainty that all is an illusion.

There is only one obstacle: a solid, horrible obstacle that holds you, hostage. That obstacle is a shapeshifter, adapting to circumstances but always functioning as a recurring pattern from the past. In other words, what's hysterical is historical. The monster is incredibly savvy about how and when to wake up the doubt and an expert on how to press on your weakest points, creating a repetitive emotional freeze within your body and mind. It convinces you that there is no solution, no medicine, and no escape from the pain. It gives you a perfect excuse for why it is impossible to move ahead, preventing you from reaching what you want in life.

There is someone who can help you defeat the monster and shake free of the paralyzing fear. You have a hero. Every child naturally has one, even if they do not label them as such. Perhaps you have forgotten your guardian angel, the one who can hold you together in rough times. Now is the time to call upon your hero. The thing is, you may not know who your hero is. You may have forgotten, but you do have one. Is it your relative? Is it someone you know personally, or a figure like Mother Theresa or King Solomon? Is it an imaginary Wonder Woman or Superman? Your teacher from 3rd grade? Your neighbor? It doesn't matter whom you pick as your hero, but it is essential that you have one.

You can ask a child, a man in his 80s, a woman in her 40s, a person who lives in Antarctica, or someone who camps in the deserts. Whether you are someone who grew up in Buckingham palace or the slums of Kolkata, you should have a hero. Everyone has a hero.

A hero nurtures your soul when you are the most vulnerable. Thinking of your hero can comfort and inspire you when you are in distress. If you quiet yourself for just a moment, your hero will come to you. She or he can talk directly to your inner being with a powerful message, beyond words, beyond mere sounds and expressive language. The message, born of your admiration of the hero's qualities, is what you need the most at that time.

Chapter 10

Bridge of Trust

Alef. Mem. Nun. .א.מ.נ

Trust אמון · Amen אמן · Trustworthy אמין · Artist אמן · Trainer מאמן
Belief אמונה · Believe מאמין

◉

Austin, Texas, April 209

"So, Thursday, April 18, we will start at nine until four in the afternoon; we might even finish a bit earlier," said Mary on the other side of the line with her southern sweet, inviting accent. "See y'all in a few months!"

I wasn't sure to whom she was referring by "y'all" other than me, myself, and I. I have never been to Texas. My love of horses is my only connotation of that wild, wild world. And now, I am invited to present a seven-hour-one-day workshop in Victoria, Texas. I feel proud and also somewhat apprehensive about this adventure. Leaving the kids and flying alone to a place far from anything I know as a city.

Victoria is two or three hours south of Austin, near the Gulf, and the thought of leaving them alone tortures me at first. It always does when I fly to lecture in a different state, but I cannot miss this opportunity.

After leaving notes filled with bullet points of duties, schedules, favorite meals and snacks, and a list of their favorite books, I am on a not-so-long flight to Austin. I land in Stetson country.

Away from the city smog, the traffic, and the noise, I drive south from the Texas capital along a highway with endless green horizons and cows on the roadsides. Driving from Austin to Victoria looks like a scene from *Gone with the Wind,* and, for a second, I want to be Scarlett O'Hara.

Thank you, God, for trusting me with giving and sharing what I love.

I am given the gift of communication, standing in front of strangers and sharing what I am passionate about, what I learned and researched and lived half of my life. Whenever I am in front of a crowd, I know I am born for this in front of people who are willing to use my information. My veins, my voice, my body all have one aim. I'm here to share, to humor, to give. When I was young, my dream was to be an actress and a singer on the stage, maybe like Madonna, who danced with me on every bus ride. I never really sing like a pop star, but yes, my heart sings in every one of my classes, presentations, and conferences. I haven't won an Academy Award, but I was given the ability to share myself with others to craft my lectures to be interesting, funny, emotional, and inspirational. It's a gift the Universe gave me, even if I dreamt about something else. The Universe has an exact plan; we need to choose if and how to manifest it.

A teacher named Sarah sits in one of the chairs, second row. Blonde, blue eyes, with eyes that hide stories behind them. She is polite yet has a tough presence. As a western woman, she shows me multiple

140

sides of the feminine spirit. Sarah listens, and her skeptical eyes follow me from one side of the room to another. Without saying a word, she questions every word I say. Her arms are crossed, her body is closed off, and she rarely makes eye contact with me. I *am not buying it. This is too much for me.*

Mary tells me the story. Sarah is not just a teacher. She is a mom to an eight-year-old boy with autism. Sarah's son is affected by a social-emotional ability that makes him different. Desperately, Sarah is looking for answers, for consolation, for quick fixes.

Can I help her? I pause.

If I could only tell Sarah that I was just like her, as I, too, am affected by someone else's disorder. Like her son, it is a disorder you cannot see. You cannot touch, but, like potholes on the road, you can feel it. I understand her. I feel her pain, her frustration, her unwillingness to give up on her family, her devotion to helping the one she loves the most. I want to scream and shout and cry with Sarah.

I know what it is to feel hopeless, faithless, and utterly distrustful of the healing process. This daughter of Jerusalem and this daughter of South Texas, who never met before, share similar pain.

I feel Sarah shift between sharing personal stories, group work, and partner drills with each PowerPoint slide. I am speaking about how to communicate with children with special needs. Eighty pairs of eyes of educators (and mothers) are looking up to me. I may be standing at the front of the room, but I am also sitting in Sarah's seat. I talk with love, compassion, and care. Sarah listens. Her arms unfold, and her face softens.

She is in tears.

I choose to say nothing. I am here fully for Sarah. I want to wipe her tears, hug her, console her. But I freeze. I know she aches. I continue with the workshop. At the end of the long seven hours, Sarah stands in front of me, and we look at each other for a long moment, like we both know.

"I want to take you home," I hear Sarah say with tears in her eyes, "you just described my son as you know him." And she added softly, "As if you know me."

At that moment, I knew I flew 1,500 miles to spend seven hours in a room filled with Texan women to meet Sarah. The Universe brought me all the way here, even if only for a few moments. I realize that there is a reason I left Lev and Liam and let myself be directed into the heart of South Texas. Sarah needs a person outside of her life to be her anchor. She needs to hear that she was doing the right thing, that she is not alone, that she is understood. Or is it me that needs to hear all this?

With a soft, loving voice, I tell her, "Sarah, you are not alone." I tell Sarah I will adopt her. I will email her, call her, and see if her hope is a spark that could grow into a flame.

I don't have a child with autism. She doesn't know that I, too, am destroyed by someone else's disease, which I cannot change. We hug. We exchange email addresses. We know. And then it's time to drive back to Austin.

If I was home right now, my mind would be racing between to-do lists – loads of laundry, phone calls, mail, dishes, bedtime, cooking, driving, grocery shopping – and schedules for a few days. I am afraid to admit that I enjoy this! I am back on the highway, back to the liberal and traffic-clogged Texas capital.

Mile after mile, one empty road after another, scattered deserted houses lead the way. No one to take care of, no one to please, no one to blame, no one to point fingers. Free, I am alone in a place I have never been to before. I realized I have no one to please. When I get to Austin, I will be able to enjoy a whole new day for myself. From deciding when to wake up, what to have for breakfast, when to shower, which places to visit, and what time to eat dinner. If I so choose to, I can eat eggs for lunch and a tuna burger for breakfast. I can decide where to go in the city and come back to my temporary home when I desire. I have no one else to create a conversation with. Just endless time. Almost endless.

I start to notice the voice from within: quite scary, quite releasing.

"Hello, Ella!"

"Hi, it is me."

"Nice to meet you. Again."

I drive through landscapes I've seen in the movies. Endless, bright spring green fields. Cows, farms, and wild horses. Slowly, I can feel my heart smiling. The single-lane road from Victoria to Austin is breathtaking. My heart pumps with pleasure. I'm far from civilization, far from responsibility. I trust the black attached rectangle box on the dashboard to show me the upcoming small intersection, which I must pay attention to.

Suddenly, the lights on the GPS box blink and go out. The app that came with the rental is broken, and I am out of cell tower range.

Almost desperately, I am trying to get back to Austin. I find myself making detours for hours, going back to the same intersection, relying on the few Texan strangers for directions. It seems like I am driving huge infinite circles, as it all looks the same. My only consolations are the stunning views and horizons of huge fields of April blossoms forming purple, pink, and yellow blankets across the land. The colors change every few miles. I see white, brown, and black cows. Oil pumps. A few scattered houses. Cemeteries before and after every town, perhaps to remind me this is where life starts and ends. Without cell reception or GPS, I drive for what seems like hours, lost and increasingly exhausted and hungry. And just like that, in front of my eyes, a little BBQ joint appears. There is sometimes order in chaos.

An old, bearded man sits behind the counter. He stares at the horizons, slowly chewing tobacco in his mouth. It seems like he sits like this for hours.

"Hello, do you still serve?" I ask, noticing the place is empty. The big trash cans on the sides are full, evidence that it was packed with customers just a few hours ago.

Taking his time to answer, the old man looks at me and just nods, "yes."

Everything seems like slow motion here. Carefully, I first browse the counter: Rich, buttery mashed potatoes, fresh coleslaw, and sizzling refried beans. My belly grumbles *feed me.* I ask if the beans are vegetarian. The shop owner's teenaged daughter comes out of the kitchen. She must have heard my different accent. She seems amused by my naive question.

"Where are you from?" she asks with curious eyes.

I don't want to go into the Holy City conversation.

"Los Angeles," I reply.

The stunning blonde girl's eyes light up. She asked me if I had ever seen a celebrity or had seen a concert with curiosity. The only event she's seen is the local rodeo.

Different perspectives on beans and celebrities are what makes this world grand.

With hungry eyes, I load my plate with beef, mashed potatoes, and sweet coleslaw. I pause next to the bean tray. Even though I eat non-kosher meat outside of my home, eating pork is a big no-no. It is, by all means, a dirty sin beyond eating meat that was not blessed by a rabbi or eating shellfish. No one sees me, but, still, I skip. I suppress my gluttony. I am breaking some rules, but not all.

The family gives me explicit directions on how to find my way back to Austin. They draw maps and make them clear and easy. They give me hugs and. They ask me not to forget to tell the celebrities I see in Los Angeles about their place with so much pride. I promise I will.

"Bless your heart!"

Full of food and full of love, I get back on my road. Within a few miles, my GPS came back to life. Probably, it was hungry, too.

When I reach a freeway and have full bars on my phone, I call Dan. I disappeared for a few hours of country heaven, but now a paralyzing fear hovers over me. It is time to tell Dan that the seminar is over, and now I'm going to take care of myself. I feel selfish. I hesitate to tell him that I booked two nights at the W Hotel. I dread the reaction.

"The hotel is located in the center of Austin, with great access to tourist places," I justify my horrific, egotistical act.

You are a terrible person, an inner voice inside me declares, repeating what Dan tells me when he is upset. I do what I do best to defend myself in advance: I play the victim. I feel guilty for not going back home. How can I justify staying two nights just with myself, away from my duties, away from my role as a mom, away from my family?

"You are selfish," Dan flares on the other side.

I crumble to pieces inside.

"You are spending our best money on you while we are going broke. You always think about yourself."

I apologize and explain it was a special deal (it was). I try to justify my acts, but the anger penetrates my very cells like a purple dye dissolving into a cup of clear water. I hang up the phone, embarrassed and emotionally defeated.

The GPS tells me I am close to Austin. I am terrified and intimidated. I believe every word Dan said. We are going to be broke tomorrow, and I am a terrible mom. The shame, the guilt, and the defeat are flooding my body. I gasp for air. For a second, I forget where I am. I am in a black hole of self-hate and disgrace. I am an awful person.

146

Flashing lights behind me glaring from the mirror. The car behind me called for my attention like the impatient teacher on a field trip. I raise my eyes, and right in front of me, I see the entrance to a bridge. A steep, white, tall, huge – and I later discovered – a famous bridge. Slowly, I start driving. I have never been on such a bridge; the railings are narrow and short. I feel I might fall. I know I will fall. I press the breaks and slow down the alienated rental car to barely ten miles per hour.

My legs start to shiver rapidly, uncontrollably. The palms of my hands start sweating on the steering wheel. I am halfway up, and I cannot continue. I want to stop completely, to get out of the car and just run, run away as far as I can. I hear my heart pounding. *Boom. Boom. Boom.* My mind is foggy, and through the heavy curtain, I hear cars honking behind me. There is no escape. I try to press the gas pedal, and my right leg shakes even more with terror. There is no going back, and I cannot go on.

Panic.

Sweat.

Fear overwhelms me.

I cannot breathe.

No air.

I was ascending higher—no control over my body, no control over my life. I am frozen from within, on autopilot on the steepest bridge, on the road to the unknown.

Steeper.

147

Higher.

Scarier.

◉

Los Angeles, December 2009

Dan and I hire therapist after therapist, and yet another specialist, to help us communicate and rebuild what we could not do on our own. We switch therapists like chess pieces, trying to continue the game. Once we're dissatisfied or uncomfortable, we drop the therapist with ease and make another move. The game continues.

The Monster of insanity hits our home just before the big crash. Rehab. In Palm Springs.

Another consulting session. I feel sorry for myself. Life did it to me. Addiction won. It took my husband and my kids' dad, and now he is trying to wash away the Monster with people who speak Monsterish and can tame it after we fed the Monster day after day.

The therapist from the rehab in Palm Springs, who knows Monsterish fluently, listens to me. I make the same accusations repeatedly, still trying to make sense of it all. As in every other previous therapy session, I try to convince the therapist that Dan's fault is this time! I'm a broken record. I am not even sure who I am even trying to convince passionately. No one cares anyhow, except my Monster.

"I want to be the sick one!" I blow fire. "I want a chauffeur, a cook, a nurse, and a cleaner!"

I glare at the therapist, swearing again that *"It is him!"* with my countless usual explanations, my perfect well-sorted and addressed arguments. I am prepared to defend myself like it's my doctoral degree.

"You are sick, too," she says firmly, almost with a yell to get into me. The armchair grows cold. The abstract pictures on the wall seem petrified. The rug stares at me. The room is perfectly quiet, as if my attitudes confront every corner.

"Me?" I stop. There was a long, painfully silent pause.

"Yes," she continues, "you need help, go to Al-Anon."

Al-Anon! I have never heard this word before.

As Good Girl Jerusalem, I am on a sudden mission. I google A-l-a-n-on and find meetings nearby. It is not a potion, facial cream, or body wash. I cannot order it on Amazon Prime. It is not a pill or ointment I can pick up at the drugstore. It is a meeting.

A meeting? Simple!

Relieved, I tell myself I need to find a meeting immediately so that the revelation and the profound cure will appear as quickly as possible. I sort the meetings by zip codes, days, and hours. So many! I find one, not too far away, starting in 20 minutes. This will prove it was all his fault; I was the healthy one. The GPS seems to agree, guiding me through miraculously light traffic. My goal is clear and singular: I need the cure they sell at this Al-Anon place. I will buy it, take it for a few days, and be healed.

Easy.

I can do it.

It's a sunny day, one of those perfect Southern California days that the rest of the world envies. Ten in the morning. The long, tall oak trees on the side street greet me with gentle rays of the sun flickering in between the leaves. Welcome to your first meeting. I hear the trees greet me with a sweet sensation of familiarity. The bird's whistle and sing, "open your heart, open your mind..." beautifully orchestrated. The world is happy to see me walking into the building. I entered from the back door, embarrassed that someone might recognize me if I chose to enter the front door off the main street.

Quietly and hesitantly, I enter a back room, probably a storage, office, and tiny kitchen all in one. It is dark and leads to another room, a bigger, brighter area. I tip-toe so that no one can sense my arrival. Tentatively, I scan the few people in the room to make sure that no one knows me. I sit down in one of the cold corner chairs, shifting my eyes. A couple of old, ill-matched, torn sofas and some battered metal chairs are circled. The room has windows with old, half-broken shutters. Tri-fold pamphlets sit on an old brown, round corner table. Nearby is a rectangular table with color-coded fliers, brochures, and books. A few posters on the wall with a few sayings I did not understand.

This does not look like the cure.

I thank the Universe and my guardian angels, to the extent I believe in them, that there were only three people in the room. I look at them carefully. No, I do not recognize anyone. I am relieved. The leader is in his fifties, white hair, and round Lennon glasses, wearing a Hawaiian shirt. He has khaki shorts and Teva sandals and holding an old black, three-ring binder, from which he reads several paragraphs aloud. The others in the room recite along with him. They know it by heart. They keep saying words like Higher Power, Serenity, and God.

This is crazy. I think to myself. *I do not belong here. Make it short. Maybe they are all crazy. I couldn't possibly belong here.*

The two other women sitting in the room are approximately my age. One of them looked very confident. She sat tall and beamed with love in her eyes. The other was shy, hiding great pain in her soul. I know they are looking at me with curiosity, too. I try to send them a sweet smile, as I always do in a new crowd, but no matter how I feel inside, I can't muster even the slightest grin.

I hear them reading from books, except the words aren't clear. It all sounds very hazy and blurry. I sat there for about ten minutes. By now, my undiagnosed Attention Deficit Disorder is kicking in. This is an hour and a half meeting.

An hour and a half? I can't do it. Okay, I came late – what if I leave early? I bargain with myself for a few minutes, just as I sometimes do in the middle of a workout class – manipulating the time, breaking it into segments of ten minutes, maybe leaving early with all sorts of good reasons and excuses. *But I need to cure myself. I need to show them that I am me again. That I am not the sick one. I* remind myself of the reason I am there. *Concentrate, concentrate.* I force myself to sit straight up. *I am Good Girl Jerusalem,* I assure myself, *I can do this.*

I struggle to focus. People share their stories. Three minutes each, timed by a timer, and they don't interrupt each other. Their words and sentences are choppy, like waves in a storm. Not one clear sentence is spoken. But then, the unexpected happens. I didn't predict this or even imagine it could happen, but tears fill my eyes—heavy drops of tears. I nearly choke, trying to hold them back. I clench my hands tightly. And then, in one breath, all of my tears gush out like a waterfall. Thick, genuine, long-awaited tears. Tears that I have collected and hoarded for years; these tears are flooding out of me. They fall on my knees, down to my feet. They fall like rocks, one by one. Each tear contains the truth, the raw reality, the secrets, the shame – but they fall with the need to be right, the need to be understood.

"This is the time for newcomers," I hear the group leader announce. They all looked. At. Me. There is a long pause. I feel embarrassed, fidgety, and uncomfortable. Public speaking is my second nature. Give me any stage, and I will perform and work with the audience. I will rule it like a courageous lion in the savannah. Not here.

I mumble, "Ummmm, I..."

"Your name?" they all ask at once as if they practiced this moment in countless dress rehearsals. They all stare at me.

My name? Why do they want to know my name? I have to think cautiously about my answer. My name... my name. My tears cover my face; my black mascara smeared, I am choked up and want to give a fake name, something popular like Jennifer or Julie. They stare at me, waiting. I think about my favorite, comforting color. I gathered my courage.

"Ella," I whisper.

"Welcome, Ella," They all chant in unison.

The meeting is over. Everyone stands up, holding hands in a small protective circle, just the four of us. Their stories stand with us as well, held within us. The woman next to me holds my hand with warmth. She knows, and I know she knows.

"Keep coming back; it works if you work it," they all repeat. Most of them close their eyes.

Keep coming back. The words echo in my head.

I am not cured at the end of that meeting. I never get my "she-is-healed!" certificate I eagerly yearn for. I keep coming back. I'm thirsty for more. I'm ready. I made a promise to heal.

You didn't CAUSE it, You can't CONTROL it, and You can't CURE it!

Have you ever built something with another person just to see it crumble and vanish in front of your eyes? Have you started a dream that collapsed in a single day, just like cards or dominos, one layer after the other, until it becomes a pile of nothing?

It is surprisingly easy to spiral down and still not have mercy for yourself. You look at everything that's happened, and you lose what you knew as your core; you lose confidence, trust, and hope. You cannot buy faith. You cannot find it or borrow it, and it is not established in a minute or ten. Faith is confidence in an unknown force, something stronger than you, which wants to and will always create what is in your best interest. It is hard to trust a notion that your five senses cannot perceive, but this blind trust is the true core of certainty. For some, it might seem very easy. *Build confidence and move on with your life.* But it requires hard work and mental persistence, and it is an individual journey.

Another way to think of faith is to imagine it like a fragrance. Different scents work differently for different people; your skin will tell you if a perfume is right for you or not. Your senses will know, and your heart will tell you. A fragrance that is good for one person is not necessarily good for another – it's important to experiment to find the scent or spiritual path that works for you.

Find your source. Call it the Universe or call it God, Source, Power Greater than you, or rely on a natural power like the ocean, forest, or a mountain. Your source can be as unique to you as your scent. Regardless of what you choose, know that this power is always there for you, and it will carry you when everything is at its most challenging. Your source will create situations that, at the moment, do not look to be in your best interest. It creates these challenges in your life to push you into making the changes you need and crave but is afraid to start. It will help the bud of your life finally blossom into a flower – a life you never even imagined. When something is demolished, another thing will be built.

Putting your faith in a higher power doesn't just transform your life. It changes things for your family, your friends, your community. Those who love you have seen you struggle, and they want better for you. Only when you choose faith can you give those around you what they want most for you: a transformed life.

Seek and find your center of trust. It is there. Perhaps you can see it with both eyes, hear it with both ears, you can touch it with your ten fingers. You can talk to it. And if you believe you can sense it, you will find the faith that is perfectly yours, showing you a brighter future and the place of reassurance for which you have always longed.

Chapter 11

Highly Gifted

Nun. Tav. Nun. נ.ת.נ.
Gift מתנה • Give נתן • Fact נתון

◉

Los Angeles, November 2011

My fortieth birthday. I had perfectly prepared my man well in advance.

"I do not want bling jewelry, and I do not want a fancy name tag leather jacket or designer high heel shoes. And no, I don't want any surprise party or some gourmet dinner with five delicious courses."

I rehearsed my speech to my husband weeks before, hoping people wouldn't get a sneaky invitation. I disliked the thought of having my family and friends juggle dates, filling their calendars with expensive obligations and thousands of unwanted calories. I didn't want to walk into my house or a mysterious restaurant and have people jump out from side rooms and behind couches, greeting me with a loud "surprise!"

"But it's your fortieth birthday!" said Dan disapprovingly. Dan, my man, who was good at surprising me.

On my first birthday we celebrated together, eight months after we started officially dating, I realized Dan had missed his calling as a professional surprise planner. It was as if he put on a supernatural creative hat and pulled out an entire celebration on my birthday. He carefully planned three days of glorious festivities. Dinner with friends, followed by a dance party. The next day, an expensive and renowned Broadway show with the best seats in the house. He topped it all with a romantic dinner in a secluded ranch in Malibu Canyon with a personalized dessert menu that included a heart-pumping poem.

I read the poem, which was all about butterflies and love.

Do I deserve all of that? I asked myself. *It is just my birthday.*

I read the poem, trying not to swoon with each verse. The last line was a shock.

"Will you marry me?"

A camera flashed. The well-prepared waiter took a picture of my man proposing (a rare moment in the pre-smartphone era). This was the most significant surprise of my life – a birthday that ended with an amazing proposal and a huge diamond ring with blue sapphires. Blue and white, the colors of Israel. Perfect for this holy chick!

For my fortieth birthday, I wanted nothing of the sort. I desperately hoped that he would not surprise me. I didn't want diamonds, or poems, or Paris. What did I want? What did I want?

A brand new kitchen.

I wanted it, I needed it, I deserved it – but mostly, I just wanted it. And I was prepared to negotiate.

"I will give up on four years' worth of birthdays, Mother's Days, and anniversary gifts, just to get a new, white, comfortable kitchen."

I replayed that tape to Dan again and again. I was sick of my thirty-year-old, brown, squeaky-floor kitchen. Instead, I dreamt of being Rachel Ray in a kitchen palace. I wanted a chef's hat for my birthday crown and my birthday queen's regalia, a cute, short, black apron. All that was secondary, of course. I just wanted my kitchen.

Forty arrived. But nothing happened overnight. No wrinkles appeared. I did not get wiser, and I was not handed a fantastic overview of my life's meaning.

I turn forty on a Saturday. I wake up at 8:00 AM, a pure luxury when you are a mom of two, even on your birthday.

It's my birthday, and I will sleep if I want to!

The kids know the second I'm awake. Joyously, my angels run into my room, jump into my bed with excitement, and cover me with tender kisses and hugs. They sing with loving, sweet voices and sparkling eyes. We spend precious cuddly time in bed, which is the best gift I could have received at any age.

Having reached my fifth decade, I feel officially like a woman. The four of us sat at the tiny dining table, enjoying colorful plates of organized fruit assembled like flowers and pouring maple syrup on homemade pancakes. As I flip the delicious sweet brown pancakes, I wished my kitchen was easier and more comfortable to cook in.

159

With a child's impatience, my daughter disappears into her bedroom and playfully runs back out with exuberance and shows me THE present. She holds a small white box wrapped with pink flowers, draped in a feather boa in her little hands. She has handmade the wrapping. How could this moment last forever? All three of them stare at me with big smiles.

"Mom! Let's open the box now."

With great anticipation, they asked me to reveal the gift.

I try not to show my disappointment.

Did I not ask, over and over again, no jewelry? How come no one heard me? How can I refuse this head-over-heels birthday present? How am I supposed to say no to this little handmade box with a precious gift in it?

Carefully, I unwrap the handmade boa, the wrapper, and slowly open the promising jewelry box. I assume it's a ring, or a bracelet, or maybe a necklace. For Dan, I do my best to look excited and happy for the kiddos for the family. The children are excited, and I am not sure if they have already seen it before or not. My eyes shine, pretending.

Gently, I snap open the little top. I see no bling. No beads. No gold or silver. I unfold a white note and see my son's drawing of a colorful flower. In my daughter's handwriting, I read: *This is not a piece of jewelry! Happy Birthday, Mommy!*

They've been holding in the surprise, and all three laugh harder than I've ever heard them. Dan, who had slipped away for a moment, emerges from the bedroom with big architect boards and blue-ink planning posters.

My dream kitchen! Dan heard me! Astonished, I am truly elated. I love my man, and, more to the point, I am falling in love again.

Kitchens don't just appear like diamond necklaces. We spend weeks remodeling, planning, moving, choosing, measuring, buying, exchanging, and designing—endless trips to hardware stores, kitchen and cabinet stores, and paint stores. We demolish, build, and continue building.

We delight in our creation, greeting each progress point with the glee of a child who just scored the winning goal in a soccer tournament. I insist on a few things, no matter what the designer, the builder, and the architect desired. Despite their opinions, I design a very narrow pantry to hold precisely the cans and the snacks I need, labels facing me, no more than three cans deep. I divide the long kitchen and build a separate laundry room to create privacy and space.

It's my kitchen, and I'll decide if I want to!

After two long months of decisions and dust, we cut the imaginary red ribbon to a radically face-lifted kitchen. Each corner in this kitchen gleams with care and tenderness. After the long cold winter of eating take-out food in a dusty house, I fall in love with my new, bright, spacious, stylish kitchen.

Dan granted my wish. He made me feel more like a princess than I knew possible. My glass slippers dance on white tiles; my happy fingers glide on white countertops and swing open the shimmering cabinets.

There were many creative ideas in the kitchen, but most of all, I was proud of my most creative, innovative idea: an electronics drawer! This drawer would be stocked with cleverly hidden wires and sockets to charge phones, hold earbuds, and storage batteries. Everything was hidden inside the drawer. There would be no wires on my new white countertop.

One week after completing the kitchen, I put on my fancy Julia Child apron, and I start baking and cooking like a (slightly mad) genius in a lab. I experiment with food colors. Bundt cakes. Mousse cakes. Pancakes are shaped in letters, flowers, and other surprises for breakfast. I realize that I am strangely unafraid of failure, certain that no matter what, it will all turn out just as it should in the end. The only thing I have in my mind is *'try, try, try.'* I test, sample, make it again and taste over and over.

The children are my guinea pigs. If they lick their lips, it's a do-it-again recipe. If they make grimaces, I know to deem it "never-to-repeat."

In that kitchen, I am reborn at forty.

I use colors and spices with zest, a response to the joy and love I feel. I decorate plates, garnish meals, and offer bee shaped cake-pops for the school's yearly spelling bee competition. I pull together wedding cakes and holiday delicacies. If I succeed in concocting an exquisite, delicious, satisfying treat, I am validated as the sweet lady.

Los Angeles, 2012

Water.

In The United States, water is not free. At least, not if you live in the Westside of Los Angeles. You have to pay for water to drink it. Children in much of the rest of the world would laugh at these ridiculous Westerners. Mineral water, freshwater, infused-with-electrolytes water, alkaline water, spring water, mountain water, blue tops, clear containers, round or square bottles. Choose your water, as long as you paid for it. You see, if you drink tap water in Los Angeles, it is not considered real water. The taste is not clear enough, not pure enough, not healthy enough.

Angelenos treat water like diamonds. The diamonds in California can never be too big, too shiny, or too sparkly. The houses in Beverly Hills cannot be too grand, too new, or too gated. Women cannot be too thin, too blonde, or too wrinkle-free. It is the land of nothing-is-too-much.

I was born into a world of multiples. Six siblings, seven houses by the age of six, one hundred and one steep steps up to our Jerusalem home, four languages. Too much? Hah! The more, the better. Try me, God!

When my children, Lev and Liam, were in their first years, we did not have a fridge with a water dispenser, nor did we have the fancy waterspout with filtered water. As shopping was one of my many mommy duties, I was also in charge of buying the water. Religiously, I hauled the water from the grocery store shelves into the cart, to the cashier, into my car trunk, and the house. Heavy cases of water bottles – thirty-six or even forty-eight bottles at a time. This was before the Amazon Prime or the Google Express era, where water can be delivered miraculously right to your doorway. I was grateful we had the right water and grateful that I did not have to carry those heavy, bulky cases up the one hundred and one steps to our home, like in my childhood.

Recycling the bottles quickly became a chaotic mess. Crinkly empty bottles ended up everywhere, underfoot like Legos. I went on a hunt for a simple solution that would make the water problem easy and simple. Eagerly, I tried those big one-gallon jugs, but those quickly turned into a logic puzzle every time I had to organize the fridge. How could I fit these plastic giants between baby food, fruits, and vegetables? I was determined, but I gave up on the jugs quickly.

Water. Isn't it supposed to be simple?

And just like that, the hoped-for answer comes into our mailbox. The flier looks promising.

"You see, this way, we will always have drinking water, cold or hot, any time we want it."

I convinced Dan to sign up for the water service, pulling out all of my charm and convincing tools I've collected through the years. He thinks about it for a few days and does his calculations. After I protest for a few days (deliberately neglecting the tedious mommy-secretary-duties), I get the green light.

Water.

A few phone calls, the signing of a bewilderingly long, small-print contract, and there it is, the happy end to my water carrying years. Water service comes straight into our house, the truck with huge blue bottles quenching our thirst and ending my quest.

Twice a week, the truck screeches to a halt outside. The sound of the brakes is an orchestra to my ears. We've started with two bottles a week, but we need five by the first hot summer. They're happy to deliver; all I have to do is change the bottle when one is due. Roll the big bottle from the storage to the back of the kitchen.

I will do anything for water. I feel like the girl in Africa who brings the water from the well. Carrying the enormous tin jug, rolling it, lifting and placing it on her head, letting her daydreams drift within her mind, away from the pressing weight and the sizzling heat. The little girl is daydreaming about taking a long refreshing shower, enjoying cold air-conditioning, and drinking sweet homemade lemonade. I do the same. I am daydreaming about wandering in Africa, feeling free, dancing in the wide-open fields talking to the zebras, the gazelles, and the giraffes.

I am hot. August is a burning month. Blissfully, I turn on the faucet and enjoy the long, cool, relaxing shower. I forget about the girl in Africa.

Water.

"Hi! I'm Freddie!" a muscular dark-skinned man came to our door with a big jug of water on his shoulder. He has tattoo sleeves on his arms and legs, and I can see the dimple on his chin behind the baseball cap. "I'll be your water delivery man!"

165

Every other Wednesday, the squeaky rusty brakes announce Freddie's eagerly awaited arrival. Courteous, generous, and polite, Freddie always greets me with a smile, fixing his baseball cap, asking about my day, and always curious about the babies. From one visit to another, he tells me about his four kids, all under the age of 14.

"These are my kids!" he would show me with a proud grin. "I love them more than anything!"

He proudly tells me about their achievements, soccer games, and the fun he plans for them in the coming weekend. Freddie loves being a dad – even his tattoos feature their names on his arms.

When you meet a good-hearted person, you feel it. Though it's not part of his job, he helps me change the house's water bottles when I imagine all he wants to do is finish and end his shift. No one pays him to stay longer. His deep dimple and kind smile give away his good heart and sweet nature.

Water makes this girl happy, just as it did my Grandma Esther, who ladled it out and made families and children happy and satisfied during the long British blockade of besieged Jerusalem. Tirelessly, she carried the water pails to thirsty souls. Water was a luxury. Ice was something that only the richest people could have in their homes. And yet, freshwater was served. Every sip was pure gratitude.

It's a hot August day. I'm packing for my brother's wedding in Israel. The brown canvas bags to help the kids count down the days I'm away are finished; all that remains is to figure out how to close my suitcase.

Screech!

Freddie is here. Water! It doesn't matter how busy I am; I go outside and say hello. We have our routine friendly exchange. I'll offer him a health bar and fruit to snack on, and he'll leave two sleeves of plastic water cups.

Something is off about him. He is shier, and he mumbles through the usual small talk about the kids... and then comes the question. It seems like he's practiced for days and finally has found the courage.

Freddie shifts from one leg to the other and then asks, "How about lunch together one day?"

A moment of awkward silence. A tiny pebble was dropped into a still pond.

I smile at him with my left cheek dimple and softly reminded him, "Freddie, I am married."

Pause.

"Just as friends," Freddie corrects himself, embarrassed.

"I am married." I was firm. I'm disappointed but a bit flattered. I never thought about any other man but Dan.

Freddie steps back.

What was he possibly thinking? I ask myself.

When the truck leaves, I notice the health bar and the fruit on the kitchen counter. This day Fredie leaves not only two water cup sleeves. He leaves four.

You cannot compare your insides to someone else's outside.

Look around you – social media, billboards, and movies tell us to be better, stronger, prettier, and greater. In this era of instant gratification, it is easy to swipe, turn, scroll in the constant hunger of what is next, what is more, what is bigger. But does it exist?

You forget that sometimes the simplest things are the best. What is pure in its core existence is what you need. No need to chase after anything else.

Water. The basic necessity of life is water. Pure, clean, fresh water that the soul not only wants but needs to in order to exist. We search for water that's better, holier, sweeter, and we forget that we are water. The purest water the Universe ever created.

You are water. You have water around you, inside you, and within you. What is your water in your life? What is the one thing that you could not survive without? Is it family? Is it money? Success? Work? Art? Kids? The answer is simple yet complicated. It contains every aspect of life, every sense, and every person. It is a quest for water that never seems to end. It is love. Unconditional self-love. This is when you stop chasing for the next gig and pause. Sip the water of life in an intentional, slow, confident way, enjoying what life presents to you because you truly do not know what is next.

The moment you pause and become aware of your brain and the chattering committee in your head, you will be able to stop it, even for a few moments. Only this way will you be able to enjoy what is in front of you. You will be in the moment and stop planning for tomorrow because no one can predict the future, and by constantly trying to live for tomorrow, you miss today.

Pause. Your life is now.

Chapter 12

10mg of Help

Ayin. Zain. Resh. ע.ז.ר.
Help עזר · Helpful עוזר · Name of a plant עזרר

●

And so round and round I go.

The lying. The deceiving. The tears.

In hiding. No one can see.

The confrontation.

More tears.

And the control in a mask of love. How it hurts.

What hurts the most? Convincing myself this is the last time.

I believe.

It's another honeymoon period. Life is brilliant, incredible, spectacular!

No lies. No pain.

I breathe again. Almost freely.

And then it sneaks back in.

The first sign of doubt. I ignore.

I close my eyes.

I'll splurge and buy a few more hours of illusion.

My denial seals me off from reality.

Maybe I'm a failure.

No, maybe, here is the proof: I drive along the same road, again.

Without a seatbelt, without enough gas, ignoring the stop signs.

The big black word shrieks from a brilliant field of yellow: "Hazard!"

And the second I let my guard down, the moment I start to trust, it
happens again.

A second time. And a third, and a 10th. I stop counting.

It's clear as day – and yet I stay blind.

But I can see it all

◉

Los Angeles, July 2013

5 am. The alarm goes off. Well trained, I hit the stop button almost before it starts. It is completely dark outside, right before dawn. The world-sun is still sleeping. I try to regulate my breath, trying to mimic my dream-breathing so that it sounds as if I am still deeply asleep. Breathe in, breathe out, listening to my air, in, out, and again. I am a soldier in the middle of battle, ready to get up in a millisecond to execute my mission. The first mission was a success.

Dan is sleeping on the right side of our California king size bed. One bed where two people sleep alone. His chest moves up and down with his breaths. I close my eyes and listen to his deep sleep, trying to match every move I make with his exhalations like an Olympic synchronized swimmer. Dan never snores; his breaths are equal, steady, deep. He is sound asleep.

Slowly, I sit on the edge of the bed, making sure not to make any sudden movements. I stop and listen to the breaths. I am careful with each movement I make, aware of every tiny pivot. First, I turn onto my side, sit on the edge, and pause to listen. I tiptoe from the room, quietly, cautiously, like a wise and expert thief – a robber in my own home. Gently, I close the bedroom door, holding the knob to avoid making any suspicious noise. My heart starts beating louder, and I am afraid it alone might wake him up. As irrational as it is, I freeze, stand by the door, waiting to hear if he heard the pounding in my chest. Ten seconds. Thirty seconds. Everything is calm, quiet, serene; everything except the race in my heart and my mind.

I continue with the dark early morning routine I have adopted for the past two months now. I peek into Lev's room and smile. She is so pure and peaceful with her little pink Lambie next to her face. Then I go to Liam's room, his sweet soft curls resting on his face, gleaming in the reflection of the night light. Pure little kids, if you only knew what your mom is up to.

My workout clothes are waiting for me in the kids' bathroom, adjacent to the laundry room. They have been waiting patiently for the mission all night. I hid them there the night before as part of my master plan for my early morning hunt. I get dressed quickly, tactically, like the soldier I once was. Black sports bra, sports top, Lululemon leggings, and socks. I don't put my shoes on, I put them outside on the back entrance last night. My heart is beating faster. I stand and organize my breaths again.

Don't think now – it is all going as you planned, I calm myself.

I hang my pajamas on the shower door softly to not make even the slightest noise, aware of every sound around me. My gym clothes become my detective cloak. I put my jacket on without zipping it and sneak out the back door next to the laundry room that leads to the patio. I am still in my socks, holding the tennis shoes in my hands.

I am out of the house. I exhale. I can breathe freely.

Yet, the very fog that protrudes from my mouth in the frosty air is the same fog that conceals me from the truth. I put on my tennis shoes one by one and feel anxious but confident. It is now already 5:20. The dawn is drawing near. It is getting lighter; the sunrise is approaching the horizon.

I pause.

I unlock Dan's car with the spare key I slipped in the pocket of my jacket the night before. The car beeps.

I freeze.

I gaze into our house to make sure no one is up. I can almost see through the sheer curtains. The fear is persistent.

I am a burglar—robber of trust.

I open the driver's side door and lift the middle console. I am on a mission; I am looking for something. I open the bottom section of the console and go through each item. There must be a reason. I know something is up, my gut tells me. Methodically and quickly, I search through old body shop papers, stale mints, work contracts, more spare keys, mailing brochures, paper clips, a few notes scrambled by hand. Again, I find nothing. I am disappointed. *Nothing.* But my gut tells me differently.

I am done with my search and sit on the side of the curb. Exhausted, but not because of the early hour.

At 5:45 a.m., my neighbor Lila comes outside. It has been three months now that Lila and I take our long morning walk. She is my alibi, and she doesn't even know it – for now. I must continue my underground quest.

I must find it.

"So early, Ella," Lila complains loudly. "How can you wake up so early?" She locks her door, and, along with her voice, the sun is rising.

Lila is beautiful, her big smile reflects her loving heart. She just had her third baby, and I am her motivator to lose the baby weight, so her husband will find her attractive again. We are an exchange of desires.

Four times a week, I wake up and search Dan's car. I find absolutely nothing. I look in the backseat, under his seat, in the back seats' pockets, the side doors. Every morning, I search another section and then meet up with the ever-smiling Lila for our morning walks, wearing a mask of a good wife like nothing happened just fifteen minutes before we shed calories to keep our hubbies' eyes satisfied.

And then, I see it. I notice there is a button on the car key I never pressed before. The trunk. The trunk? That is not just a click of a door. This is noisy, noticeable, and much more dangerous. My heart beats in ecstasy like an African drum in the middle of a full moon drum circle.

No! Are you crazy? I ask myself as if I am sane.

Did you lose your mind? Dan will hear for sure.

My insanity weighs the risk of Dan waking up, and my plot is revealed in shame and disgrace.

As Lila loses weight, I grow crazy with my secret. I become my enemy, thinking, rethinking, and analyzing the hunt again and again. I was not a trained intelligence officer for nothing.

This is too much of a big secret. Before the trunk expedition, I decided to share my secret with "smiley" Lila. I confess my morning quest to Lila. I confess my insanity, my feelings, my shame. Lila, still smiling, hugs me. Her love handles hug me like a mama bear.

"Ella, it is probably nothing," she reassures me.

"I will be here with you when you open the trunk," she continues with her dimple.

After all, she is losing weight, feeling great, and wants to make sure we put an end to this nonsense and keep our a.m. marching. I look at Lila and admire her positivity; her life is devoted to her husband. I secretly wish my life were as simple. I wish I could erase all these thoughts as easily as cleaning the teacher's whiteboard after every class.

Like every other morning, I follow my plan to the letter. I set the alarm to 5 a.m.; I leave the room, check the kids, put on my gym clothes quickly, and leave the house. I look at the spare car key in my pocket and almost press the trunk button, taking the risk that my plan will be exposed before I even find something.

I pause.

I wait for Lila to come out before the trunk endeavor. Maybe her smile will mask my face as well.

Ella, it's one click. Do it. You know there is something you must see.

"Just press the button," Lila prompts, drawing close to me.

I look at the picture of the trunk on the key and press the button. With a long slow whoosh, the trunk is now open – exposed. My heart stops.

I prepare for the worst. I imagine Dan is coming out of the house and seeing it all.

It's quiet. Nothing happens. The pre-dawn silence remains. The birds are sleeping on the big oak tree next to our home.

I lean into the trunk. Hesitant to touch, I slowly search with my eyes. Papers. Shorts. Shirt. More papers. Socks. But these socks seem huge, folded into a big elongated ball.

The socks!

I take the white gym socks and unfold them.

And there they are. A vial of pills – dozens of pills.

It's here. *It's real.*

My body shakes. My knees begin to buckle under me. My quest is over. This is what I was looking for. I press the key button, and as the trunk door closes slowly, I feel my entire world collapsing.

I didn't want to find anything!

I shake so much I cannot even stand. Lila holds me as we sit on the sidewalk.

I try to regulate my last breaths. I pant like a wounded puppy.

The devil again.

Lila, not smiling anymore, takes out one pill and reads, "WATSON 853", otherwise known as Vicodin, the opioid painkiller.

The secret stays with Lila.

She takes the vial and guards it in her house like a rare work of art.

I say nothing, waiting for Dan to ask me if I saw the vial. But he says nothing, two adults playing hide and seek. The shame hugs the white picket fence's perimeter and stuffs what's inside with fear and sadness. I am afraid to share. I am afraid to tell. I am afraid to confront. From there, my life gets smaller and smaller.

I feel as if I am standing here in front of a huge intersection, lost as to where to go next. Should I go right, left? It's not just me standing here alone, it's Lev and Liam beside me. I've been responsible for them for ten and seven years, and I must take them with me on this road. The intersection is confusing. Signs, lights, signals I know and recognize from driving school, some blurs that I do not remember at all.

Does red mean "no" every time? Can the yellow change to green, or is it red right after? The errors flash before my eyes, one after another. A billboard of a happy family, another rehab, and a happy comeback. A sad wife, depression, and chaos. Slogans and sayings echo inside my head.

I am lost.

I try to navigate my way in this intersection by fear. If I go this way, I will get lost. If I go that way, I will get run over. I need clear instructions.

And then Dan arrives home with the smell I once knew so well, with his big arms, with his usual look in the eyes telling me he missed me. I scrunch the instructions into a paper ball and shoot it into the closest wastebasket. His eyes promise me the moon, his arms protect me from hell, and I see one road, the very narrow one that promises the four of us access to a fantasy land that is labeled "family and love forever."

I hold onto the vision of that road for a few hours, or a few days, until the fear comes crawling again, reaching into my being, my bones, and my heart. I see long yellow stripes with big words: DANGER ZONE.

"No!" I once again ignore the warning signs. I am blind to the yellow barricades and flashing lights.

I manage until I see the familiar, unmistakable signs he is numbing his pain again. Another pill, another day in bed, another argument, another put down, another error or arrow in my heart.

Logic versus feelings; a test I never feel prepared for. My heart is heavy once more, and the debate rages on.

Give me an answer! I beg. But I don't even know whom I am asking.

I refuse to accept it, but I know I have to. Not because of Dan. He has his road, his journey, which once was connected to mine. The fears that come with getting back on the same road are so immense that failure seems assured before we take a single step. I will blame him for any little bump in the road. I will close him off and won't let him be.

Dan needs to be there for himself. I need to be there for me. Our roads have to separate.

"God," I scream as loud as I can, yet without words. "Why? How is it that two people can fall in love, create two lives, create one world, and then... you break them apart?"

I am looking for logic again. Something to explain to me in convincing yet straightforward words this great mystery.

I mourn. My brain dusts off the memories and only fixates on the happy ones. My memory log highlights the good times and forgets about agony. I live in L.A., and I'm as good as any experienced film editor in the Hollywood studios. I summon up images of trips: Palm Springs, Italy, Mexico, New York, Hawaii with the kiddos. I want to run back in time, and I'm willing to leave the bad memories on the cutting room floor.

Except I know that there will be a fourth time, another cruel relapse.

My sadness is so deep that it isn't about Dan or the children. It is about me, encompassing everything I am.

There are no shortcuts to pain. It comes when it must. There are no shortcuts to life.

I look ahead; the intersection is there. I need to take one turn at a time. There is no one "right" road. It is hard to choose: do I stay, do I leave? Each turn will lead me to the right place where I should be. Because they say, there is no right answer.

What follows is the desire to escape, too much or too little sleep, the sudden desire to drink like in the movies until I pass out, though I never do. If only I could find the magic eraser, I would use it.

Retail therapy doesn't work. Purchasing is an empty promise. Brand name watch, a fancy black and gold purse, a tight dress to show my curves, which are craving a hug – a genuine hug that says, "you belong to me." And don't forget that halter top to show off my shoulders and biceps, which are so toned yet so weak at the same time.

My legs hurt from searching every store, reaching out for anything that might bring some joy, distraction, or color to my life. With sore feet, store after store, forgetting to eat, or even to drink, I continue to hunt, dragging myself along, hands aching from the heavy bags. When I arrive home, I look glamorous, but the illusion of relief is fleeting.

Even if I am drop-dead gorgeous for the day, my eyes tell a different story.

Nothing numbs the pain. The void is so gaping; the openness cries so louder than any song, conversation, or anything the universe could offer me. Nothing could cover the vast hole.

My life fell into it, and I became lost, wandering my roads. I was lost in oblivion.

> *Insanity is doing the same thing over and over again and expecting a different result.*

That Monster loves to win, loves to conquer at any price. The addiction wins if not dealt with at its core, every hour for the rest of our lives. If one doesn't deal with his or her terrible conniving addiction and simply lets it take over, the habit does what it does best. It reigns over us with an iron grip. There are three, and only three, outcomes when we surrender to our addictions:

Insanity.

Jail.

Death.

All are dreadful. They rarely come instantly, though they can. The slide towards one of these three terrible ends is more often a slow one, the result of one bad decision after another – decisions made by the addict's brain.

Death. I almost touched it. I almost let the Monster eat everything I had, taking hostages in every direction, conquering my stomach, life, relationships, family, babies, and everything I treasured. I was so busy with what was around me and ignored what was in me. I nearly lost my own life. I had given up. I waved my white flag. I surrendered to what was bigger and stronger than me. I found myself living the life of someone else, claiming it was mine.

If you want to change something, start by doing only one thing. All you must do is take the first step. Make the decision to change. Even if the road is unclear, try to let go of your obsession with how it will happen, when, or who will help you. Too often, we linger in our process of change because we are not sure who will help us or how the hell we are going to make the change. How do you even start? Paralyzed by worry about how the change will happen, we blame, accuse, and point fingers. We tell our friends the horror stories and the injustices, convincing others that the world is conspiring against us. We wait for someone else to change, cure themselves, and make the transformation we desperately need. We dawdle and sit in the mud, in the cumbersomeness, in the chaos of life. It all comes from one fear—the fear of creating change.

There is no manual for change. The great mistake so many of us make is that we think we need one, a detailed guide, each step written out, illustrated with helpful diagrams. Your brain will tell you that you need a timeline, graphs, clearly established goals, and bullet points. You need precise objectives and a clear path.

All of that is a lie. You do not need any of this. What you're listening to is fear. Fear's goal is to create anxiety and confusion so that you will be afraid to make any change. Chaos loves fear, and fear is derived from chaos. You truly need only one thing: a decision. A promise to yourself that you want to transform and become better. Look at yourself in the bare, exposing, neutral mirror and gaze deeply inside your pupils. Do you see turmoil, or sadness, or disappointment? Know it is coming from within.

If you take the first step, the next step will present itself. You won't get to see the road ahead, and you'll stay frozen if you demand a map. You do not have to know where you'll be six steps from now. Just have the inner willingness to admit your faults and accept your participation in this madness. See how you, just you, feed your Monster. I promise you'll be astounded by how your life has changed once you make the pledge to stop living your life the way you have done in the past. The question is, are you ready for it? If you are indeed ready, the gifts you will receive will be beyond anything you ever thought you deserved. You cannot prepare yourself. Just know it is there waiting for you. Just as you will decide, the Universe will provide – but it will always be in that order.

Do you want to live your life differently? Commit. Like a mother commits to her baby at birth, saying, "I am here for you." Be there for yourself.

Chapter 13

Courage to Change

Alef. Mem. Tzadi. .א.מ.צ.

Courage אומץ • Brave אמיץ • To make an effort להתאמץ • Effort מאמץ

◉

Israel, August 2012

The flash of summer heatwave welcomes me. The heat outside of the airport is unbearable. I forget how scorching it is here at the height of a sizzling summer. After a fourteen-hour direct flight, I am exhausted but mainly excited. This time I flew by myself without Lev and Liam with me. LAX to TLV, kids free, bags free, toys free. It is the first time I've used my frequent flyer miles, which I saved for this special, exciting, and unforgettable event of the century: My baby brother is getting married!

"Finally!" My mom is relieved. My youngest brother, the boy filled with hyperactivity and hormones since toddlerhood, and the city's famous playboy is getting married at last. This is not your average summer wedding; the sixth sibling, her youngest son, is getting married. The celebration of my brother, who is fourteen years younger than I am, is going to be huge.

Sasi is hugging me at the airport. "Sis!" He hugs me for a whole, long minute. I allow myself to collapse in his strong arms and wide chest but just for a few moments. I feel love, true love. I am loved. I can trust for a few days.

I don't tell him. I keep my secrets with me. He is getting married in a few days. Sasi -- the short version for Sasson (happiness in Hebrew) -- is fourteen years younger than me, but really, he is my twin. He understands me without words. I try to hide my heavy heart between the walls of my soul as I have since Lev, my second child, was born. I am ashamed. I fight between hiding my secret and yearning for his raw opinions, which Sasi always gives me. But only if I ask.

Sasi gets me my diluted cappuccino in a paper cup from the airport vending machine. We escape the coastline heat and drive to my home city, Jerusalem. Sasi puts on the radio, the one radio station that plays my childhood songs and reminds us that it's Shabbat soon. Sasi rolls down the car's windows. Jerusalem's calm breeze was welcoming, fluttering gently across my face. The well-known steep inclines on the way to my childhood city, passing by old tanks from the forties abandoned on the side of the road, reminding me that you need to fight for independence.

I look at my wise and loving brother. I am calmer. I am safe. This is unconditional.

As each day goes by, I feel my soul healing from my heart's long-standing neglect. Here, there are no routines, no responsibilities. *What a crazy thought for a mom!* Music, dancing, gathering, meals, celebrations, loud conversations, reuniting with family and high school girlfriends I haven't seen for more than a decade. Spotting new wrinkles of wisdom, each one of them has created a whole new world, with new careers, love stories, white picket fence houses, and three kids. With mama duck pride *(Here are my babies!),* we take turns showing family pictures on our phones, collecting all the beautiful compliments. It tames and soothes my aching soul, who desperately misses my little ducklings.

I stare at my phone's screensaver since I already miss my Lev and Liam. They smile at me with their brown, wise, innocent eyes, which seem to understand everything, especially love.

I'd been racked with guilt for leaving Lev and Liam. Ten days away– how could I still claim the title "devoted mom" if I leave them to go to a different continent? Trying to conquer my worry, I had diligently searched for a crafty project on the creative moms' blogs. I was on a mission. I need to help my babies cope during my ten days' negligent absence, or, rather, help myself with this separation anxiety. I needed something to stop the "What a horrible, horrible mom you are" thought that came the second I booked my ticket and only intensified when I packed the suitcase.

Browsing Etsy for days, I found the perfect DIY art project that would explain and show Lev and Liam the trip duration. I handmade ten canvas bags and decorated them with pastel colors. On each canvas, I wrote a number. The number represented the number of days in descending order until mommy comes back: ten, nine, eight, all the way to one. I inserted a little surprise for each bag – a cute picture of us, a little riddle, a joke, a love note. A little something to tell them, "Mommy is here, and mommy misses you a lot. Count the days. I will be here soon!" I hung all ten bags on a long raffia rope from the living room's curtain rod. Each unique bag declared my immeasurable love.

The love bags assuaged my guilt and made it much easier to enjoy ten summer days and ten hot nights with my family, the all-nighter celebrations of weddings, and the before-and-afters. In all this happiness and warmth, I feel at home again. Thousands of miles away from what is now my new home in California, I feel real happiness once more, real safety, real sanctuary. However, I do not allow myself one thing – I cannot afford to waste this precious two hundred and forty hours on sleep. I am, at last, surrounded by simplicity and truth.

I miss my sweet princess dancing baby girl and my blond baby boy. I miss the soft touches, the hugs, the innocent goodnight kisses, the pure, gentle smells. I miss them both! And here in my homeland, I feel like a baby myself, just for a few hours, for a few days.

It is day eight. Feverishly, I'm packing in love, storing it for the long trip home as best I can. I am stuffing in every last morsel of treasured kindness, of listening, and of strength. I want to bring home with me the gifts I received and collected these days. Learning how not to be embarrassed for who I am, embarrassed by my tone of voice, of my loud laugh, of my you-can-call-it-OCD, of "my way or the highway." I've been put down for a long time now, been ashamed, been criticized, ignored, and corrected. I put my wishes in a hidden box so no one will notice. But here, I allow myself to dare, to laugh out loud with arms open to the side, to be silly, to <u>be</u>. I thought I forgot how. I fill my suitcase like a thief, stuffing, pushing, compressing as much as I can in every little pocket, affection, hugs, and attention. I pack to the maximum extent that the zippers and the pockets of my suitcases can hold. I know I'll have to pay overages, extending the fifty-pound weight limit; freedom is expensive.

And then, my stomach.

My stomach is in pain. *I am too excited to go back to Lev and Liam.* And then, when my stomach continues its independent twists, the next thought hits me. *I probably ate something spoiled at one of the endless wedding parties.*

I find excuses to tame the sharp needle feelings, not allowing any thoughts of sickness to crawl and interrupt the last few hours of my bliss in my homeland, but my stomach aches. I feel the discomfort getting worse and worse like a woodpecker that pecks on a thick trunk. I don't say a word. I visit the lady's room frequently. Every other hour, and then every hour. I am in denial. *No time to be sick right now!* I order myself, like a tough drill commander. *My babies are waiting.* There are only two more canvas bags left on the rope at home. Two. One. The children were counting them down with anticipation.

"Soon. I will be home soon," I promised them on the phone. I am bringing presents and local goodies, waiting to hold them close to me, to my heart. For me, they are the ultimate present in life.

My sister gives me an antacid, but my stomach still fights me with a sword, sharp stabs daubing me over. I agree to try a few home remedies. My grandma instructs me to rub hot cognac on my belly as her great-grandma taught her. It will warm my stomach and cure it. My grandma is wise from a long line of wise women. I warm the cognac, rub it on my stomach, I stink like an Irish bar, and wait. But nothing helps. It's probably the stomach flu. I hide it. I brush it off. I ignore it.

Go away, stomach flu! I again demanded. *Your babies are waiting.*

During the last couple of days of my trip, I stayed in a suburb next to Tel Aviv at my sister Lee's home, the second eldest of us six children. We decide to go shopping, and while she is browsing the shelves searching for another deal, I stop in the bathroom. Afterward, we sit in a coffee shop, and I drink herbal tea. She makes me laugh. I look at her. Soon, it is time to leave the comfort and safety to which I have grown accustomed over the past several days. I protest like a toddler stamping his feet. *No, I do not want to leave! Five more minutes, pleeease!*

Lee feels me. She looks at me with her pure, honest smile. Her two deep sweet dimples and long, dirty blonde hair in a bun and her deep almond eyes can get the immediate attention of any camera. Lee is only a year and a half younger than me, but her spirit is older. She's never taken a New Age class and knows nothing about yoga or meditation. She has no clue who Tony Robbins or Marianne Williamson is, but Lee's heart speaks before her mouth. She is connected to the Universe, to God, to Love.

It is time. It is ten o'clock at night, and we wait for the taxi driver to arrive and pick me up.

We sit on the curb next to the entrance to her condo building. It is late, another hot summer night. Without words, she hugs me. I pray as her love, her warmth, and her arms envelop me. *Don't stop,* the little girl inside me whispers. Lee hugs me, keeping me close to her heart. She feels me, and her lingering hug becomes warmer. I want to stay in her encompassing arms for just a bit more. She knows. The taxi pulls up, telling us it is time to separate – again. She looks at me as her tears fall one by one like heavy raindrops. Ignoring the awaiting car, Lee holds my face with her sweet soft hands. We are forehead to forehead, and her pure eyes drill right into me. She gazes into my soul.

"I love you," she says softly, with confidence and comfort.

192

Pause.

"Do not be afraid!"

She slowly unwraps from her left wrist the light brown braided bracelet she handmade. She crafted it for weeks, carefully choosing each gold-plated charm with attention and love – a hand, a heart, a peace sign. She is continuing to unwrap the bracelet. As the tears fill her eyes, one by one, a tear falls through each loop. She then winds it onto my left wrist like a ceremony of pure, honest, and absolute love.

"Do not be afraid!" she says again when she completes her ceremony of love.

I quietly cry. So does she – her tears are on my cheeks, my arm, on my hand, on my wrist. My tears are down my face, my throat, my shirt.

"No fear," she reminds me again.

Her words seep into my soul, into my body, and through my veins, into my heart. I scream without a voice – *Don't leave me! Don't let me go! Come with me!* – but it is too late. I am in the cab. The flickering lights are on the horizon. I am on my way to the airport, not to the happy greeting of the arrivals, but the grimmer, good-bye-for-now departures. I touch the bracelet. I feel Lee's love on my wrist with each pulse inside the little chambers of my heart.

My stomach is burning.

The tall flight attendant offers me the tray with a forced smile. I refuse with a smile back. I find a brilliant stomach solution for the sixteen-hour flight: I do not eat a single bite. It is the only way to save myself from frequent visits to the smelly, tiny, stuffy airplane restroom.

Sleep, sleep.

Fighting the turbulences inside and outside, it is always a more extended trip back to the US from Israel than traveling to Israel. From one home to another, I soar; from the first home that gives me endless, raw love to my newer home, where I am the giver, thirsty for the loving embrace.

Los Angeles, August 2012

With sparkly eyes and wide-open arms, Lev and Liam jump on me, crying out, "Mommy, you are home!"

My heart is beaming. Every hug, every kiss is precious. My children are the reason I come back. They cannot even fathom the need I have for them.

Stay close to me. My heart crumbles again.

We all lay together on the living room carpet, hugging each other for hours, unwrapping gifts big and small. They taste every piece of new candy and chocolate. Sweetness flows in the air as they tell me innocent kids' stories about school, about Grandma and Grandpa shopping with them, and about Daddy being silly at bedtime. They share the colorful notes and the happy pictures they discovered in their little treasure bags on the rope. I am whole again. No matter what else, they are my one real motivation for what I know as life. I feel better, and I even forget about my stomach just for an hour or two. I kiss the kids goodnight on their forehead and leave their bedroom. I can feel the jet lag fatigue slipping into my eyes.

I manage to hide my sadness and my rumbling stomach. No one should know how much fear I'm holding inside.

My stomach has a life of its own. Everything that goes in quickly comes out. I hold nothing down. The bed whispers to me, *"Come to me,"* seducing me to enter, lay down, and sleep. But I can't sleep. Everything comes up to yellow from having nothing in my stomach. I am now familiar with every scratch and nick on the toilet rim and the lid. I am exhausted from all the impulsive purging.

Make it stop!

You cannot will yourself not to vomit. Again and again, I drag myself from my bed to the bathroom and back. How is there anything left in my system? Hazy and weak, I am a fragile leaf. I sleep and wake up frequently, not knowing if I am dreaming or in a dark reality.

Tiny footsteps enter my bedroom. The little ones come for a hug.

"Mommy, we love you!" This time they don't have bags with numbers.

"When? When will mommy wake up?" They ask with their sweet, soft, worried, and innocent voices.

They disappear into another room, to school, to the backyard. It's quiet for a while. And again, I hear their echoing voices come in and out of my bedroom. First, for a few hours, then a day. Two days, maybe three. I lose all sense of time. I try to drink water, and it all comes up again. My body rejects life.

Dan enters our darkroom to check up on me.

"Are you okay?" He asks. He's desperate to stop this torment, *Bring my wife back to health. Bring her back._*

Between taking care of the kids and working full time, he is exhausted and looking for answers. I miss being the wife who used to do it all with perfect command and productivity. I dive back into a deep sleep.

Dan gives in to his mom's advice. He leads me into the car and takes me to the local hospital, so we do not have to wait for hours in the crowded, world-renowned Los Angeles hospital. The local hospital's waiting room is freezing to keep the germs out, but not the fear that has built itself walls inside my heart for years. I crave him to hold my hand, but he is busy with his phone, responding to emails. *Hold me.* Luckily, we don't wait for long. Within two hours, the doctors connect me to an IV, to essential life.

"She is dehydrated," the doctor tells Dan, finally relieved.

Drop by drop, and I feel alive again. The fluids replenish my body and my soul.

I am once again breathing life. As the fluid rushes into my veins, Dan makes jokes – he is always funny when he is nervous. This trait is one of the reasons I fell in love with him. Like a third grader who is in love with his classmate but does not know what to do with himself, he makes me laugh. When my worried, type-A personality comes to the forefront, powered by two Duracell batteries of ruthless efficiency, Dan throws the funny hat on his head and serenades me from the window. "Don't cry for me, Argentina....." and acts like everything is not such a big deal after all. He reminds me, "It is not a hurricane, nor an earthquake. We will survive if no one washes the dishes before bed. It would be okay if we did not pack four different kinds of snacks or apply three layers of sunblock every morning." His wise sense of humor is a cure—a cure we both need, but one I often pretend not to need at all.

For the next two days, the world is dancing and hopping once more. My morning routine renews. Dishes. Emails. Take kids to school. Meetings. Lunch. Laundry. Dusting and sweeping. The usual. I even managed to edit another chapter of my first book, discuss ideas with my app developer and still pick up the kids. An afternoon of fun, we create an art project on the patio. When the kids are in bed, I started planning Liam's upcoming birthday party at the reptile center – the entertainment, the decor, the food, the goodies bags. I am busy again; no time to think. I feel alive again. I'm back to being my conductor. I am happy. I feel love. I see the butterflies. I smell the flowers.

Order seemingly restores. But inside, I am still afraid of the truth.

I am terrified to speak about it.

I know full well that if I dare to bring out the truth, it will certainly destroy me. It will create violent chaos with no way back. It will be better to pretend, hide the fact, and shove it deep into a hidden cabinet so no one will find it. But the truth keeps growing, and I need to block the door because it is in danger of bursting off the hinges.

I am scared. I push on.

The weekend is here, and we decided on a family day at the aquarium. We admire the beautiful creatures, the sloshing water, the happy sea lions—Lev and Liam are joyful. They are so innocent, flapping their arms like wings. They are the happiest when they see Dan and me together. The truth doesn't need to exist. Not today: I will ignore it and sink it in the deepest part of the aquarium. What does exist is running around, petting the starfish, and feeding the seals. What is real is a happy family, a beautiful day of love, and more pictures for our family album. Six hours of the most beautiful bubble exists, one hour away from home.

"Mommy, Daddy, we are hungry!"

Famished from the long and exciting adventure, we find the nearest family restaurant. It's a nearly unbearable forty-minute wait time as we clutch the black round buzzer, which finally cheerfully vibrates when it is our turn to sit. We are one of many starving, exhausted, and desperate families at the end of a family Sunday-Funday. Silverware is dropping, kids are yelling, adults are losing their patience, the table is a sea of crayons, kids' menus, and lemonade in plastic cups.

And then, I can feel it coming. Again. I rush to the bathroom; my stomach is rejecting it all again. I hate this. I am disappointing my babies, who look at me with worried sweet eyes, wanting to hold on to the day we just had.

The drive home from dinner feels longer than the flight back from Israel. I collapse into bed, my mind wanting to hold onto the sun, the beauty of the day, the giggling, and the curious eyes astonished by every little detail, but my body is desperate for rest. I disappear again.

I plunge back into a deep sleep.

White flashing light. I wake up in a cold white room. I look around and hear rapid voices: two nurses are around my bed.

"Call Dr. Nelson, the head of the cardiovascular department. Her pulse is under fifty beats per minute." One of the nurses checks my blood pressure, "Have him write special permission to lower the monitor's alarm to thirty-five beats per minute."

The beeps stop. I fall and dive into my darkness until the next nurses' routine checkup shift.

Finally, a calm comes. The heavy-duty medications that probably could tranquilize an elephant not only dim the pain in my stomach but also take away the heaviness in my heart.

Again, I am thirsty for his hand, for his touch, for my man's love. But Dan's visits are short, mechanic, robotic, almost seems automated. I look at him, standing restless in the room, his fingers fidget obsessively on his phone keys.

He is busy; He has a lot on his mind; He needs to take care of our family.

I understand my husband.

I am sorry I put you through this. I will be home soon.

He doesn't touch me. I am an object—an object with no purpose.

My file, placed in the edge of the hospital iron bed, is getting thicker, full of more speculations, blood tests, and signatures of changing doctors. My weight is now only two digits, and my color is white, just like my sheets.

A week goes by. Liam's birthday is tomorrow, but his mommy is in a white, sterile hospital. I give directions on what to tell the seamstress about making the tablecloth, the gift boxes filled with goodies for each child, and which friends to invite.

How can I miss one of the most important days of my baby boy's life? I cannot bear this thought. *He will remember that. Liam will never forget that his mommy wasn't there to hug him and sing happy birthday to him while he blew out seven candles.*

The immense guilt, sadness, and fear soak into my heart. With every last ounce of strength I could gather, I sign the hospital papers to be released against medical advice, promising I will not sue them if something happens. Nothing matters. It's Liam's birthday party!

"Mommyyyyyyy!" A big hug from with his voluminous locks against my heart. The sparkle in Liam's eyes is the wonder medication I needed the most. It is unconditional reassurance, and I offer him the comfort he deserves in return.

Mommy is here. Mommy loves you no matter what.

Hiding my bones under a long, white skirt and putting extra blush on my cheeks so no one will notice the pounds I shed, we arrive at the party as a united, loving family. We sing "Happy Birthday," and Liam blows the candles in one fell swoop, foo. Flash.

"Smile." We take a family picture. Everything is perfect for another photo album.

Bigger.

Brighter.

Whiter.

Shinier.

Take me.

I am almost there.

The Light is expanding, getting bigger, wider, stronger, mightier. It was pulling me into it. The Light is vibrating. The closer I am, the more I feel its inviting warmth, endless energy, and intense magic. It is heaven. I want to enter it, to be a part of it. Forever.

Call for help, says the Light.

It is not the words that I hear; it's the Light's immense thought. I feel Lev and Liam close to my bare being, as if they are back in my womb, together. My babies.

Nobody.

No thoughts.

No feelings.

Just the Light.

Bigger. Brighter.

Shinier. Glowing.

I am almost in it.

Brighter.

Whiter.

Shinier.

Calming. Comforting. Almost there.

But then, the miracle. I whisper, *h e l p*.

Dan just came in the door, rushes to the bathroom. He finds me on the bathroom floor and takes my pulse, just like he used to when we used to workout out together before kids; twenty-seven beats per minute. He dials 911, cradling me in his arms while he talks to the paramedics on the phone. Four desperately long minutes later, a fire truck and an ambulance enter our street with loud sirens.

Whoosh! I feel an unexplained sharp, spikey whoosh in my chest. It's blue. It's sharp. It's shocking. A massive plunge into my heart. My real heart.

Shaking, cold as ice, I hear beeps and people talking, but their words are not audible. I shiver. I am on my daughter's soft, pink bed. I am not dreaming. Paramedics are hovering over me. I close my eyes. The loud siren wakes me up. I am strapped. I am in an ambulance. I cannot stop my body from shaking. Warm hands in blue gloves place a gas mask on my face, checking my pulse, and working with automated efficiency. Lethargic, I close my eyes again. The ambulance stops— sharp rays of sunshine in my eyes. I feel the wheels of the cold metal bed move beneath me, and grey doors swing open.

Blue Eyes.

"I am the doctor," the deep blue eyes say.

Blue Eyes opens my own eyes with one of his fingers and looks deep within with a warm smile. "Did you play with drugs?"

I don't play with drugs. Not me. I am a Good Girl from Jerusalem. I want to yell.

But I just nod my head. *No.*

Ask him, not me. I keep saying mutely. But no one has heard me for years now.

I did not listen to my almond-eyed sister when she said, *"Don't be afraid."* Ignoring her loving wisdom, I stubbornly chose fear. It seemed like the easiest way. I let my stomach take over and lead me into complete darkness and then into the mighty Light. I allow my immune system to deteriorate, and I almost gave up on life itself. My immune system surrendered, defeated by the bacteria I brought back from my trip. Bacteria of immense fear from the truth.

I let fear take over.

Los Angeles, September 2012

Whoosh. Whoosh. Whoosh. The big, grey regulator machine that sits next to my wheeled bed makes loud, steady and measured huffing sounds. Breathe in. Breathe out. Breathe in. Breathe out.

It is cold. I am shivering under the thin white sheets, covered with only one thin layer of a fleece blanket. There are twisted wires connected to my veins, stuck to my chest, and applied to my mouth. I am nearly naked, except for this papery cotton gown, dressed mostly in cold plastics and tubes.

I lie on my back, arms beside my limp body resembling branches of a leafless tree in autumn. A thick, rigid, white pillow supports my head. Slowly, I open my heavy eyes and scan the dark, almost-empty room. No artwork. Sterile. On the wall, there is a big white clock in front of the bed, with long, black hands, ticking.

Tick. Tock. Tick. Tock.

A small flat-screen TV hangs in the ceiling corner, and a dry-erase whiteboard is opposite my bed with handwritten phone numbers and other digits in green and black ink. The curtain's shadow decorates the sidewall and the arm of the only chair in the room, dimly illuminated by the light in the corridor.

Everything feels so dense.

Ligaments. Bones. Veins. Muscles. My forty-year life now depends on a metal box connected to the wall by a thick plug. *Whoosh. Whoosh. Whoosh*, the machine continues.

With an immense desire to vanish, I close my eyes and wander nowhere.

No thoughts.

No dreams.

I disappear.

The beeps of the alarm and the bright fluorescent lights wake me up. There is a frantic commotion in the room. Nurses in tight ponytails and light makeup come in and out of the room. They urgently press buttons on the heart monitor, which is now hysterically warning the whole cardiology floor. *Beeeep. Beeeep. Beeeep.*

"She's dropped below 50," one nurse in thick braids informs the other.

The nurses are distinguished in my head by their voices, some harsh, some melodic, some guttural. I wonder if this is how they talk when they are with their girlfriends or husbands or find a great pair of shoes at the mall.

Completely ignoring me, they bark short orders from one side of the bed to the other and make decisions about the machine next to my head.

I am here! I am here!—they do not even notice me.

Here. Look at me!

The nurses are at an emergency pace. The heart machine indicates that my pulse is too low and has set off a series of alerts. Without looking at me, they push an oxygen mask onto my face.

Look, I am here!

My heart rate stays below 50 beats per minute, unwilling to rise. The nurses wake up the famous on-call cardiologist. He faxes a special handwritten order allowing them to set the alert down to 35 beats per minute. The nurses go back to their station, and the doctor goes back to sleep. One nurse stays for a moment to write another message on the whiteboard for the morning shift, this time in a red marker. The machines fall silent, and the lights go off; I go back to my peaceful, nowhere land.

This internal pumping machine of mine needed an adjustment for years, but I ignored it out of fear. My breaking heart gathered orange-yellow-brownish rust, and finally, my body said, "Enough!"

Ignorance didn't make things better. Sweeping troubles under the thick rug did not make them magically disappear. They instead slowly bunched up. I felt these hard lumps every time I walked barefoot on the carpet, the coarsely piled fabric of my life. I was there for everyone else, except for myself. I looked at everyone with a magnifying glass yet refused to look into my mirror.

And now, important doctors with diplomas from prestigious universities, years of residency, and impressive CVs are taking messy, scribbled notes about my inner workings, analyzing them twice a day. I am a box, an object, perhaps an airplane with some faulty parts that need to be fixed and replaced.

I stay tucked into the industrial white, crisply ironed, rough sheets. They continue to talk over my head, deciding what I can and cannot eat and drink and what my ideal heart rate should be. These rivers of wires connect to me, hooked to machines that keep pace with my heart and adjust my breathing.

I am still here.

I did not touch the light.

Whoosh. Whoosh. Whoosh. I am eight thousand miles from my Holy City. I am at the mercy of many dedicated and experienced nurses and doctors who whisper in a language that is not my own.

The regulator reminds me. Everything starts with a sigh, the long sound of a breath. It's the first letter one must write. The first letter of most alphabets. *A. Alef. Alif. Alpha. Ajab. Ani.* The concrete basis for the highest flights of our existence.

It is the darkest right before the dawn.

The dark is there so you can see the Light. If you don't experience the darkness, the painful dimness, and gloom of life, you will never find the Light. You will never come to appreciate it. Find it. Find the darkness in your life and stare at it. Listen to it. Listen to what it has to teach you.

If you turn on a lamp in a bright room, you will not notice the light from the lamp at all. It will disappear, absorbed into the existing brightness. But if you light a match in a dark room, you will see that light, even if it is dim, tiny, and humble. The darker the room, the brighter the light will be.

Running from the darkness won't work – it is your gift and your key to finding the brighter things in your life. Even if it's scary, even if it can be paralyzing, look into the darkest of the dark as best as you can.

Thank you, darkness. Thank you for showing up in my life. Thank you for making it all dark, because now I know this is the only way I can see. I will experience the Light. You came into my life at just the right moment, and I am ready for bright, shining, clarity, and change in my life because there is no fear; it is merely an illusion.

Right at the moment when you think it is the darkest, that mighty, glowing, embracing Light will arrive.

It is always darkest before the light of dawn.

Chapter 14

Monster's Promise

Bet. Tet. Chet. .ב.ט.ח

Promise הבטחה· Trust בטחון· Insurance ביטוח· Reassurance הבטחה
Confident בטוח· Safe בטוח· Of course, חם· Security בטחון

◉

Los Angeles, October 2012

I am confined in the hospital for what seemed like endless days
and nights, covered with heavy, starched linens. They smell of sterility,
neutralizing any remaining feelings—white nothingness. My only
luxury is awareness. To simply *be!* Time nearly stops. Every minute
seems to stretch like playdough in the hands of a curious child. It hits
me: I do not want to leave my life now. I won't let the bacteria win
and ruin my life, the lives of my babies! There are beautiful things I
have not seen. There is so much that hasn't come to fruition. I haven't
celebrated my children's weddings, I haven't smelled all the beautiful
smells of nature, I haven't heard the magnificent music that hasn't yet
been written, I haven't visited all the fascinating places in the world, and
I have not learned all the words I have wanted to say. I will rise again,
walk away from this bed, away from these long disinfected corridors.
I will experience more. I will choose to see the light within this world.

Dan and I had killed our relationship. We had done it slowly,
giving up in stages, blaming each other, and pointing fingers. We each
ran towards our well-hidden addictions, refusing to look in the mirror

and into our own eyes. Gradually, the funny, smart, sensual relationship turned into a walking-on-egg-shells duel of suspicions.

Today, I know. Today, I can admit it. My addiction was Dan. My addiction was judging him: looking and finding his faults, his blameworthiness, searching with extreme delight for his rotten skeletons in hidden closets. I became an archeologist digging ever deeper into the darkest places of the past.

In my mind, the secrets I uncovered were giant, too horrible to expose to the gossipy world, so I kept them tucked in my brain and deep within my reckless, emotional, weak heart. I kept long, tidy, creative – or so I thought – journals. I played a private investigator, and it nearly destroyed me. I kept it in, waiting for the perfect moment to declare it to the world, pretending someone cared. But really, no one cares. People are busy with their own stories, lives, and agendas. They forget. Still, I became addicted to the next clue, the next hint that would show the whole world. *This is **his** fault!* I was blind to what I was doing, addicted to his addiction. This Monster fed us both with illusions, sweet lies, and bitter deceits.

I could not get out of my detective role. The treasure hunt was too thrilling to quit in the middle. Between kids, cooking and baking gourmet cakes and pastries, business meetings, and writing my first book, I somehow found the time. That's the thing about addictions. You can always find the time to feed them. Otherwise, the empty hole is too vast.

This Monster was even bigger than I had imagined. It required meals—heavy, fatty meals with oils and cheese and thick sauces. This Monster was more prominent than both of us, far bigger than the little family we had created. Willingly, we let the ravenous Monster into our home, allowing her to sneak in the back door. She ate upon whatever her eyes landed. One person wasn't enough to satiate her; she ate us all. Divide and conquer was her method. This Monster divided us quickly, each to his or her addiction. We were too busy obsessing. We forgot about why we had come together: to create a new life, to build a happy home.

There are moments where I missed Dan's youthful manner, his pure wisdom, his unique, raw sense of humor. With togetherness came the birth of two beautiful babies. However, the addiction made it toxic and unfocused. We forgot. We tried to fix things, but that worked only for a few weeks, or a few days or even just a few moments until the Monster reared its head again. Once again, our vision of each other, and our outlook on the world, became blurry.

As I was buried in that crisp, white, disinfected bed, glancing out the window that exposed a tiny sliver of blue sky and a few puffy clouds between the tall hospital buildings with their mirrored windows, I promised myself to heal. I vowed to heal my stomach. I would care for that stomach that stored and hoarded the dark history and gaping wounds from every step along my path. Firmly, as if I were in a ceremony, I pledged. That moment, between blue and white, I made a deal with my naked self. I made a covenant with my soul under the wires and long tubes, surrounded by bulky machines that counted my pulse, monitored my heart and examined my whole body.

I will take care of myself. I will fight this compulsion. I will find myself in all of it. I will deal with this obsession, I will go back to my children, and I will choose life!

Los Angeles, October 2012

It's my first morning since my release from the hospital: no beeping, no IVs, no harsh lights, and endless conversations between nurses. Lev and Liam are in school, and I can lie in bed and relax. Serenity. Suddenly, I hear the familiar sound of screeching brakes outside.

Freddie!

I'm nervous, but I'm also eager to smooth over the awkwardness. If I can give him the bar and the fruit, if we can laugh and make small talk again, maybe I can wash away the embarrassment of his last visit for Freddie.

I see him from the kitchen window, fixing his baseball cap as he clambers down from the truck, a heavy bottle on his shoulder, heading towards the backside of the house.

Freddie lost some weight, I think to myself. I stroll to the door, open it, and my heart sinks. It isn't Freddie.

He is so embarrassed he changed his route after three years. There's no other possible answer.

"Where is Freddie?" I ask the driver, who is a bit taller, slimmer, and does not smile at all. I miss Freddie's gleaming face.

"Freddie!" the new driver stares at me with stunned eyes, "You don't know?"

I stare back, mute, looking for answers. *What is it that I do not know? What do I need to know?*

212

The driver takes a deep breath, "Freddie died two weeks ago."

"Two weeks ago?" I freeze, my disbelief and my shock holding my body hostage.

The driver nods.

"How?" I almost yell.

"He had a brain aneurysm two weeks ago... he never regained consciousness."

"Two weeks ago?" It is as if I've lost the power to do anything other than repeat what this Freddie substitute tells me.

"The funeral is tomorrow," the driver continues, interrupting the beginnings of my bitter argument with God.

Two weeks ago, I was lying on the bathroom floor, my heart rate at 28 beats per minute.

Bigger.

Whiter.

Brighter.

Two weeks ago.

I did not follow the light to its end. But Freddie did.

On the same day that the Universe decided to give me life, it took Freddie's. We saw the white light at the exact moment, but only one of us came back.

From the lowest point of my life, I got the courage—the courage to change.

Pain comes and goes,
Suffering is something to which we hold on.

The message I grew up with was simple: you are always there to assist the person who is in need, who is sick, who is weak, who cannot help themselves. But I'm not the only one. Perhaps it's you, too. Was it the constant spoon-feeding of others' beliefs you received when you were a child? Your parents, movies, songs, commercials? Subliminal messages to become the bravest hero, whether that meant wearing capes, badges, bulletproof vests, or nurses' outfits? Is it the healthiest thing you can do? Is saving others at any price the wisest choice? Even if it costs you your emotional health?

When you help someone, consider if they can help themselves first. If the person using you as a crutch is repeating constant excuses as to why they haven't healed, victimizing themselves, and helping you feel essential by saving them, why would you accept them handing you heavy sandbags dressed as trophies? Why take these weights that are so heavy that they will end up bringing you down? If you feel that someone else's exhausting weight of life is pulling you deeper into the cold depths so that both of you seem to be drowning in an ocean, then you must abandon the heavy, sinking patient and swim for yourself. It's not cruel to leave someone who chooses not to save themselves; it is cruel to abandon yourself. If you realize that you worry about them more than yourself, then you must turn around and start reclaiming your life.

It is much easier to save others rather than save yourself. You might concentrate so hard on the act of revitalizing and healing someone that your own life diminishes. What are you trying to do? Are you hiding from your pain and trying to be the hero for others? Are you being someone else's Higher Power, diminishing the idea that they need to go through their journey and healing?

If you collapse, if you find yourself gasping for air with what feels like heart failure, it is not the end. Instead, it is the beginning of your life. It is time to be your nurse, to pick up the real hero outfit and wear it with pride. *Save yourself first.*

This transition out of rescuing will not be easy. It will not be smooth. You will probably go back to old habits, wanting to save other people, ignoring yourself and your own needs. You must face your truth, your pain, your past. The temptation to forget that pain by focusing on others will be immense.

Looking into the mirror, you may see that you are the sick one. You are the one who needs help the most. It is the beginning of a beautiful journey filled with pain, with tears, facing the truth. When you finally accept that you're addicted to taking care of others to avoid your healing, then you can begin – without pride or ego, but with determination – to put your emotional health first. Believe it or not, you will soon be showering immense love on your beautiful, perennially youthful soul. That soul is the one who needs you the most.

I promise you; you'll know that facing the truth is worth it when you breathe freely at last.

And most importantly, there will be no more whispers.

Chapter 15

Let's Play Nurse

Jerusalem, 1980

This blessed city of Jerusalem treasures thousands of years of history in its every corner and turn. My city. The strict municipal law requires all the stunning ancient material known as Jerusalem stone to cover all structures, giving the city a unique, magnificent look and feel. Any structure in this city, my city, small or large, from its hotels to schools, apartment buildings, supermarkets, storage spaces, bars, and brothels are all made from this unique golden stone. It is the classic symbol that distinguishes this city from all the others in the world. This ancient stone reveals white, beige, and pink colors, which makes the city shine in a glimmering golden color during magnificent sunsets.

In the middle of the city rises the Holy City's hospital, built from the same stone, the holy stone, proudly named Gates of Justice. This city is where I was born. Where else would this "Good Girl Jerusalem," this "Holy Chick" be born?

My mother, her mother, and her mother's mother all worked at Gates of Justice hospital. Three generations of hard-working women, three generations of dedication to helping patients, and assisting big-name doctors build their prestige. Three humble women were so busy with other people's lives that they forgot about their own. My mom, grandmother, and great-grandmother were strong, competent women who worked – and collected wrinkles – in the Holy City's hospital.

When my great-grandmother retired, the hospital went through a significant facelift. I was in the second grade, and I could feel the immense excitement in the city. It was the talk of the town—new structures, new walls, modern automated doors that opened and closed with smooth sliding motions.

The stories in the newspapers were exciting and filled with promise. The new hospital building had not yet seen war. The blood of terror victims had not yet soaked it. It had not yet seen injured soldiers. But this is Israel. As I grew, I saw this hospital become stained with blood. As those years passed, the big sign outside, the one that proudly proclaimed "Justice," faded away.

Gates of Justice was my mother's workplace. While the other kids went to their mother's offices, I went to the hospital. I was permitted to play with all sorts of bottles, sponges, hats, hoods, clamps, long tweezers, and silver "throw-up" bowls. I even ate the industrially-conceived hospital food in scratched plastic blue and white plates on big white trays, still steaming hot from the giant commercial dishwasher. I didn't eat in the visitors' cafeteria, but in an underground one, which we reached by hidden elevators, passing corridors that revealed the ceiling's air conditioning ducts. This cafeteria was always noisy. Clanging dishes, metal chairs scraping against the off-white vinyl floor, competing voices clamoring over the din of the cafe. White, green, and blue scrubs all pushing in the queue, trying to get served quickly before their break was over. I watched them all, making up stories about their homes, their real clothes, and the person upon whom they had just operated on in a spotless fifth-floor room.

While other kids went to their doctor's clinic, I got an appointment with an expert in the field on the spot. We had the shortcut to the elite physicians. "Personal" was the magic word. Doctors were gods, and nurses were angels. All had the same smell of sanitation, the coppery scent of scrubbed metal that holds your heart frozen.

My unconventional romance with the hospital started young, in that world of white gowns, tags with identifying photos, first and last names, quiet clogs, green hats, and white scrubs. I was always fascinated by the long labyrinthine hallways stretching out in four directions. I never knew where, or even if, they ended. People opened and closed mysterious and impressive heavy doors. No matter how many times I visited the hospital, I was always curious to see what was behind this door or that one. I felt like Alice in Wonderland, interested in peeking. I had the marvelous idea that every room could capture and take me far away to a different, dazzling land.

Then. There was—the whispering.

Whispering, murmuring, and inaudible conversations: each hospital passage contained endless numbers of secrets. The nurses, the doctors, the employees, the visitors – all leaned in close to each other's ears. My mom reminded me to also whisper at her work. I knew the drill: always keep it quiet. In my visits, I did not say a word. I just followed the adults with their swift movements with my big brown curious eyes, looking up, following their hands, guessing the emotions by their facial expressions, by their shoulders. Often, they did not even notice me, the quiet, tiny girl with smooth, dark brown braids beside her mommy. I learned to read so many things.

I never understood why my mom never whispered at home. She used her voice loudly and clearly – even by Israeli standards. We are not a quiet people. Perhaps she felt she had finished her daily limit of whispering and was going to go to the opposite extreme for some relief. Can you imagine whispering all day long? It is like holding in a big secret but not knowing what the secret is all about. Conspiring and worrying all day, gossiping about patients, tests, results. In my mother's world, only the sickest people are allowed to yell. And when they do, they are immediately quieted by a magic pill or the prick of a needle.

Three generations of nurses in my family – and, as it turns out, I am the worst nurse ever.

I should get a medal, a certificate, a glorious blue ribbon: Worst Nurse.

You are warned. I am impossibly anxious until you heal yourself. If you're sick, I want results, and I want them now. I cannot wait until your fever dips, your cough subsides, and you smile again. Don't expect me to feel sorry for you, to stay there until you beam again. Your pain is my pain, and it will be until you get out of bed. I take it all in, all on myself. I love you without end, and your sickness becomes mine.

Heal! Now! I will cook my chicken and vegetable soup that fills the house with the best aroma. I will give you this with a warm fuzzy blanket and fresh hot mint tea with honey. I will drive you to the pharmacy and find three or four remedies to make it all go away quickly. I will write you a card and draw a smiley face next to it. But there is where my nurse duties end.

Sick people scare me. I am restless when anyone is sick next to me. I tiptoe so no one will hear me. No one will call me. No one will need me. I hear moaning, pain. I roll my eyes. Can you heal faster? How long will it take until this is complete?

Physical pain causes emotional pain within me that I cannot handle. But when the ill loved one finally gets up, takes that cleansing shower, and says, "I feel much better, that was living hell!" only then do I feel my soul relax with relief. Health has been restored, and I am free, home happily once again. The burden of expectation disappears.

Either too embarrassed or too proud, I stopped the legacy. After four generations, the matriarchal line of nurses in my family ends with me. The white-ironed uniform will be forever hiding in my closet.

◉

Los Angeles, 2013

Within twenty-four months, our kitchen had collapsed. Shut down. Now, the cupboards are empty of secret ingredients. The oven is cold. The scent of baking no longer blankets the house. I had no clue I would bury my phone in that same magical, innovative drawer we created together, hiding from it so that I won't have to read the nasty texts from my beloved man. The separation and the loss freeze me like an old packet of peas in the freezer coated in frost.

Dan and I had built a dream, and now it is a nightmare. We're not the only ones doing the smashing. We are both caught up in the cruelty of lawyers and the corrupt, Byzantine family court system.

I believe every word the lawyers and the mediator tell us. They incite hatred between us and maliciously convince us that we will be left with no money unless we take aggressive action. They plot to get us to sell our house so that they can share the grand prize. Day after day, they drill these hate-filled, destructive ideas into our minds and hearts.

I have to close the kitchen. We must sell the house and uproot; move the kiddos to another school, go to another home, and other bedrooms – to another kitchen.

I am going to disappoint my babies. That thought haunts me.

I miss our Friday night Shabbat dinners. Every seven days, the entire family comes to the table without presents. We do not need Santa to appear to say, "I love you." My mother cooked from Thursday night to Friday afternoon in my childhood, inventing meals and creating recipes, trying to satisfy each child's different taste buds. Yummy smells and flavors that exude family togetherness (and calories) fill our home. What I miss the most is not the food or everyone sitting together; that is a bit of a cliché. What I miss is the simplicity, the innocence in each one of us six kids.

The part of Friday dinner that I loved the most is when we sat around the table and speculated about each other's futures.

"Your kids will buy shoes every day and will run away from

home," we used to joke with my sister, Lee. To this day, Lee adores shoes and hides them in little cabinets in her house.

"You," they pointed at me, "your kids will read Shakespeare, play the piano, and remember the math chart by heart at age five."

Ten kinds of foods—Moroccan fish, cooked salads, challah bread, schnitzels, meat, chicken with potatoes, and finely chopped salad—filled the Shabbat table. Every Friday night, fifty-two Fridays a year. On Shabbat, we, kids, are also allowed a particular soft drink, an excellent green soda that became the taste of Friday night. All we had was time. All we had was us. We were the TV, the comedy, the big cry, the memories. It was the sweetness in the chaos of six kids dining together and appreciating what we had, fighting over whose turn it was to do the dishes: at least eight glasses, sixteen plates, seven pots, and countless bowls and silverware. The click and clank of the dishes, the laughter rising and falling. This soundtrack described my childhood.

I am in search of the sun again.

Divorce is not just separating our communal property. It is like painfully dying while watching it happen in slow motion. An increasingly dark screenplay written by cruel fate traps me. What started as a love story has become a horror movie. I'm trying, desperately, to do a last-minute rewrite. All that I come up with are various tragic endings.

We built a kitchen. And now we are destroying it together. I try to convince myself that the Universe is planning a better future for us. A place where no one is blamed and criticized. A place where we will not fear anyone else; a place where hugs and music, and kisses are free and abundant. A home where we can wear any clothes we want, a place of trust and honesty, and one of unconditional love. A place where a girl who once trusted someone loved her can cook and bake the happiest of meals in her kitchen.

Put down the magnifying glass and pick up the mirror.

Living someone else's life is exhausting. Whose life did you try to live? Whose life did you try to correct, enhance, and guide? Over whom did you obsess? You want to protect them, save them, and make their lives better because they suffer, and you're sure you know how to change and build a better life for them. If only, if only they would follow what you say, if only they could see what you can, but they cannot. Their problems, their anxiety, their chaos consumes you. Slowly, you forget about your own life because the only solution seems to be taking over another's. You will never leave them to be eaten by the wolves of their own bad choices. The responsibility is heavy and real.

Enmeshed in someone else's life, you embed your journey with theirs. They teach you how to pretend, how to lie along with them, how to put aside your desires, your hobbies, your smile so that they won't suffer alone. Codependency is crawling at your skin, wearing the mask of a hero.

Their life is always more critical because their suffering is more significant and more profound than yours. They compare their lives to all others, and they foster guilt. You are made into the strong one, the capable one who can handle it all and save them.

If you find yourself afraid of a person's reactions and find that they manipulate your responses, then you are living for their life. It is not always clear that you're doing it from fear. It may seem like it's out of needing to give or receive love. It can happen with a family member, in a work situation, in a romance. This situation is a form of addiction or codependency. The notion of ceasing to take care of someone else's emotions scares us because then disaster will inevitably follow. The person will fail, collapse, or break down, perhaps dragging you down with them. The responsibility is as immense as it is false; it's rooted in the lie that you are powerful over someone else. Without you, this person will fall deeper into depression, sickness, or another disaster.

This is an illusion. When you stop, the person must deal with the turmoil all by themselves or find other friends or family members to continue the codependent dance. This is their addiction. Like every dance, this one has two participants—each dance forward and backward at a different time. One is needy, and the other is the savior. The longer you dance, the more you become something that is not your plan – certainly not at your age, and not in your circumstances. You neglect your emotional life for the health of another.

This is the most challenging chain to break. The obligation, the self-blame, and the fear seem so real.

As with any addiction, the first step in recovery is admitting you are in it. Then, ask for help and refrain entirely. This is harder than giving up alcohol or drugs, as the person will still be in your life. A bottle of vodka doesn't call you up to say it misses you, but the person to whom you're addicted will call you and insist that, without you, they cannot make it to the next day.

Know that you are more than their salvation.

Nothing is more satisfying than living your own life and making decisions that are created upon self-respect and love and not upon others' manipulations. You fail, you succeed, you try again, but this time, it is *your* life. This is how you grow, as you experience what is in your hula hoop, your circle, and no one else.

The bitterness, the sweetness, the whole rainbow of taste – it's yours now. When you love yourself, and what you have, creating it one experience at a time, without anyone else hovering over you, then, at last, you are free.

Chapter 16

Attitude of Gratitude

Yud. Dalet. Yud.   .י.ד.י
Admits מודה • Thanks תודה • Gratitude הודיה

◉

Los Angeles, 2014

I don't mind the creaky doors, the peeling color from the walls, and the rusty chairs. They tell my story. Three times a week, like a baby who requests his milk in the morning, I come back. I find my seat in a room, perhaps in an old church, a city recreation center, a hospital. I join the same souls, say the same prayers, feel the same consciousness of the Universe. The format is in a binder, the one where they use the term Higher Power instead of God. I listen. I drink every word. I still feel a stranger among new people who are starting to have familiar faces.

Once, I regarded those rooms as foreign and far from what I was.

These are weird people, probably grew up in the streets or with crazy parents.

I once labeled them as if I were different and an elite.

I am better than that. Do not judge me.

Fear. Fear comes from ignorance, and I am getting over my ignorance, or at least I am trying.

Ella, stop! I wake myself up as I stare at the shoes, the shirt, the blending fashionable, and no-fashion-at-all nameless people. It's been a few weeks since my first group meeting, and I still soak in every word. I collect all the experiences I hear. These memories and stories are not mine, but they tenderly hold my soul and allow me to be who I am without shame or embarrassment.

I am not the only idiot addict in this complicated world.

I am relieved to be among others, no better than I am at figuring things out. Nope, I am not unique; I don't have any superpower.

My addiction to other people's feelings is not something unusual. I should not be embarrassed.

Like the others, I am seeking answers, liberation from this horrid race to blame myself. I am discovering that there is a different way. I am learning to trust the Universe.

Gradually, I let strangers carry me and take my heart without knowing who I am or who they are. This wondrous experience is love as I've never really experienced it. Unconditional love. Self-love. In the first weeks, all I bring and can bring is my raw pain. I carry pain that I hide deep inside. In the rooms of Al-Anon, they teach me to talk about it, to express it, to laugh at it, without being a miserable victim. With snot running down from my nose, I giggle, cry, and act silly. I make sounds I never knew existed inside of me. I am like a child who first cannot speak and then learns to make noises by gulping in air and letting it out all at once—a few syllables, and finally a word. Giggle, hum, chuckle, snort, shriek. I try it all, my feelings pouring from my soul out into the world for all to hear. I am healing.

I stare at the black on white words—family court. The day I dread arrives. Dan and I are in family court. The divorce is proceeding. I scream on the inside.

We had been two adults who once were each other's entire worlds. And now we are allowing three men in dark suits to dictate our future – and our kids' futures: two lawyers and a judge. Our home is cracked open and broken up into two incompatible halves. A tangle of codes, obscure regulations, vicious declarations, and a stack of threatening forms are swirling around in each of our lives. I have nowhere to hide.

The shame and guilt reach to my core.

Why did I have to start this? The regret and the grief hector me. *It's all because of you; you ruined your family!*

The days leading up to the hearing are awful. Our lawyers are ready to tear into each other in an expensive opera. They will eat everything we built, every penny we worked for and saved. They mean to bring out the worst in us, to show us how monstrous we are. They capture the portrait of being mortal enemies.

Can I run away? Where to? How can I get there, and who will help me?

The phone rings.

Don't answer the phone! One voice has my best interests at heart.

Maybe I should listen to the message.

Ding—another email in my mailbox. The other voice wins, and I skip another heartbeat. Another email makes me feel faint. I learn words I never knew existed. I feel like a dyslectic girl in a very chaotic class: *Stipulation. Ex-Parte. Declaration. Mediation. Four-way meeting. Ruling.*

Stop! I beg.

It doesn't stop. More emails. More chaos. And I want to disappear even more.

Another email. This time from him. No, it's a text; it's filled with accusations and yelling. My brain reads and repeats, "this is the truth." I knew on some level that it was wrong, and I needed to prove it. But I couldn't. He had a spell over me. Whatever he said was always the truth.

I lost myself. I lost myself a long time ago.

Help.

Yes, I can help myself. I always could. My brain is best when overthinking what will happen. I can think clearly and find five different solutions. This is especially so when I'm talking.

This time, like many other times, I try to control each scenario. If this, then that. I draw up plans and more plans. I write hundreds of emails and texts in my head. Some I send, some I don't dare.

All that happens is that the pain becomes sharper. I get more tired. I take up less space in the world – and that's what I want more than anything. To shrink away and let someone take over.

Friends. Family. Consultants. Anyone that knows something about life, I'll follow and listen. Just help me, please. I'm so tired and so lost. Something inside me is still calling for help, but I can't help myself. Something massive has paralyzed me. The pain is vast, and soon I can't cry anymore. I'm stuck.

H E L P.

I finally ask for a different kind of help. I'm not specific. There's no wish list, no bullet points, no suggestions. Just help me. I'll do whatever it takes.

I genuinely don't know who I'm asking at this point – God, a Higher Power, the ocean, the mountains, myself, somebody, something. It's not even desperate or needy anymore; it's more calm than frantic, this pure, true calling for help. I don't know what I need, but you do, whoever you are. I choose to trust that.

I am in one of the rooms, surrounded by love, but I cannot be present. I sit up front, a spotlight entirely on me. I try hard not to let my undiagnosed attention-deficit disorder take control. My soul strains to listen to everyone's horror stories.

I have one thought spinning in my head, *Hearing Day.*

My head calculates how many more hours there are until I have to sit in the hellish court. I have two painful days and no one to accompany me. I want to erase time, to wipe it out. I am frozen in my chair. God sometimes tells us things through other people. More and more, I happen to listen. I suddenly hear the word "courage" spoken with clarity. I turn my head to the back of the room.

There she sits in one of the chairs; she is like all of us, but so different.

She is an elegant, tall, and slim woman; she has gathered her long shiny black hair in a silky ponytail. She has beautiful soft white skin and wears red lipstick, and her outfit looks like something you'd see in Vogue. Her thin high-heel shoes match the belt and leather purse. Her accessories are beautiful and bold, signaling complete confidence and exquisite taste. Her presence wraps me with confidence. Her name is Ronnie.

You would never guess that she once was also in a relationship that was overwhelmed by addiction. I dream of sitting like her one day so I, too, can be cool, calm, and confident.

Does she belong here? I wonder.

"Being in the past is depression; being in the future is anxiety," Ronnie opines. I am in the future. I am in the past. I am in Ronnie's sweater.

Ronnie continues, "...but being in someone else's thoughts is slavery."

Ronnie is the perfect mix of strength and softness. She looks at me lovingly and knowingly, with wisdom in each eye. She knows what I am going through.

234

Come and talk to me, she calls me without saying any words. She holds me with her gaze.

Seriously? What does she want from me? My instinct and my fear buzzed,

My frightened ego had kept me from approaching her after the previous mee *'Don't trust anyone, Ella. Remember what happened last time when you trusted?* 'tings, but today my body ignored that yelling ego, and here I am standing in front of her. She is taller than I thought. Her skin glowed, and her words did not matter. What matters is that she was there, strong, confident, and knowing. I shyly approach her with hesitance; she looks at me with understanding eyes. She opens her arms and hugs me with all her immense patience as if I were a baby. I break into pieces. This is what I needed. The Universe has sent me an angel, an angel named Ronnie.

Trust is not my strong suit, definitely not with women who were not my sisters. My mom taught me how to be suspicious before I even walked. And when I trusted, I heard "I told you so" more than once. But with Ronnie, I did not even ask why she cared. She poured her magical love into me. *'I am here for you.'* She puts her hand on my hand, her quiet confidence calming me. For a few moments in the chaos of my anxieties about the court, lawyers, and paperwork, I feel safe. Like I belong.

But I have nothing to offer her in return.

Every meeting, I hear another person share, a young woman, a student, an older man, no particular age or gender, no specific culture. All are the same. Sometimes I take notes; sometimes, I ponder what they said. But today, Ronnie moved the furniture in my soul and shifted the heavy grandfather clock in my heart. *Bam.*

After the meeting, I drive home, in-between the past and future. Ronnie's words resonate inside me. I want to have what Ronnie has – I want to sit calmly in one of these meetings, wearing the world like a loose shawl. I want Dan to leave my mind, my thoughts, and the little corridors of my brain. I want to drape a long sleeve, brightly colored cashmere sweater over my shoulders.

I park my SUV in the driveway. I secretly miss my pre-motherhood two-door sports car. Dan and I were practical when the babies were born and decided to switch from a fast and daring sports car to a safe, big, sturdy SUV. How boring! Shifting the gear stick to "P," I wish I could put my worry and obsession into "park" as well. I always obsess about what Dan is thinking about me; I fixate what he says about me and how he describes me. I forget to live my life the way I want and deserve because I am craving Dan's approval. I am thirsty for his acceptance. Dan has become my God.

The keys in my hands, still sitting in my car, staring at our charming 1940s house, dawns on me. It wasn't Ronnie talking to me at the meeting today. It was the Universe looking into my eyes and telling me the truth. I am now parked in more ways than one.

◉

Los Angeles, 2014

The Universe has shown me the tiniest light in the darkness. I was waiting for my daily conversations with Ronnie. She is there for me, listening, enlightening, and teaching me how to breathe—showing me what self-love is. What guilt is – and what it's not. It is not self-love. Today, I know that guilt is a wave of anger at yourself. It doesn't serve you. It harms you and weakens your soul.

She promised me, day after day, that one day my fears would dissolve, and the Universe would bring the solution. Honestly, I did not believe her. I could not even see a glimpse of hope, of light, of clarity. I listened anyway.

Court day arrived, and she asked me if I want her to drive me there.

"Just for support, Ella," she reminded me, "I won't be part of it, nor take sides, but I will be next to you."

If I ever was doubting the benevolence of the Universe, this is when I knew it was real. I was sure of its love.

Our hearing was at two o'clock in the afternoon.

"What are you going to wear?" Ronnie asked me that morning. "How are you going to do your hair?" She continued calmly, "What accessories will you add?"

Not one word about the lawyers, about the brutality of the process, about wrong and right. Fashion got me distracted, like distracting a kid from their hurt knee with a fun toy.

"I will pick you up," she softly offered, her words caressing me like I was her baby.

Ronnie showed up an hour and a half before hearing time. She was wearing an elegant black blouse and a chic long skirt with high heels, contrasted with red lipstick. I wear a simple white dress, with pale light brown lipstick. We talk about fashion, our children, how we think of God, and how a real lady walks. There's not one word about fear – it's gone. She blew it away.

As we get into downtown Los Angeles, my stomach crumbles. She feels it and reminds us both that the Universe is with us and that, no matter what, I will be fine. Love wins out over my crippling fear, even for a few minutes.

We arrive at the long, old, brown corridors of the Superior Court. Time stopped there a long time ago—every footstep echoes. I wonder if that is the sound you hear on your way to hell, anticipating the mighty flames. I sit on one of the old benches, waiting in the hallway to be called. Ronnie sits next to me and chats with me about random things: no fear, no gossip, no worries. I am in the moment. When Dan arrives, I can still hold myself together. Two months earlier, I was in the same corridor all by myself, and my monster inside me was so afraid that it dissolved me into pieces. But this time, it was different. Our last name is called. Ronnie stays in the hallway while the rest of us go into the mediation room. By law, the court needs to offer mediation. The lawyers already prepared us for this stage, as it is a pure waste of time and the government's money. It is brief. I do not let any feeling gush out, remaining a lady as gratitude would have me be. Mediation fails after a few moments, and we leave the room, separate, disconnected, and divided. Dan's disgusting look shakes me, but Ronnie was there to remind me that he is afraid, too. He, also, is worried.

This first mediation hearing is just a preview of what is to come. I dread the return to court even more as if I were a little four-year-old girl about to get her vaccine shots. Ronnie offered to join me again, and on this challenging day, she's ready in front of my house first thing in the morning, elegant as ever. In a babysitter's care, the babies sleep in while I head off to fight for them.

"A real lady always arrives on time," she explains.

This hearing day isn't as smooth or as short as the mediation. Dan looks at me as if I were a murderer. I can sense it; his anger pours from every inch of his body and face.

A lady. A real lady you are, I remind myself.

Ronnie sits beside me, asking me questions about which man was Dan's brother and which his attorney. She does not interfere. She is not taking any part in the game, just supporting me with a constant, colorful, loving dance.

It becomes chaotic. The lawyers push for mediation, again, this time in a different hallway. We do not know that both are just going for attorney fees from our savings accounts. Nothing else matters to them – only money as if it wasn't enough that we are paying with our souls and families. It grows darker, and Dan loses his temper in the hallway.

"You are a psycho!"

Ronnie says nothing. She just gently closes her eyes and touches my arm with confidence. I think she is praying. I do the same. Dan doesn't get what he wants: my reaction. I remain calm, sitting on the bench with Ronnie and my Higher Power.

I am safe.

Dan switches gears in his frustration, yelling at my lawyer.

"You are a crook!" Anger and shame, boiling over.

Look around you. Where is the love? I remembered being in love with Dan, and he with me. So long ago.

I get through this because of Ronnie. It is Ronnie who shows me how to smile rather than turn my head away. Ronnie teaches me how to smile and say hello when I want to scream and turn my anger into compassion. Ronnie teaches me that asking for help is a strength, a self-loving action that our fear destroys, but our love conquers all.

I learn to trust. Again.

"I am afraid to say goodbye to the kids next to his car. I am afraid that he will talk to me or look into my eyes." I am sharing with Ronnie my shameful secrets.

I whisper my anxieties to her. It takes me a while to realize I am afraid of myself. Deep inside, I know the fear was my own making. My quick reactions, reactive responses, and hyper-sensitive weakness – these were my creations. There are only a few feet between our front door and his car. Whenever Dan pulls up to take the kids for their special daddy time, it is awful to see them walk those few steps. Every time Dan's car arrives, I feel my soul scratching; I am convinced I am hurting my kids who were yearning for a whole family. Dan does not come inside the house; I don't come outside to say hello. I am embarrassed, ashamed, and apologetic. These feelings are hidden very well inside me, and I certainly don't show them to Lev and Liam. I need them to see a strong, determined Mom who builds a tall wall to hide all of her emotions. I guard myself, afraid of his reactions, put-downs, and insults. I hide behind the white half sheer curtain, waving goodbye.

Ronnie tries to show me how to love myself, but I don't know how.

"The first step is to stop obsessively reading Dan's texts and emails," she teaches me.

I admit, compulsively, every night I read his repetitive words filled with blame and shame.

I love and respect myself more. I won't read it; I won't participate in this game.

The urge is unbelievable. I want to read each word, analyze it and fight it in my brain. I am a cutter. Reread it, knowing it hurts, and it cuts like a razor blade where I am most tender, sore, and vulnerable. It stabs where I am exposed.

I remind myself of Ronnie's words, "You do not have to read all these. Show yourself, love."

For the first time, I fall asleep hugging my spiritual book instead.

A few hours later, I wake up and read the emails.

I relapse.

My heart sinks. It is hard to tell Ronnie, but I can't be anything but honest with her. I tell her about my mania. She is not disappointed; she doesn't lecture me, she is not upset. Lovingly, she understands and waits. And just like that, one day, I stop reading it all. It doesn't matter. If it matters, the Universe will find a way to let me know about it. I have freedom.

Ronnie had the love and the patience to listen when I could not even listen to myself. Slowly, she encouraged me to approach Dan's car, to take those dreaded few steps out of the door when all I want to do is hide.

She guides me, "No comments. No demands. No threats. Just love and understanding."

I am lost. *How do you show love for someone who continually hurt you, made you cry, and stole your trust?* Instead, I'd run a half marathon, clean three houses, or make cupcakes for all the kids in the school.

Honk. Dan is the most punctual man you will meet. He doesn't arrive five or ten minutes early, nor even one or two minutes late. He comes on time every time. *Honk, honk.* He is here, my babies running outside with sounds of joy.

"Daddy is here!"

Maybe they are excited to see us at the same time, even though we are awkward yards from each other. Once, their parents shared romantic love, and, today, they are two strangers.

If I told you that I became Mother Theresa in one day, that would be a lie. This process was long and agonizing. At first, I took a single step out of my doorway. Just as quickly, I retreated to my safety zone, into my home. I closed the door and locked it, checking it three times over, only in case. Eventually, I went forward the first two steps, three... and then I was standing next to his car, and I felt entirely safe. I was still alive.

Did I just look into his eyes? Nothing dreadful happened, I am still here, and it is all in my head.

I could see at last that Dan behaved like that out of fear. Like a bully kid putting down the weakest child next to him, I was the target of his anxiety, not of his confidence. I realized I didn't buy into his drama anymore.

I do not hate you, Dan. I am not afraid of your anxiety.

Later that evening, after the kids' bedtime, I realize that I know what to write to Dan. I am sharp, decisive, and straightforward. I open his text trail from the past few months, scanning the long chain of hurt. But tonight, I am stronger. Tonight, God has stopped the insanity. Tonight, my vision is clear. The fog has burned off. Instead of rereading his communications, nitpicking each word, twisting reactions to this direction or another, my fingers type one short, concise sentence.

"What you think about me is none of my business."

I have waited more than a decade to say this, without mumbling—no apologizing.

I read it once, and I hit the send button.

No fear, no hesitation.

Ten pounds of heavy mortar and bricks fall off my shoulders.

My spirit is free.

I bury my phone in the electronics drawer in the kitchen. It is ten-thirty at night, and I do not want to read his response. I need to be in bed. I take care of myself and pick the color of my next sweater.

My mind doesn't make up a million scenarios like it used to. It doesn't matter if I wake up to read the stern, abusive, and horrible responses. I am proud of the little girl that said, *no more abuse. I am not accepting it.*

The morning after, I don't jump to check the phone. It can wait. Prayers first, meditation, then coffee. I wake up the kiddos, fix breakfast, make snacks, and make their lunch. I do my makeup and wink to myself in the mirror like I found the new me. I do my hair differently, letting the tight ponytail loose. I put on my tennis shoes slowly, first the left shoe, then the right, to break the habit of putting on the right shoe first. Today is all about breaking habits. I will sweat in a good workout to remove the remaining fear.

It works. This morning, Dan's phantom was not standing next to me in the bedroom, bathroom, kitchen on our way to school.

At last, I'm ready to pull the phone from the drawer. I scroll to the text messages—no response; Nothing at all.

My text didn't send. I didn't press the send button.

I am not ready yet. I am still in Dan's mind and thoughts.

We rise by lifting others.

If Ronnie had shown up in my life in a different time and different place, we would never have met. I would have been too afraid or too judgmental to approach her. The universe brings people into your life when you are ready, and Ronnie could only be my anchor when my boat was about to sink. A stranger who saved me from me. In this world of giving and taking, do you trust strangers? Would you give your trust to someone else? We pay lawyers, insurance agents, doctors, psychiatrists, and accountants; we give them our life, health, money, legal issues, and secrets. They start as strangers, and yet, sometimes, they, like Ronnie, turn out to be angels, too.

Find a Ronnie around you or be a Ronnie for someone else. The universe is there for us; it never yells at us, holds grudges, or hates. It's patiently waiting for you to invite it in to help. The light cannot come into your life if you insist on staying in the darkness. Miraculously and consistently, it will find its way to you if you are willing to get help; if you are ready to stop blaming yourself and see that there are other ways to live rather than in immobilizing fear.

When you exemplify gratitude and treat yourself with love, you will attract the Universe's hand to your life. Help never comes without your inner surrender and acknowledgment that you need help. The Universe is there to offer everything you truly need if you only stop the cycle of blaming and shaming yourself and those who look like your enemies. When you see that all hate is an illusion, then you can wake up – wake up to love.

Chapter 17

Drama Junkie

Mem. Chaf. Resh. מ.כ.ר.

Sell מכר· Sale מכירה· Addict, Junkie מכור· Addiction התמכרות
Acquaintance מכר · Familiar מוכר · Known מוכר

◉

Los Angeles, 2014

The business of cleaning is always loud. Carwashes. Dishes. Hot showers. Nothing is still – the flowing water, the harsh scrubbing, the sweeping brushes, the slapping sound of slippery soap, the broom that pops out of your hands and hits the floor with a bang, vacuum-cleaning, washing, and humming with declaring its job.

When I clean relationships, it is the loudest. The noisy thoughts that run through my mind, the dusty shelves stocked with yes and no answers, hard decisions scratched across the blackboard of my life's story, the greasy pain that seems impossible to scrub off.

How can I reject my best friend of thirteen years? How can I finally say "enough" to the person with whom I shared my body, my kids, my life, my bed, the fridge, and the bathroom for half of my adult life?

No store sells the magic solution strong enough to clean my life of this grime and caked-on crud. I think about Dan, again and again, my thoughts about him try to clean him out of my head, but they spin in a forward illusion mode, like the wheels in the car wash tunnel. Everything about him always seems promising and brilliant. He is handsome, thoughtful, and considerate. He is my knight in shining armor. I didn't see the dirt in pain, the lying, the deception. The insanity of our relationship cycles:

He is nice. I feel complete.

He is mean. I fall apart.

He is accepting. I feel calm.

He disrespects me. I feel alone.

He is acknowledging. I feel free.

He is inconsiderate. I cannot breathe.

He is approving. I feel alive.

He disapproves. I plunge into oblivion.

I wonder which is more confusing, living with this chaos and being afraid of the next outburst, or living in his good graces knowing the ambush of his sudden explosive anger is always just around the corner? I cannot find the formula, but I sense the random schedule of fear. The thoughts "he" and "if" intertwine, creating mantras in my new American vocabulary. I find myself trying to stay ahead of his actions by contemplating *What is his next move?* I am at the ready in my familiar role as a soldier, guarding the camp.

When you live with an addiction, you perfect your obsession. The fear, the questions, and the suspicion control any speck of space in mind. What did he say to his friend on the phone? To whom did he talk? Why is he staring at me? Why is he happy? Or sad? Is he sleeping or staying up all night? The obsession over someone else's life takes over. I order my obsession to stop, putting in earplugs so I can't hear myself. I want to live my life without being afraid of someone else's reactions without being a slave to the whims of another. I am tired of feeling compelled to act, react, analyze, blame, cry, cry more, cry a lot, do, do more, do again. Feel Guilty; Promise; Repeat.

And yet, I still love him.

I love him.

I love and depend upon his approval. This is the only way I feel alive.

Circles. Half of our relationship is in my mind, tracking the past and calculating the next cycle of progress and catastrophe. I hear the far-off drumbeats of war. They echo deep within the nerves, stretching around my heart and unsettle the thoughts in my brain. After the constant analysis and intuitive strategies, I forget who I am, where I start, and where I end.

Like a madman walking in the streets searching and begging for his sweet words of approval, I am lost, which will help me remember who I am. I pray for his words like a panhandler hoping to scrounge the change to buy myself a drink.

I am exhausted from the trials, from make-up sessions, from tests. Just show me the truth, the reality of what is.

He is my magnet, and I am his. Hard-headed iron magnets are endlessly pulling and pushing energies.

And yet, we are soulmates. The attraction is captivating. I want to inject into my veins the drug of passionate love every moment. I cannot get enough of it. It comes every morning in the form of conflict. I do not know how to be with him. I wake up, and I want to kick him out of our bed or jump on him. I do not know how to just "be" in his presence.

I am a junkie; I get high when I stay with him. I get high from thinking about him. I obsessively crave every word he says. And when it scares me, I run away, but not too far. I take a break, sweating, out of breath. This craziness is my barometer. Stay? Leave? I have all the options in the world, but they are all tainted with sharp excuses, neediness, and intense fear.

Like Ken Jennings, the polymath Jeopardy winner, I presume to know every detail of what will happen if I stay or separate. I have multiple scripts running in my head, playing out different possible futures. I am a fortune-teller. It is utterly inevitable. I build up these harsh but varying scenarios like pyramids in the desert. My sadness is built from mortar, brick by brick, with a strong shape, a sharp point, and a weathered look.

This fantasy of "they lived happily ever after" has been purged. It has poured from my eyes and down my face, washing away my carefully placed makeup. It has swirled down the drain of reality. It has been cleansing, it has been painful, and above all, it has been loud like a bulldozer in a construction zone.

We are both emotional swingers, bound to one another, yet share each other with another vice, at least in a different sense than the usual. We swap feelings. We love again, we hate again, and then we love-hate, and then hate-love. And so, we spin around, loving to hate and hating to love.

Drama is our drug of choice. It gets us off more than sugar, cigarettes, booze, cocaine, or heroin. I am addicted to each of his words; I hunger for his look and thirst for his manipulation with desperate compulsivity. The more secretive and criticizing he behaves, the more intense his anger, and the more shocking the surprise that knocks me down. The crazier I get, the better the rush. I feel like I am on a cliff's edge, blindfolded. I know I will fall. I like teetering on the precipice. I delight in the anticipation.

I leave, put up the STOP sign, and then retreat to the other room, but only for an hour and then come back. The danger is playing games with me. I crave the torture, the chaos. I want to feel like someone is shooting me through my heart after being tossed into a pit.

The cycle repeats. That's what the addictive cycle does. Again, I walk blindfolded, again and again, telling myself to trust. Perhaps this time, I will be safe. Or maybe not.

◉

Los Angeles, 2014

It's the birthday of our daughter. Exactly a decade since I became a mom. No doulas, no helpers, no parents. Only Dan and I were in the delivery room. Just the two of us, waiting for our creation to arrive. After twenty-seven long hours of labor, she came into the world at 5:25 a.m. on a Saturday. Sweet, innocent eyes staring at me from a hospital blanket folded like in a cocoon.

Mommy, I am here. I am yours!

I got a new title: Mom. I looked at her with a heart that just opened up to new expanses it never knew before. In a life-changing moment, I was immersed in a decisive, indescribable, immense moment of love, unconditional love, caring, and worrying more than I had ever thought possible. I couldn't have done this with anyone but Dan, I thought.

We created.

Life.

Together.

The alarm goes off earlier than other mornings. I hit snooze, trying to remember why I put it half an hour earlier.

Then it hits me. *It's Lev's birthday!*

As with every birthday, I get up earlier to set the special birthday surprise breakfast table. Twice a year, I get to make sweet homemade pancakes, with each pancake in the letters' shape in their names. I decorate the plates with fruit and prepare the dining room for the festivities. Flowers. Balloons. Cards.

The delicious smell of pancakes inevitably calls the kids out of bed earlier than usual. With half-curled hair, happy eyes, and long-sleeved flannel pink pajamas, my daughter comes out of her bedroom excited to celebrate. I love to see those innocent eyes open wide when she comes out of her bedroom. This day is supposed to be all about *her*, her unforgettable moments of growing another year learning and experiencing.

This birthday is different. She comes out of her bedroom, and only Mommy is here to sing Happy Birthday. Daddy will not be here this year or any future year.

Her parents are both so self-absorbed that they turn their daughter's birthday into a conflict between themselves. I think about how cruel we are.

Am I selfish? Are we all selfish? This day is about my daughter. But somehow, we manage to make it about us.

I find a solution! I decide in my head that Dan must call right when she wakes up. I will control her loss, my loss, and the reasons for our family breaking apart. He will call *right now*. The commanding officer in my brain barks the order and demands compliance. I am a champion chess player who will read my opponent's moves. I am ready.

Dan doesn't call on my time. Everyone else in the family calls, one after the next, singing Happy Birthday in two languages, bringing smiles and laughter. Lee, Sharon, Libby, Sam, and Sasi.

It is almost time for school, and I am still waiting for that one phone call. It doesn't come. My baby looks at me. Her intuition tells her that my thoughts are not only here but also far off in the future, letting someone else's choices define my world.

Her dad is not present, and for a moment, neither am I. I am in Dan's mind, in his brain, trying to find the answers.

I am addicted to understanding, controlling, observing his behavior.

"What happened? Why are you sad?" she asks with puzzled eyes and mouth filled with colored sprinkled pancakes.

I hug her. I want to tell her that divorce is not her fault, that she did not cause it, nor can she control it. On her special day, there is nothing my daughter can do to change what has happened.

I want to tell it to the little girl inside me.

I let the highs and the lows control me. What is, in fact, only five brief minutes last hours in my mind.

Finally, just as we're about to leave for school, he calls. I am relieved. Our daughter is the happiest princess in the world. Or is it me that feels happy and content? I project my feelings onto my ten-year-old daughter. Both of her parents love her. She basks in comfort, just like the day she was born.

Dan asks to stop by "just for a second" after dropping the kids off at school. He sounds like an excited child. Intrigued, I let him come by, trying to hide the thrilled girl inside me. I straighten my hair, fix my make up, and put on my favorite shirt. I spray on his favorite perfume.

It occurs to me: we needed two lawyers, four assistants, a four-thousand-dollar agreement, and a court order to allow us the space to date again. The price is astoundingly high, but the effect is beautiful. I see the flowers again; I smell him again; We have sex again, And the court agrees; I agree. I let him splash like a teenager on my body; I devour his smell. I eagerly await a text, flirting my way into his world and his mind. I quench myself with his flattery. I am in love. My body rests in the sky. We no longer live together, so now we date.

He finally arrives.

"I went to buy our little girl a gift, and I got you a jacket," he says, "It's a little cold outside."

I try out my new black, fashionable warm jacket. It wraps me with secure love. I feel the blood running with satisfaction; Dan's approval is enveloping me. My addiction is at its peak.

Ten minutes later, we are on the floor, kissing, grasping, touching every part of each other's bodies. This situation is familiar like it used to be between us a decade or more ago. We breathe. I am in heaven, and I let him lead the night. For me, that is the key to a powerful man. Give him control. Dan chooses a classy restaurant to dine tonight with our daughter to celebrate her special birthday. It is all about her. Presents, cake, candles, dessert, love, giggles. Are we a family again?

Our children see their two parents together, talking, smiling, breathing together, not making crazy scenes. On her tenth birthday, our daughter can relax, gather her presents, and let go for a few hours while her parents are together.

Dan is sweet again. The sweet, sugary, unhealthy candy is on the counter again. I taste and grab for more; I am a glutton. I can't take my eyes off him. Once again, I love him, and I loathe him.

The confusion is tearing a hole in my reality. Being in a relationship with someone who does the unexpected at any minute is intoxicating. This is my rollercoaster and one I ride blindfolded, not knowing which way it will turn at any moment. Slowly rising to the top, you anticipate the rapid drop to the bottom. The adrenaline is pumping even during this slow ascension. Soon, there will be screaming from both terror and joy.

Inevitably, the ambush comes.

"Are you seeing someone? I know you are." He asks twice.

He looks at me contemptuously. Suddenly, he is hollow, distant, and judgmental.

I did nothing!

I want to scream out loud for the world to hear. But what's the point? It is too late. I know this look on his face too well; it is coldly familiar. I feel ripped and emptied.

How can he ask me that immediately after we just immersed our bodies in passion again?

I let him in, and he promptly built a wall between us. His investigative questioning is making my skin crawl. My boundaries are being trampled again. I want to push him away and scream at him, *Do not ruin this party!* Over and over, he builds a beautiful, sophisticated sandcastle just for me and then suddenly destroys everything with a bucket of water. I feel betrayed, as if I helped build each sandy, wet tower, only to see it demolished.

I do not answer his question. It's not because the answer is "yes." It's because my heart is aching. He *knows* me. How can I be with him and someone else? It is not possible for me. I am Good Girl Jerusalem. And why would he ask me this question in the middle of a happy moment of our lives, on our firstborn's tenth birthday?

We return home. I lie alone under the covers in our bed. The balloons in the living room are slowly deflating, saying a long goodbye. They will be back next year. Our family won't.

As I lie there, the rain starts to pour. I can hear the drops hit the windows, heavier, louder. Nature is cleaning the streets but not washing away my feelings; feelings are not facts.

The rain outside gets fiercer. It is a downpour, and it is incredibly noisy. It doesn't often rain in L.A., but it floods the sidewalks, turning the streets into rivers when it does. It feels scary, all this plummeting rain that scrubs every stone, every road, every street. There is no mercy from the angry sky; it comes down and cannot be stopped. The business of cleaning is at its fullest.

A bright, sharp lightning bolt hits, and the thunder warns of more strikes to come.

Rain is real, Cleansing is real, and change is real.

After a storm, there is a chance of a rainbow. The day when our firstborn, our daughter, was born, a vast and magical rainbow filled with the richest colors I'd ever seen filled the sky. It foretold a colorful, magnificent, fulfilling future.

Sometimes, I think that we came to this world with one goal. We come here to experience facts and feelings, to sort them out like the colored blocks we played with in kindergarten. Which ones are big, and which ones are small? Which ones are blue, and which ones are red? Which ones belong to me, and which one belongs to others?

After the long night lying awake, listening to that rain, my brain is on fire, and it is hard to get out of bed. I drag myself to the shower, watching the water beat down on my body, a body filled with the complexity of torment. Each bone in my body feels damaged. The drugs that soothed me are leaving my body, and now it aches with the pain of detox.

The little girl in me desperately wants to see her family. They are eight thousand miles away from where this Good Girl Jerusalem was born. The fantasy about love and support enters my heart. I spent fifteen hours on a plane, followed by love, hugs, and kisses. I can feel my sisters and brothers, mom, aunt, grandmothers, and childhood friends. I can smell the scents and feel the serenity. I want to be hugged. I want the promise that everything will be perfect forever. But instead, I'm stuck here in the shower, aching from withdrawal, already thinking about my next hit.

I am, after all, a junkie.

Feelings are not facts.

Drama. Do you like drama? I'll bet you immediately said to yourself, "I hate drama!"

Somebody else, or maybe a group of "somebody elses" may come to mind. All that vicious energy, thievery, gossiping, bullying. In your sensitive heart, how you hate drama! But there's another part of you that, deep down, probably craves it.

Drama can be like chocolate cake – so sugary sweet; it's a sin. Drama is a single dark chocolate truffle. You may start with one tiny taste – just a small bite; it cannot hurt. You do not get to enjoy this rare truffle every day, so you savor what you can. The taste lights up your mind, hooking you into another bite. And another.

If you are like me, real chocolate is too raw, too rough, too predictable, too easy. My drama is much more complicated. It's more like cheesecake.

Yes, cheesecake. Fresh, creamy, cheesecake baked to perfection.

There is something about baking cheesecake that requires careful skill. In the end, its consistency is soft, with a sweet and salty crust, the complex texture making the experience dramatic. All those textures melt together into one thrilling sensation after putting it into my mouth. And no, it did not start in New York. Its origin is from ancient Greece, the birthplace of drama.

You see, I am a junkie. I will start with one bite and then another. I will slowly savor and enjoy every single bite and the fateful swallow. I continue taking bites to send me over the top with pleasure. Then, inevitably, the sickness sets. It's always sudden, even if expected. My stomach turns, and I cannot eat another morsel. I reject even the simplest and most nutritious remedies that might help. I am lost.

Are you like me? One moment, you enter the land of milk and honey, indulging in its richness, but it doesn't take time for everything to turn bitter quickly. Before you know it, you're screaming aloud, hoping to break out of what should have been your promised land, desperate to flee into the dark, dry, hazardous desert. Sometimes a few precious drops of happiness fall from above, and you try to hold onto them. But they always slip away. You find staying is impossible.

You know you deserve better than to live in fear and pain, spending years serving as a minor character in someone else's self-centered epic. You know you should have never built your life upon another person's agony and depression. You can't ever please or heal a sad, desperate person who ignores your wishes, your feelings, your desires. It's easy to see other people's realities and be blind to your own. You are a slave to sorrow, stuck in your own personal Egypt. Pharaoh will not let you go, not without a full ten plagues and divine intervention.

Changing course and voyaging into the unknown seems very dangerous, but there is always a moment when you must walk away. Take responsibility. Release yourself from misery. Trust that God is there with the best plan for you – a future you can experience with all five senses, a future where you will never feel threatened or ashamed –, and the sweetness endures.

Chapter 18

The Big Dip

Tet. Bet. Lamed. ‏ט.ב.ל.‏

Dip ‏טבל‏ • Immerse ‏טבילה‏

◉

Los Angeles, 2013

It is the beginning of the end, my brain tells me. I need to let go of what I once knew as "my life." I need to surrender the fantasy of being happily together as a family. *Letting go* is now my mantra. At the very least, I try for it because my heart tells me otherwise.

I am in an upscale, closed-door, invitation-only meditation event. I don't want to be here, but I'm sure this will help me "let go." I can also bring Lev and Liam, who are now ten and seven, with me. I hold onto them like a security blanket.

I put on the most beautiful flowy dress I own and gather to meditate with a hundred strangers. It is a non-religious place, foreign but still familiar. Speaker after speaker, I hear spiritually profound messages. I hear more about God, who seemed to disappear lately from my life.

Are you ready? I ask myself, doubting everything in my life. I act like a robot, doing what others told me to do, believing in what I am supposed to believe. I am numb.

They tell me fear is an illusion. It is temporary. It comes and goes like a cloud drifting in the sky. But I have lived in fear for a long time now.

I'm sitting in a big theatre filled with people intently focused on being in the present, in the moment, and my thoughts race like the feathers of a torn pillow in the wind. I close my eyes and try to calm the unknown, the fear, the anxiety from the D-word. The divorce. The cruelty. I open my eyes again and look in front of me – I see her.

Seven rows ahead.

She's sitting with her children: one smiling, shy toddler in her lap, a dirty blond-haired boy on her left side, and her right side, her fourteen-year-old firstborn with two long black thick braids. She is here to meditate, looking to do what we all need to—letting go.

It's Madonna.

Madonna Louise Ciccone. Madame X.

I look again and again. Madonna accompanied me morning after morning, afternoon after afternoon, to school and back. She showed me that giving up wasn't an option. She taught me how to dance with the fullness of my heart.

Before the meditation, I play with the thoughts like a ping-pong in my head during the break. Should I approach her? I gently ask Olivia, who is one of the organizers and my mentor for the day, to approach Madonna. I'm surprised to get a smiling nod of permission.

Slowly and respectfully, I approach the first row. Secretly, I am praying that the announcer will ask everyone to sit down, but everyone is still chattering. I stand right next to her. There is an empty seat next to her daughter. *Is it the Universe that has emptied it for me?*

"You saved my life," I say to Madonna, feeling dumb.

Who says things like that to people?

Her daughter glances at me, perhaps thinking that I might be yet another weird groupie. Who wants to be chased by a crazy fan?

I am different! My entire being wants to convince her.

Madonna looks at me for a few seconds and finally replies with a very suspicious look, "How so?"

Madonna Louise Ciccone looks at me, and I quietly answer, "You truly saved my life."

What I want to tell her is how she held my hand, how we took bus rides together, how she helped me forget about the chaos of my parent's divorce. With a press of a magical button, I could daydream about everything that I wanted to do. Dance! And not just dance, but live without rules, queues, lines.

"Thank you. I hope you will continue to empower teenage girls and young women to be who they are," I hear myself tell her, trying not to take more time or space than what I dared.

Quietly, I go back to my seat before the meditation starts.

My immediate thoughts are about how she regards me, about how I interrupted her and her family, although I did apologize for intruding. I worry that she might think me crazy. What did I expect? That Madonna will hug me and tell me that she is proud of me? That she will announce that I am the girl whom she saved? That she will introduce me to her children? I just did what I was afraid to do the most. I stepped out of my comfort zone.

Putting my hand over my heart, I tell myself, *I did it for me.* This is not about proximity to fame or another selfie with a star. It is not about getting a signature or being admired for thirty seconds on social media. It is a dedication to the young teenage girl who found a *Lucky Star* on the long bus rides running away from the drama. It is for her. It is for Ella.

I close the circle.

I did what Madonna taught me to do when I was her young age.

Be honest.

Walk and talk my truth.

◉

Los Angeles, November 2014

It is Sunday afternoon, and the kiddos are with their daddy. After years of dedicating every Sunday to my family, I have one day – a full twenty-four hours – all to myself. There was no early rising, no breakfast preparation, no sideline patrol at the soccer game, and no kids' entertainment for the weekend. I do not have to take care of anyone but myself. I love my quality time with Lev and Liam. When we are together, it is impressive. But I must quietly and secretly admit I also enjoy the time I have alone. I have me – all to myself.

"Good morning self!"

"Good morning to you, too!"

"What should we do today?"

"Today?"

"Fun!"

"Well, that's a great idea!"

"AMUSE ME!"

"Me?

"Make me laugh!"

"Me?"

And that is how the conversation goes for a few minutes, as one tosses the ball to another self. I look at my watch again. And again. I have plenty of time today. Dance class, a movie, shopping, breakfast, a walk, organizing the closet, ideas are flowing one after the other. Start knitting, clean up my email inbox, take a hike. I wish I could go back to bed, but no, I am a Type A Personality. I cannot make the bed a destination on a Sunday morning. Let me do something productive. I am something that requires thinking, planning, and maybe spending money.

While I am arguing with myself and going back and forth in my busy mind, Rachel calls.

With Rachel, you do not merely ride to the mall and go on a shopping spree. You don't waste your money on an $18 glass of champagne, and you do not whine about your current body mass index and calorie intake. With Rachel, you are in the moment. She doesn't try or plan. Things magically happen when you are with her.

The "selves" do not even have time to argue or think it over. That is it. Whatever Rachel decides, we'll do. Jump!

Two hours later, I stop by Rachel's. She doesn't say much. She isn't like an ordinary girlfriend. With her, it is not about fashion or jewelry, romance, and sex, or a spicy secret from the past. When Rachel's eyes speak, you listen.

Simple, humble, beautiful. Soft almond eyes, pale skin, and a slim figure that flows like wheat in an open prairie. When you are with Rachel, you do not want to be her. You want to be the immense connection and devotion she has to the Higher Power. Rachel doesn't want to be you or anyone else. She has wholly accepted who she is and where she is. Rachel has no reliance on glamor, fame, or wealth; she is simply herself, Rachel. That is her glory.

This Sunday, we venture out to a Korean Spa. A little quiet women's spa in a swirling city, just Rachel and me.

We pay $20, adding $3 for yellow square sponges to scrub ourselves and start a four-hour journey from one quiet room to the next. Sauna. Himalayan salt room. The hot room, hotter room. It is sweltering. I suffocate. I need air, cold air. It's too hot. It is strange how Rachel can stay in the heat twice as long as my soul will allow me to remain. It is unbearable. I need to escape from the room. I crave the soothing air outside.

Have mercy on me, screams my body.

And just like that, Rachel leaves the sauna with a smile. I stumble out, following Rachel to the next experience. She doesn't say a word.

Ice water pool.

No! My entire body shrieks.

I am not going to put even my little toe in. It is far too cold, but I keep quiet. Like a kindergarten girl for the first time, I obey Rachel as she shepherds me from one humid sauna to the next. I pretend not to see the ice water pool.

Do what Rachel says, commands the voice. I try to avoid the very thought of ice water on my sizzled, red-hot skin.

Right when I thought there is no escape from this "pampering" torture, a miracle happens! Right then, Rachel skips the ice water pool. My body is relieved, but only for two seconds until she walks towards the hot green tea pool.

Now we will be even hotter!

From the fear of freezing water, I dread the heat again.

Don't panic! I order my confused body.

The extreme temperature agitates each one of my tiny cells. I pray that Rachel will forget about the green tea pool and the ice water pool, but I know it's all coming soon.

We immerse ourselves in the green tea pool. Indeed, I will be hotter now than if I went walking barefoot on Tony Robbins' coals. To my surprise, we do not turn green or brown. We just get very hot, and our bodies are flushed red. We are steamed like dumplings.

I feel heavy, sleepy; my breathing slows in the present moment.

Women sit and wander casually around at the spa: young women, older women, skinny women, curvy women. No one is comparing their figures; everyone is naked, wearing the Universe's chosen suit.

"Now, let's dip in the cold water," suggests Rachel.

Before we even step towards the glacial pool, my brain freezes. My body is shaking before we are even near the pool.

No! I refuse.

I dare to disobey Rachel.

"No!" I continue with determination. "I am not doing it! I am not putting my toe in this freezing water!"

The thought of the freezing water on my steamed body is like listening to the scratching of long fingernails on an old chalk blackboard. It grips my mind with dread.

And yet, it is so easy to refuse Rachel. She is never upset nor disappointed. She simply accepts you. It's a fact. That's it.

Her acceptance oddly makes it difficult to refuse her. I want the person, whom I just said "no" to jump up and down and prove to me that I just made the biggest mistake in my life.

Fight for me.

Rachel is quiet.

Without me, she continues with her mission, quietly and humbly. She goes into the icy water. She starts dunking herself, one dip after the other. She stays calm, ignoring my protest. She dips again and again.

Her soft kind eyes look up at me, and she whispers, "Come in, Ella, come in. Just one dip. No need to hesitate. Just jump in."

But this?

Rachel ignores my refusal and patiently waits for me to join her. She smiles.

After a moment of silence, Rachel softly continues, "Do it for you; you will feel great after."

I must do it for myself.

It is not about pleasing Rachel. It's not about making her love me more. I know she does. She accepts me. I want to do it for myself.

Without further thought, I immerse myself in the water.

It is icy. A polar bear would shiver. My body solidifies into a stiff block.

Without having any time to think, Rachel starts to dip her full body in, her head below the surface. Ten times. Every time she emerges, she says a word in Hebrew. Ten words.

"Keter." *Crown.*

"Chokhmah." *Wisdom.*

"Binah." *Understanding.*

"Chesed." *Kindness.*

"Gevurah." *Discipline.*

"Tiferet." *Beauty.*

"Netzach." *Eternity.*

"Hod." *Splendor.*

"Yesod." *Foundation.*

"Malkuth." *Kingship.*

I recognize them. It's the Ten Sefirot. I do exactly as she does. This is what some call a mikveh – ritual immersions.

Ten. Ten dips. I hardly dip down the second time; I tremble on the third. Oddly, on the seventh dip, I feel better. It is somehow bearable by the eighth. By the tenth dip, I am comfortable. I do not even feel the cold water. I can stay longer. So, I do. We are one—the water and me.

Intuitively, Rachel emerges from the pool, allowing me to feel the water all by myself, letting me go through the experience. I am by myself for a few more seconds until I come out as well.

"Mind over matter," Rachel looks at me with her sweet eyes and a smile that glows with unconditional love. "You did it."

I feel like a baby who has rolled over for the first time all by herself. I feel like I have just written my name by myself for the first time. I feel like I am in Paris for the first time, like I am in Rome, in Prague. I feel like I am just diving for the first time into the Red Sea. It is clear. It is real.

We repeat the ritual again, going from one sauna to another, one room to the next. Increasingly, it feels good. She changes something within me; she is creating this moment. I silently tell her how I love her. My heart beats and pumps with compassion.

Rachel is half-God to me. Rachel is the connection to the Universe, the rope to a faith that I needed long ago. Maybe it is because she prays more often than me? Is it because she knows the morning blessings by heart or the reason for each holiday? No. Rachel has something solid you cannot measure in any quantity or standard. Rachel has faith. Full, knowing faith. She understands that, even though I keep questioning the process, I also had strong faith inside me all this time. That faith, as powerful as it was, was always obscured by fear.

Rachel awakens the spark that brightens my certainty. She's the one from whom I need to acquire a spiritual map, that treasure hunting map that says how to change my mind, without fear, without objection, without making a hundred-mumbled-excuses until I say... "yes."

Half an hour later, Rachel and I are sweating again in the sauna. I'm heavily breathing like I am climbing the steepest mountain. This time, my body doesn't want to run away from this maze of temperature quest rooms.

With a sweet smile, Rachel looks at me and says, "Now you can go into the cold water pool."

I stand up, waiting for my guide to get up and come with me. To my surprise, Rachel doesn't move. She remains behind, calmly lying flat on the hot wood, relaxing, half smiling. I think she is talking to God. I want her to talk to Him for me, too. Maybe she can find out some answers.

Wait, I have to go by myself? Rachel, this is insane! My mouth shouts, yet I retain complete silence. *I need Rachel by my side.*

I feel the steam pouring into my body, into my brain, into my heart. Once again, my mind feels hotter than a boiled potato on a wintery day.

Rachel, who somehow hears the words in my mind, keeps smiling, and, with her eyes closed, simply says, "Yes, this time by yourself."

Like a toddler who just had a long, cathartic tantrum, I make my exit noticeable. I puff, and I stomp, not because of the boiling steam, but because I let my automatic reaction control my being.

Rachel says we have the magic of making all the other women leave the pool when we approach it, so it will be all for ourselves. Alone, I get out of the sauna, and, as I walk towards the empty cold pool, I command my thoughts to stop arguing. I ignore my fears of the freezing water. I ignore my toes, which are warning me away from the ice. I calm my heart. I approach and, as if I am brushing my teeth, without thinking about each step, I take off the very small towel they have provided, place it aside, approach the ladder to the pool, and I climb in.

The water is perfectly pleasant.

I know what to do. I dip ten times for each of the ten Sefirot, not exactly remembering the words for each dip, but I have the intention of letting go with each breath.

In. Out. One.

In. Out. Two.

In. Out. Three...

Nine.

Ten.

The water covers my body, hugging my soul. The water is there, promising me I will never be alone. The water touches my feet, my ankles, my thighs, caresses my curves all the way up my back. It lovingly covers my stomach, my glorious breasts, my smooth round shoulders; it engulfs me up to my neck, my mouth, my nose, ear and eyes, and every follicle of my brown-black hair. While my body is resonating with the water, one simple word emerges from within TRUST.

I have done it by myself. On this quiet Sunday afternoon, in this little spa in the heart of Koreatown, I have changed my perspective, infusing myself with bravery. I may not have walked on hot coals, but this feels as if I did. I let myself feel fear, but those fears no longer shape or limit the thoughts within my mind. They cannot touch the deepest part of me, the part so connected to the Universe that transforms reality.

Take the contrary action.

How many times have you let your body dictate what you need, what you desire, and even what you think? Every craving is based on your raw physical desire. *I need a bigger car; I need a man, I need a woman. I need a new title in my career. A bigger house. Luxury vacation at a five-star hotel.* The hunger for more is relentlessly blaming you, reminding you with the loud voice of an impetuous dragon that "You are not enough! You don't have enough!" Only by fulfilling the next craving can you have any relief from that feeling of inadequacy, except that the fulfillment vanishes as soon as it arrives.

Beneath our deepest craving, there is one entity controlling every decision we make: fear—the immobilizing fear that provides the illusion that you cannot do something or cannot refrain from doing something. I cannot stop eating certain foods. I cannot stop talking the way I do. I cannot end this relationship. I cannot take this course. I cannot dip my body in freezing water after my body is scalded from a sauna.

Fear immobilizes us. Fear will stand at the door like a gigantic ugly bouncer, making sure you do not try to enter what might be the most beautiful experience in your life. Fear makes you move away from fulfillment, muttering "no, no, no" under your breath.

Think about the last few things you did not even attempt, that you perhaps didn't even dare to think about because of fear. You contemplated and decided against the next step just because of what *might* happen.

Fear will send you alarming warning messages that feel very real. Sometimes it even seems so scary that the threat to your body feels valid. The immediate reaction is paralysis, and the secondary response is procrastination. Panicking and procrastinating, we stay stuck in fear. Sometimes, that fear hardens into an ongoing panic, other times, into enduring depression.

The only way to step outside of fear is to first question it, ignore the fake warnings, and teach yourself to silence the nay-saying chorus that your busy mind creates.

Start.

Not tomorrow, not later, not in a month.

Now.

Open the door.

Turn on the light.

Take the step.

Jump into the water.

Cultivate complete certainty that things will flow and magically come together because *it is all already given to you* by the Universe. You are the only one who stands between what you could have and where you are in your present life.

Fire this cruel, degrading bouncer who mocks you and blocks you. Tell him that you will be brave and move forward, no matter what.

And if you ever feel that the water which surrounds you is too cold or uncomfortable, you can always come out of the pool and dip into it later. You will not forget that you have tried – and you can, and will, assuredly try again.

Chapter 19

November Miracles

Nun. Samech. Samech.   .ס.ס.נ
Miracle סנ • Wonder סנ

⊙

Brentwood/Los Angeles, April 2014

Calendars. Clocks. Countdowns. Reminders. There are so many significant moments in life I wait for with excitement. The first day of school, graduation, the daring, intercontinental move, college graduation, the new job, the big trip, the glamorous wedding, delivering my first baby, becoming a mom, delivering my second baby, moving to a new house – the first day of anything.

Tomorrow is divorce mediation. This is not the excitement I yearn for. This is absolutely dreadful.

Over the last two weeks, chaos has erupted, and everything has been thrown into turmoil. Dan is controlling the roller coaster, and I am strapped down inside it, unable to get out. We have already had one horrible divorce mediation meeting. During it, he treated me like I was the scum of the earth. He called me names, accused me of cheating, of being malicious gossip, of being promiscuous. He became increasingly upset as he built his case against me.

Flash. Someone takes my horrified picture at the peak of this roller coaster. I am pale white. Fragile. Scared. I am going to throw up. Get me off of here.

No matter how disgusting Dan's accusations are, I refuse to offer any external reaction. On the outside, I remain quiet, stoic, trying to imagine there's a brick wall protecting me from harm. I attempt to lift a great shield to make sure nothing pierces my heart. But now it doesn't work. My body is torn and exhausted; I want to scream from emotional agony. And here comes still another corkscrew twist on the frightful ride.

For the second mediation meeting, I have packed the right papers with clear charts, spreadsheets, a confident list of desires and needs – and a brown puke bag. I have prepared my reasoned and impassioned speech, making sure I have the best opening.

I am utterly terrified.

My mother told me God created the universe in just seven days. How is it that no one can manage to separate a quarreling couple within seven months?

I arrive in Mr. Mediator's plush office, near the top of an impressive high rise building on the west side of Los Angeles. Glass doors, a big meeting room, a round table, comfortable black rolling seats, wide glass windows with a breathtaking view of the ocean – all attempts to distract from the harsh reality of divorce. I feel stripped and naked in the middle of this office. My face betrays pain; my agony is apparent. No one can hear me.

I am dividing our family into rows and columns on spreadsheets. Now there are two homes, doubling our children's lives. Each has two rooms, two beds, two nightstands, two toothbrushes, two showers. How can I do this to my kids? The guilt is spreading. I can feel it in my veins. It is intolerable. I want to smash the glass that encases my domestic tragedy, glass that seems to have my family on display.

Mr. Mediator, wearing a finely tailored suit, welcomes me with a peculiar, crooked smile. Slowly and confidently, he places a blank white pad with light blue lines on the glass table. He tries to joke with me, perhaps hoping to alleviate the panic in my heart.

Mr. Mediator takes notes. We're talking about assets.

"What did you accumulate? Who is the person who made it, bought it, and saved it?"

I try to distract myself and look out the great big window. I want to be in the ocean. I want to go into the deep, curl up under the water, and forget about the world. The dream that I once had of the world, which we slowly built together, is crumbling.

It's been crumbling for a while. It started a long time ago when my trust fractured. I lost myself in somebody else's feelings, and then I forgot that there were other feelings besides fear: Joy, awe, sadness, excitement. These evaporated without notice – it took me a long time to realize that they were gone.

I stare at the distant ocean from Mr. Mediator's office and feel mesmerized. Softly, I whisper to my best friend, the one whom I now blindly trust: my Higher Power, the Universe. I need the added strength.

I have done my research: all the websites, books, other people's stories. Truthfully, nothing can prepare a person for divorce mediation. I feel clueless, my fearful mind constructing devastating and catastrophic futures. I see myself unemployed, homeless with the children, perhaps living in a tent. We'll be lucky to get by on canned food. This terror drives me, forcing me to rehearse what to say, what not to say. I feel petrified as I imagine how he will react, but I must push forward.

The clear blue ocean stretches across the horizon. The vastness of the Pacific comforts me.

I put my life into your hands, Universe. I am doing the best I can.

Ronnie, with whom I speak every day, believes in me. She holds my heart every day, knowing that under the pain, under the drama, under each sentence that starts with the word "he," there is me, a strong me. I wonder how she does not give up on me, how her faith moves me from brokenness to rising from my bed when the sky seems painted black, and my mind is screaming, *you are worthless!*

Some days I am convinced that she will stop caring. Ronnie will disappear, or worse, be upset with or disappointed in me.

Long ago, I learned to fear people before they had the chance to unsettle and scare me. This is a fear engraved on my soul. I've always felt that the more I am connected to anyone, the greater the risk that they will leave, radically change, or ruthlessly betray me. As a firefighter on duty on the fourth of July, I was ready for anything at any moment, standing next to the cold metal pole, ready to slide down into a disaster zone.

The night before the third mediation session, I decide to sleep with God. I sleep with my spiritual books surrounding me on the bed; I have built a moat around my castle. And I have prayed to the Universe to come with me.

The morning of the day that will bring Dan and me physically together yet rip us soulfully apart, I leave the warm comfort of my bed, and I feel radiant with faith and trust. God is here, standing close, hugging me, telling me I am safe. The Universe is walking alongside me to the resolution meeting.

Dan and I enter the high rise building together. We haven't seen each other outside of Mr. Mediator's glass office for months, our interactions limited to brief phone calls. We are now two aggressive strangers in a cold metal elevator. He presses the elevator button. Time passes in slow motion. The elevator seems to be hauled up by a long rope.

I avoid his eyes. I stay close to my Higher Power, the only place I know that is safe, and I allow myself to breathe. I quickly glance at Dan without making eye contact. Grey fitted suit matched with a blue striped button shirt and shiny black shoes. He is standing tall, a beige manila folder in his hands.

Is he shaking?

Incredibly, beyond all reason, I want to hug him, to snuggle into his arms, against his wide chest. My body screams, *I love you, let's stop this madness now!*

The words are stuck, lost in a dense jungle of feelings. It is a very long elevator ride.

When I open the door to Mr. Mediator's office, I pause. I say a prayer. I let the Universe enter first. Each step. Each breath. I simply follow.

We sit in Mr. Mediator's waiting room. I want to stop the train, or at least jump out of this speeding car like a dashing hero in an action movie who always manages to create that happy Hollywood ending. I want to find Dan's lips in our darkness and kiss them. I want him to promise me he will never suddenly hang up the phone, never call me terrible names, and never accuse me of being promiscuous, or a liar, or mean-spirited, or dishonest, or sick. I want to rediscover our Italy – our passionate, magical land. I want to run with him to the beach and into the sunset, hugging side by side. We will laugh like two kids that never want to grow up.

My cheeks are now wet. The big heavy tears are spilling out of my eyes, running down, washing my face. My white pants now have black spots from my water-proof mascara. Nothing is tear-proof.

I can't stop thinking that this is the man to whom I once said "yes" with a beaming, joyful heart. Now, I am running for my life. I am willing to pay a great price for freedom. I am willing to break a house in two. I am willing to put two children through the misery of a nasty separation.

Mr. Mediator comes into the waiting area. He shakes our hands and offers an espresso or a cappuccino.

"Thank you, coffee," I hear myself reply. The truth is that I do not want American coffee. I am just buying a few more moments before the mediation.

My soon-to-be-ex-husband is getting up. He is taller than me by more than one foot. He approaches me, and he gives me a consoling hug. He is human again. I feel comfortable in his arms. I am vulnerable.

"It is going to be ok," he quietly reassures me.

I

Believe

Every

Word.

Within our marriage, I also believed him when he told me that I was miserable, that I didn't deserve any friends, and that I was crazy, just like my mother. I believed him when he promised me that he was sober, that he conquered his addiction. I craved happier days, but honesty isn't what he offered.

As we enter the cold mediation room together, perhaps for the last time as an official couple, I look out over the city. I spot houses with red tiles on the horizon. Under those tiles, there are couples who are married or perhaps just living together, some with babies. Under those roofs, some families are in chaos, and some are joyful. I imagine all of the drama, the lives that are constantly created, destroyed, and recreated in the houses within my view.

Mr. Mediator, my soon-to-be-ex, and my rushing mind are ready to conclude the deal today. Four seats are gathered around the round table. There is an empty seat in the room, right in front of me. I know it is reserved for the Higher Power protecting us all.

Mr. Mediator speaks slowly and clearly as if we are his students.

"There are four people in this room."

I am surprised. Can he read my mind?

Mr. Mediator continues, "Your history together is the fourth person, but we are not going to address him today."

I know what he must mean. But our history together is an Italian fantasy, a fiery passion that slowly burned out, and now the lifeless smoke is a mere phantom of what was.

I don't want to compromise. Giving in is not an option for a soldier or for a firefighter. But today, "compromise" must be part of my vocabulary. If we cannot come to a consensus today, I will forever regret it. I gird myself. *I am ready.*

We push through no fewer than three one-and-a-half-hour-long meetings with Mr. Mediator. We push through arguments, heated discussions, and bursts of tears. But we do it. Our release from mutual bondage is almost over.

Like I tell Lev and Liam, "Almost doesn't count." I need finality.

After the last meeting, we slowly descend to the ground level inside the cold elevator. We drop ten floors in frigid yet screaming silence. You can't cut this anger, not even with the sharpest knife.

It's a rage masked by fear. I am used to it. I have experienced this conflicting whirlwind of emotion during the ten years of our marriage. It's the hysteria that deforms our words so that they take horrific shapes. I am used to cursing, blaming, accusations, the judgment of what I wear and how I move.

I am a strong woman who can move mountains and valleys, who has been to war, who moved to a new country alone. I am a true, brave, undaunted warrior. And now I am afraid of a man who uses words as weapons, words that stab me in the flesh without mercy. He is sharp, unforgiving, crude, and intensely hurtful. He is convinced I am unfaithful, and no amount of evidence to the contrary will change his mind. It is impossible to defend myself from his irrational rage. I know it's his addiction talking.

I wish I could beg him to throw the final punch, to release the poisonous tension once and for all. All the black and blue marks from his words are deeply impressed in my mind, and these injuries cannot heal.

Wednesday. This was the day of the week when I was born. Noon, to be exact. My mom tells me the sun came out the moment I first cried.

This Wednesday is the fourth mediation meeting. Mr. Mediator tries to be efficient, with a sterile and calculating heart. No coffee is offered, just three bottles of water on the table, probably to clean up the scattered debris and dirt. This meeting proves to be a miraculous parting of the Red Sea. We manage to separate all that we have built together. We divide the house, the money, the sofa, the bed, the toys, books, albums, pictures, birthday cards. I insist on having the pictures from Italy. All these things are the puzzle pieces that had once fit together, granting a clear, cohesive picture. Now our puzzle is efficiently shattered, and no one will be able to put it back together.

The meeting finally ends up with a solid agreement about the separation. All that is needed to do is to have Mr. Mediator write up the formal court agreement so we can sign the forms. We quietly shake hands.

One life.

Four meetings.

The end.

I feel relieved. I need to escape this meeting room and live in peace and serenity.

Ronnie has generously walked with me step by step, helping me rehearse before each meeting. Most importantly, I learned to practice silence. And with her training, I now know how to peacefully leave the room before I lash out reactively.

After the repeated experience, I have realized confined elevator rides expose blind madness. I now choose to use the ladies' room to my advantage. Instead of taking the same elevator together, I wait at least ten minutes inside the spotlessly clean bathroom after each meeting.

I get on my knees in the stall and say a prayer to the Universe:

Thank you, Universe. Thank you for helping me finish this nightmarish ride. I am tired. Thank you for helping us come to an agreement, whatever it may be. Thank you for not letting me say the words I wanted to say because these words would come out of me with a mean spirit.

After leaving the building, I drive aimlessly. Without conscious intention, I manage to find my way home. It is still Wednesday, and it is Spring Break. A time for fortunate kids to splash in the water, collect memories with their family and learn about new exciting places. Dan takes the kiddos to Santa Barbara, their first one-parent-vacation. Welcome to the world of divorced families. I talk to the kids on the cellphone, and they put me on speaker. Dan is present but quiet in the room.

After some animated chit-chat, he suddenly interjects, "How come we never came here with the kids?"

I am breathless in an instant, shivering and broken-hearted. We are so close to being divorced. *How can I respond to this?* I can think of nothing to say in reply, so I quickly hang up the phone. My heart is heavy. It sinks in that we will never have a family vacation together again.

How come we never took the kids there?

Now that the phone call has ended, I am safe to say the truth aloud for the Universe to hear.

"Yes! I want to go with you to Santa Barbara, Dan! I want to travel. I want to hold your hand, to be with you. You are the father of our kids. You are the man who gave me the most precious thing in the world. I want to crawl into your arms so you can tell me everything is going to be okay again. It will be just fine. Forever."

I sit in the soon-not-to-be-our-shared living room, which was once filled with stories. My eyes land on The Kiss Box. His parents bought this beautiful gift for me for the first dinner I hosted at my condominium after we met. It's a large wooden box featuring a print of *The Kiss* by Gustav Klimt. The colors are deep yellow, brown, and green; the image is of a couple in love. The man covers his woman with his big arms, protecting her from cold evil.

I open the box and take out the sequence of our love story. Like a masochist, I go through the caring letters, cute notes, birthday cards, and tiny mementos we wrote to each other throughout the years. I eventually find myself sitting on the floor with all my photo albums, boxes of letters, postcards, and printed pictures: big boxes, small boxes, pictures from the pre-cellphone era. I study each moment, each movement. A big hug, our hands on each other's shoulders, smiles, laughs.

And then, I see the picture. It's a photograph from our trip to the Disneyland Adventure Park before our kiddos arrived in our world. The big, blue, glittery mural behind us reads promisingly, "Happy Ever After..." I look at this one for a long time.

There is so much obviously missing: there are no pictures of the yelling, the discomfort, the emotional abuse, the accusations, the profound loneliness, the dependency, the co-dependency, the addictions. We are like film editors, leaving the unhappiness on the cutting-room floor.

I finally finish torturing myself with the happiest moments of our relationship. I put the albums aside and sit up. I pause. I realize my Higher Power is sitting next to me. I do not need self-destructive distractions. I do not need wine, or shopping sprees, or chatty girlfriends, or even family. All I need is God sitting with me on the floor, browsing through my history. This moment with the Universe will be a part of my history, too. Perhaps even more important than my history with Dan.

On Thursday, I get up to a beautiful morning. I don't have a Thursday therapy session. Lev and Liam are away on a short trip to Santa Barbara with their dad. The consequences of this trip are deep and will carry themselves throughout my life. I miss my kids. And I miss my husband.

I want to go to fantasy land—the long drives. The hand-in-hand walks, running on the warm sand, finding another unique shell to add to our collection.

I get exasperated with myself. The universe, why did you create fantasies?

I fill the kettle with water and put the coffee grounds in the filter. I choose my mug, which today says "Follow Your Heart." There is a small red heart at the bottom of the mug, reminding me to keep pushing forward until I see the heart. I smile. It is Spring Break and a beautiful April morning. No school. No cars. Quiet and peaceful. Everyone is away.

I am grateful for the sky, for the birds. I am grateful that the kiddos are with their dad. I am grateful that I am healthy. I am grateful that we agree. There will be no more court. It is finished.

And then an email notification pops up on my phone.

From Dan to Mr. Mediator.

I am copied.

I read.

I gasp.

My body shakes.

"Mr. Mediator," Dan writes, "I am changing the agreement. I want the house, and I want the kids 50-50."

My heart sinks into the darkest abyss, far below bedrock, below the magma beneath the ground, below the crushing pressure, into total darkness. There is no breath. There is only insanity.

I frantically call Mr. Mediator, hoping he will tell me that it is all nonsense and that our agreement stands. Mr. Mediator is cold and curt.

"I cannot help you. You can probably arrange it in court."

Court! I am hysterical. My heart races with anxiety. *Didn't we just have a full agreement?*

In one second, in one email, we have instantly returned to the chaos of hatred and indirect communication. We have returned to paying lawyers with money we have yet to earn.

I rack my brain for a reason. *What just happened? He is with the kids in a hotel. He should be busy enjoying their time together._*

I dig and dig in my mind but can't answer the *why* that torments me. I gather that it must be my fault. I wasn't appreciative enough, or I wasn't verbally grateful for his efforts. And now I must harvest the punishment.

Hyperventilating, I call Ronnie. I need a paper bag, too, and can barely speak for a while. Ronnie helps me breathe.

The universe, where are you?

In the afternoon, I get another email, this time directly from Dan. In under 12 hours, I have been portrayed as the monster. Again.

I have fallen back into the trap. I feel the strong need to communicate with him, to pick up the phone and ask him what is going on. I want to be nice, to apologize for something I cannot comprehend. But it doesn't matter. I need to fix it.

I am a monster.

On my knees, I call out to the Universe, begging for all of this to stop. Yet, in my mind, I am beginning to doubt myself. Maybe it is a mistake to pour out my heart to God – maybe it's a distraction. Maybe it's making things worse. But at this moment, I cannot breathe. I desperately need the relief, to be released from the fear of what he thinks about me, what will happen, and how I will handle it all. I want to scream, to let him know that I am exhausted from playing these games.

If this follows the familiar pattern, Dan will take full advantage of my eagerness to make everything better. My addiction to Dan is taking over. As they say, I am looking to buy milk in a hardware store.

I call him.

He answers.

He apologizes.

I exhale... And then he attacks again.

I cannot hear his words. It doesn't even matter what he's saying. It all moves to the back of my mind. With his voice fading in the background, I feel a sudden, great upwelling of unexplained strength.

I have had enough! I'm taking back my life.

At this moment, like a lightning bolt, I wake up.

I will not be a victim. I will not be a slave to drama.

No more telling stories for pity; no more chaining my soul to sob stories and tragedies, my addictions. Dan did not do this to me. *I did it to myself.* Now, I am getting off the ride, leaving the lawyers, the courtroom, Mr. Mediator, victimhood, and the chaos behind.

Epiphany.

◉

Los Angeles, November 2014

Christmas is a month away, but it's Christmas time, nonetheless. Not like the kind seen in Europe or in old movies. People are approaching the dizzying heights of their consumer craze. Brown UPS trucks line the roads, and smiling Amazon Prime boxes fill the blue recycling bins. The malls and the stores are packed with eye-catching items that loudly claim, "I truly care about you. I want you to have fun." Soon, they'll become wrapped in red ribbons of debt and a perky bow, saying, "I will return you the day after Christmas." Children write up long fantasy lists of things they demand from Santa and try to put on their good boy or good girl outfits. Women pray that their husbands and kids won't be home when the flow of packages arrives. They have all lost the meaning of family: real dinners together and good conversations every night. Robotically they repeat the same routine again, year after year.

Today, I pre-wrap, not one, not two, but sixteen presents. *Here, my kids, indulge!* You are entitled to splurge because I took away the one gift every child deserves more than any other: a family. Hanukkah is in two weeks, and my guilt propels me through a series of expensive stores and compels me to do hours of research on Amazon for the best-reviewed gifts for my Lev and Liam. Sixteen presents minus four this year because they will spend two nights with their dad. I do the math, change my plans, and end up wrapping twelve.

When I was a child, Hanukkah was all about the oil. The fat. The calories. The big doughy, round, sweet, forbidden things covered with sugar. Not chocolate, not custard, and never the sprinkles. No options. No gluten-free, no sugar-free, and never different types of jelly inside. There was one filling, and it was red. You will love it, and you will eat it.

In my childhood, gifts were rarely given for Hannukah. Maybe a few real coins, not chocolate gelt, from a sweet aunt or a guest who does not have any kids of her own. But gifts? This is an economic innovation aimed at compulsive consumers who are easily seduced by colors, numbers, and sales.

I already got my gift this year: Dan and I are divorced. I am free.

It took Dan and me over a year and a half to realize we were fattening our already plump lawyers. It took us eighteen months of anxiety to lose the home in which we raised our babies. Eighteen months to scrape the last of our savings so we can make each other miserable. We spent our children's futures on rich lawyers so that they could enjoy even more champagne and caviar on another luxury cruise. It took me living in shame and fear, sleepless nights, endless worrying about what was to come, and the constant embarrassment. I was ashamed that I had no more money in my account and had to scrounge for quarters to buy milk and food for Lev and Liam. I required seven or eight Al-Anon meetings a week to turn my life over to the Universe. And then, six weeks of daily Al-Anon meetings when we divided the kids into two homes.

After crying for more than a year, going in and out of court and mediation, after declaring myself the most hurt victim in the world, and after hibernating in my own damp cave of emotion, I became determined to turn my life around. No more victimhood. No more retelling painful stories with ever-increasing horrible details. It was like quitting coffee or sugar, or any habit people think they cannot do without. Victimhood was my drug. I was addicted to being his victim. My mind skipped, again and again, *he did it to me!* But the simple truth is this – I did it to myself.

"You will probably receive the signed court order from the judge early next year," said Joanna, the paralegal with her nasally, sweet voice.

Sporting a red '80s hairdo, Joanna wrote and deleted sections to rewrite our agreement several times. Done with us at last, she clips the summary and the agreement, hands each one of us a copy, and sighs behind our back as we leave her office. After arguing for six weeks on the last few details of our life together, we are going back to two separate lives. Or so I hope.

December's miracles started in November this year.

Less than six weeks after we delivered our divorce papers to the court, right before my birthday, I was legally divorced by the State of California. What usually would take three to four months took only a few weeks. Dan and I finalized our papers at the end of October, and the judge approved them on November 4, 2014. The fastest divorce turnaround in family court. The judge simply didn't want to see us again. He was sick of the insanity, and so were we.

To seal my status as a divorcée, we went to the local rabbi, who declared I was "allowed to another man" in a humiliating ceremony. Dan allowed me. He is the man, and it was his decision, not mine.

It's over. No more long, exhausting court hearings. No more lawyers. No more stipulations and preconditions. Eighteen months of shame are behind me. Eighteen months of fear. Eighteen months of refraining from joy. For that long, if not longer, I was compelled to only talk about one subject in all its nasty permutations: divorce, mediation, meetings, a broken home: no social life, no friends, no work. My heart couldn't carry it all. My body nearly collapsed under the stress and pressure. They call it the "D diet," and it took its toll. I starved physically and spiritually. My body couldn't take food. All I craved was an escape from the harsh, oppressive loop called Family Law. I was like a horse with blinders. I had only one route.

Don't distract me; I am getting divorced.

And now, for the first time in years, I allow myself to laugh. I dial old friends. I breathe air. From now on, no more suspicion, spying, or hyper-vigilance. It is just me in a field of freedom.

I wake up in the morning, and it is my new life. Time is a gift now. People spend months and years building a home, and it is cruel to destroy what they built. But now that my official, civil, and the religious title is divorcee, now that the long statements, excel tables, and draft agreements are buried in an archived storage unit somewhere, I can be me.

What is it to be me again? Sipping a coffee while focusing on the foam; working out, without wondering about what meeting I have after the class; driving from school back home, being present, holding the steering wheel, and noticing the roads. Listening, truly listening, to my kids, my family, my friends, without the heavy fogginess that clouded my brain and heart.

Having friends.

I suddenly remember my small, black, pocket telephone book. I've had it since I was eighteen, but for years it's been packed away in the top shelves of our closet, inside the boxes containing my previous life, along with personal items and old journals, well-hidden with the picture albums of my bikini twenties. The little plastic telephone book is packed and discarded along with my pre-married pictures. I open and here it is, my life in alphabetical order. Its pages are a bit tattered. There is my neat round handwriting in pencil. All my friends and family in order, numbers upon numbers with area codes

I forgot existed. Emma, Bob, Josh, Iris, Lucy, Miriam, Ronit. More names. Another page, another smile. With each entry, a beautiful story emerges. A flow of crazy, sad, fun, amusing, heartbreaking, and unforgettable memories stares back at me each time I turn a page. This is the real book of my life.

This the last page before the end.

Ethan, my playful "son."

I turn to the last page. In my confident handwriting, I had placed my favorite poem in a stream of blue ink:

אֵיךְ זֶה שֶׁכּוֹכָב אֶחָד לְבַד מֵעֵז

אֵיךְ הוּא מֵעֵז, לְמַעַן הַשֵּׁם

כּוֹכָב אֶחָד לְבַד.

אֲנִי לֹא הָיִיתִי מֵעֵז

וַאֲנִי, בְּעֶצֶם, לֹא לְבַד

נתן זך

How is it that one star alone dares?
How dare he, for God's sake.
One star alone.
I would not dare.
And I, in fact, am not alone.

Nathan Zach

Don't leave before the miracle happens.

Is it true that December is the month of miracles?

According to tradition, the little tiny oil pitcher for the seven branches of the Menorah said on its little tiny label, 'will last for one day only.' There was just enough oil for a single day of light in the Ancient Temple. One day of hope during the war, not one drop more. And yet it lasted for another day. One more day to enlighten, to quietly proclaim, "I am here, I did not leave you, yet." And there was yet another miracle; another day and another day. Day five came, and after that, day six—a full week. And now a week and a day. Just enough time to replace what was left with new oil.

Is it a miracle? We all crave miracles. You find a creased $5 bill on the sidewalk. Is it a miracle for you? Probably not. For a hungry runaway teenager, it might change everything. Or perhaps that same teenager gets pregnant. Is that a miracle for her? Maybe if she has been trying to conceive for a long time. But if she is fifteen and she just had sex for the first time while on the streets, the pregnancy might not be received with the same joy.

A miracle is in the eye of the beholder. Only you can define your miracle. One thing is certain, though: miracles occur when you least expect them. They simply happen. You can feverishly look for the logic, for any explanation, for a reason. When you cannot find any reason, perhaps you should accept the mystery. Be brave in your lack of knowledge and define it as a miracle in your life.

Here's the other thing: when you are too busy, you may overlook the many miracles in your life. Pause and pay attention to what is happening; the miracle is here, right now. It is here in the wind blowing into your face. It is glaring at you in the hot sunlight on your body. It's the green that springs up after rain. Notice it! If life passes you by, you will miss the miracles, and you will miss the power of gratitude. You'll miss the magic.

When we focus too much on the past or worry about the future, we will miss what is, in both senses of the word, the present. We'll neglect the opportunities which life continues to bring. The miracles are there, and the secret to getting them is simple: be here now.

If you think about it, you'll realize that you've noticed life's inexplicable synchronicities time and again. You can only explain these by calling them miracles – these synchronicities cannot be rationalized by logic or simple explanation of nature's rules. True miracles endure past the moment they manifest. When you acknowledge the miracle, observe it, applaud it, and are grateful for it, then the Light will shine upon this moment and transform it into a lifelong memory. You will always be able to look back at this moment, drawing strength from the recollection. You can then share the story with others to give them strength and hope.

Watch for the miracles. Let them change you.

Chapter 20

Three Degrees of Separation

Los Angeles, December 2014

    I need to wait a few hours to summon the courage to dial the nine numbers to another continent across the world. With anticipation and a yearning heart, I dial Ethan's number as entered in my phonebook. Making myself smile, I play with my words. *I haven't talked to my "son" or seen him for more than twenty years.* There are so many questions. *Will my son remember me? What will he think of me?* Before I got married to Dan, I saw Ethan two or three times during my short visits to Israel, or when he moved back from the U.S., We would catch up on our busy lives and promise to stay in touch.

    Toot. Toot. There is no answer, and I choose not to leave a message. Anyhow, my number is blocked from being recognized by the other party, a paranoid move I made during the divorce. I'm not ready to unblock it yet.

    I console myself. *I will call him later. We waited twenty years; another day or two is fine.*

After dinner with the kids, my cell rings with an odd number. The caller ID shows the caller is from Orange County. I pick up the phone, wondering if it is another sales pitch or a scam, and yet, to my surprise, I hear the most comforting, sweet, loving, familiar voice.

"Heyyyyyy..." It is Ethan. He had no idea I just called a couple of hours ago.

Twenty years after he left with a red-haired girl to Las Vegas, my so-called son came back into my life. Our souls seem deep, timelessly connected. Lev and Ethan, my two first-borns, share the same birthday: February 28th. What are the chances?

Ethan doesn't speak often, but when he does, he says a lot.

Our conversation flows; he tells me he tried being a chef and then a sailor. After a series of daring adventures, Ethan moved to Australia. He is now the CEO of a successful technology company. His descriptions are short, his emotions are controlled, but he pays caring attention to every word I say.

I open the front door of the house and walk up and down our street, cell phone in hand. Finally, I sit on the sidewalk curb next to the house entrance, breathing in the fresh night air. I tell Ethan about the wedding, the kids, my career, the divorce drama, and the final emancipation. He listens with patience. As I speak, I am not aware of the passage of time. He hears pain, and he promises a sweet gift.

I can't imagine his gift will be life-changing.

"We need to celebrate your new beginning!" Ethan says, and I can see his smile over the phone, with his deep dimple only on one side. "I will be in San Francisco in January for a conference. I would love to see you." He added "Mom" just to be funny.

With my new title of "single, divorced mom," my vacations and days off are not simple. I share my two kids with a marked calendar, strictly planned for the next ten years; holidays, weekends, vacations, Mother's Days, Father's Days, Labor Day, Passover, Cesar Chavez Day. Our children's lives are cut in two nearly equal halves.

Before we say goodbye, Ethan asks me two questions.

"What days do you have off in December and January?" and "What is your email address?"

A few hours later, I receive an email from my lost son with a complex airline ticket in my name.

I open the email and browse the details—dates, hours, airlines, not one flight, but several. I look again at the airports: ICN, then on to BKK, and the to HKT. This is not a quick flight up to SFO. I need to Google the airport codes; I am shocked and elated at the same time.

Destination: Phuket, Thailand.

Say what?

Twenty years later, Ethan has given me a beautiful gift. Is this just a thank you for allowing him to stay two months on the old, battered blue couch in my first American apartment? Is it a tribute to our friendship, rekindled after twenty years? Or perhaps is it because we are truly connected like family, a bond that is forever?

The holidays come and go. The morning I leave on the trip, I wake up to a text: "See you in Thailand."

I feel like I am about to touch the sun! I am on my way to an unknown reality. The only thing I know is what to pack: three bathing suits, four pairs of shorts, and five tank tops, and two pairs of flip-flops. One tiny suitcase is enough. I had to bring my entire makeup assembly, which a girl like me cannot do without. Not even in Thailand.

LAX – Seoul, January 2, 2015

It's Friday night, and I'm on board an airplane surrounded by people for whom Shabbat dinners were not the foundation of their childhoods. Flights always fill me with the sense that I know nothing. I rest in the hands of something larger than me, which gently pulls, pushes, turns, and rotates my life. I am crossing a threshold. Sitting next to the window, I know that in seven days, when I return to Los Angeles, my life will be very different. Something will be created inside of me, warmed by the sun.

I officially fill in "divorced" when asked for my immigration status.

I am flying into a mystery. I am giving my life to the Universe, to a power that is far greater than myself, a power that graciously holds my tender heart.

Source, I know this is a gift You gave to me. I know it because it just happened without any effort or struggle. It's your magic. I trust You, Universe. I want to peek into the window of my future, moving the clouds like curtains.

I leave all anxiety behind me as I peacefully fly over land and vast oceans.

A minor miracle: on the fifteen-hour flight to Seoul, no one sits next to me. I'm able to think and then sleep without any disturbance— just me and God, up here in the twinkling starry sky. I sleep peacefully almost half of the flight, a full eight hours, like a contented child. I have such wonderful dreams!

I feel free in a tiny economy class seat on an airplane, freer than being alone in a big house in Los Angeles. I have missed myself for too long. I need this time because a new nest, a new career, and maybe even a new love awaits me when I return to The United States.

I feel like I am looking into a mirror, finding the best parts of me, parts I'd forgotten. I am a lover of life and hard work. I am bursting with energy and enthusiasm, like a kid running from a candy store to a toy store and back again. This is not mere fantasy. This is reality.

God, thank you for holding my hand in this adventure.

Connecting flight to Bangkok, January 3, 2015

I know nothing about what will happen. I am preparing for a surprise, which is a wonderful oxymoron. What will this place be like? What people will I meet? And Ethan? I am feeling elated to have this opportunity that only You, Universe, created for me. What needs to happen, I trust, will happen.

Gerard's words echo in my mind. Gerard, a famous face reader from Miami, came to visit L.A. and, for a substantial amount of money, looked at people's faces, ear sizes, and the wrinkles around their noses. He smiled at what he saw and told them of their bright and promising future. Of course, I said, "Sign me up!"

After staring at my face and examining it for three long, embarrassing, silent minutes, nodding his head with an expression that said he had taken it all in, Gerard told me I would fall in love with someone I had not yet met. "This man would come with a surprise after a divorce, and he would transform your trauma," Gerard promised.

I never met this man in my life, I think to myself, trusting Gerard. Is this mystery man here on this airplane? Will he tan in the sun next to me in Phuket? Or will he be waiting for me with a bouquet of flowers when I am back in L.A.?

Packed in a stuffy, crowded airplane filled with so many strange faces from all walks of life and from all over the world, I rekindle the love for myself.

Thank you for joining me on this trip, Universe.

Bangkok, January 3, 2015

From one airplane to another, two airports are behind me. It's already Saturday. Time is being kneaded, stretched, smoothed, and rolled just like twisted challah. I realize, when I am miserable, time is painfully sluggish. When I am joyful, time goes by so quickly.

A sneeze. I suddenly start sneezing.

The night before I left on the trip, I had taken Lev and Liam to the ice-skating rink, which now seems like it was a week ago. As much as they love ice skating, their mom suffers every time we go. Every trip to the snow, or a winter visit to the fake ice rink in the center of warm Los Angeles, Lev and Liam love to tease me.

"Our mom has hypothermia." I stare at them from outside the rink.

They turn and circle, leaving tracks on the ice. They laugh and fall and rise and fall again. They are fearless. Meanwhile, the chill gets into my skin, my bones, my joints. My toes become numb, my nose turns red, and my body shivers.

While Lev and Liam dance in circles, pretending to be in the Olympics or the Stanley Cup, I comfort myself with the thought that, within a few days, I'd be basking in the sunshine.

Sneeze.

In the Bangkok airport, I have a three-hour wait until my flight to Phuket. I cough, feeling my lungs hurt. I fear I may be coming down with a cold.

I browse the big black screens, searching for my flight among the long repeating lists of cities and flight numbers. There is an earlier flight to Phuket that leaves within the hour. I don't want to wait another three hours. Frantically, I search for the right terminal. I pass A3. Back to information, A4, back to A3, back to information, A4. Even if I have to stay for my original, later flight, waiting another two and a half hours, it is going to work, but after a day and a half of flying, being lost, and feel I am getting sick, I need a miracle now. My way is not working; I keep going in circles. Exhausted from jumping from one terminal to another like I'm stuck in an endless Pacman game, I finally give it over to God.

Higher Power, show me signs that You are here with me, that I am in the right place.

The maze game is over; no more dots to chase. I find the airline help desk.

"The flight is fully booked," the lady at the desk explains with a lovely smile.

I cannot give in. I insist that I speak to the manager. I do not accept her sorry-we-are-fully-booked answer.

She keeps explaining to me in an authoritative-leave-me-alone voice, yet adding another courteous smile, "Legally, madam, you cannot fly without your luggage."

I reply with politeness, yet with perfect certainty, "Miracles do happen!"

As I wait for the manager to show up, I notice that there is a very large Jordanian Muslim family beside me. I am fascinated. Three or four women sit together, while the men sit on the other side of the waiting room. I observe how they talk to their kids and to each other. One of the ladies takes out a purplish orange oval fruit I have never seen before. She peels it slowly and shares it with the patient kids. The woman sees me gazing at it and offers me a whole fruit. Although I understand Arabic, I choose not to say a word. I nod and thank them with my eyes. I hold the fruit and turn it over. I have never seen it before. For me, it is exotic.

That's how it starts. The world is round and plump with sweetness. I squeeze it and taste it. It is sweet, luscious, and delicious. There is so much love when we see the person as they are, without reservations or defenses of the heart. No walls, just freedom. This is love. This is light. This is life.

When the Universe made for us abundant fruit, it was made for all of us. There were no questions, beliefs, differences that drive wedges. We are humans first. We eat, we enjoy, we share.

The manager calls my name. I go to her computer station.

"We will look for something, but I cannot promise a seat." The blue-uniformed lady keeps looking, and five minutes later, I receive a new boarding pass with a confirmation that I will have my suitcase as well.

After boarding, I am met with an absurdity: I have an entire row to myself.

I insisted, and the miracle happened. This is the magic I have been waiting for. I did the work and let go of the results. I let what was meant to happen simply flow – letting the Universe guide me, take my hand, take my heart, and move forward like a river. The river knows the ocean will not refuse it; it knows it will arrive at the proper time. It flows in certainty.

Phuket, January 4, 2015

Thirty hours of travel, done at last.

It is 1 a.m. At the Phuket airport, a driver with a big sign bearing my last name waits for me. When I see him, I feel my vacation has started at last. Gently, he takes my suitcases and carries them to the black limo. I already feel relieved. The Thai driver opens the back door, and I sit like a princess. I realize he is sitting on the right side of the car, like in the UK. Who says the world needs to follow the same rules? We drive along the curvy roads to the stunning resort on the shore.

It is the middle of the night, but Ethan is waiting, and he welcomes me with a very warm and loving hug. We stand there in front of each other as if not one day has passed. Same me. Same him.

His dimple and his charm are as I remember. He has less hair. We changed, but, in the most significant way, we haven't changed at all.

January 5, 2015

Monday. A whole day was swallowed in Thailand, and I am now sick as a dog. I probably have a high fever, my eyes burn, and I sneeze and cough incessantly, choking on my own phlegm.

Ethan is a germaphobe – and despite that, he takes tender care of me as if I am his child. He brings me hot, spicy Tom Yam soup; its broth burns and heals my throat. This is how he teaches me about acceptance. This is not romantic love with an expiration date – this is true love. The way Ethan is present, without getting upset or stressed by my weakness, teaches me something I hadn't yet known about the potential purity of the human mind.

312

I'm not sick because I took my kids to the ice rink. I'm sick because, after eighteen months of anxiety, discomfort, high alert, worry, and shame, my body is ready to purge all the toxicity out, here in a place I feel safe.

It is already evening. I take one sleeping pill and sleep throughout the night, letting my body heal itself with love and serenity. At dawn, a loud rooster wakes me up. It reminds me of Jerusalem at my mom's house. I rise with gratitude.

I am giving my day and night over to You, Universe. Whatever comes, I accept it. I have no expectations.

I pause and think about what I'm saying to my Higher Power.

Is that my lesson from my years with Dan? Is that what I need to learn from other relationships? Be in the moment as it comes to me. Give me what You can without having it overwhelm my soul. Have it be beautiful and flowing. If it no longer flows, let it go.

I feel better. The sickness passes through me. In just one day in Thailand, I have sweated out the chaos and the anxiety. I am healed. It's time to start a new chapter in my life.

My second morning in Thailand is my first healthy one, and it is time to explore. Ethan and I go downstairs to the breakfast area on the shore. The mesmerizing water is a deep aqua color. The sand on the beach is golden, soft, and thin. The few coconut trees nearby are tall and wispy. The air is crisp, and a light breeze caresses my face. I breathe it in. Warm air fills my lungs with love and serenity. There are a few small islands across the bay. I feel as if I am in heaven.

January 6, 2015

Day three. I sit next to Ethan in our secluded cabana on the roof. We are sitting quietly together, watching the calming, turquoise horizon. Ethan is a comforting, loving, whole-hearted soul. I'm lucky to have this special presence in my life. No one can understand our relationship but us. Everything I need, everything I ask for, I receive with joyous gratitude. For now, that includes coconut juice, a warm pool, a beautiful view.

I'm feeling closer to you, Universe. You take care of me. And I thank you.

I become aware of my emotions, my thoughts, and the effortless movement of the ocean waves. I can hear the little ripples along the wet sand, undulating in a sensual rhythm—the gentle sound, like touching, like making love. I close my eyes, and the wind has its own conversation with me. It touches my skin, my hip, the curve of my belly. My orange Brazilian bathing suit leaves me exposed to the touch. My body responds to the sound of nature's waves; the coconuts in the swaying palm trees dance with the soft, pulsing wind. It's a quiet symphony of harmonious music. I can hear the engine of a small boat, and kids are laughing. Forks and spoons clang like percussive instruments in this orchestra. Nature and man appear in one frame of this movie of our lives. The birds fly above it all, basking in the rays of the sun.

I know I may forget the details of this vacation within a month, but I'll forever remember this feeling. I come alive again.

Making love starts with the fingertips and draws in mind – at its essence is the focus on presence, on "being here and now." It's not in

314

the future, not in the past, and not five minutes from now. It's not even in an orgasm transporting one away. Real lovemaking creates ripples in thoughts, in the body, to lock you fully, completely, into the now.

Phuket, January 7, 2015, 2:00 p.m

Awareness! When a prayer is inserted into life, it is always heard. My prayer is to do something that has deep meaning, that moves me, that creates waves in my life and the lives of others.

I'm walking on the beach. Barefoot kids are playing soccer in the wet sand. It is low tide. They use sticks as goals. They see nothing but each other, and the whole world is theirs.

I walk to my daily Muay Thai lesson. I'm ready to kick, punch, hook, conquer.

Muay Thai is my miracle. It is the science of eight limbs, which confuses people who think it's just kickboxing. The latter focuses on only four points of contact, with its punches and kicks. Muay Thai utilizes all eight points, punches, kicks, knees, and elbows.

Ultimate Muay Thai is incomparably intense, pure, and strong. It is the one sport that fills me with energy and might. I methodically push, kick, and scream to release all my aggression. The light is green, and I punch the metaphorical accelerator, elated with the power of *GO*. My body shouts with every cell. Red marks on my knees and shins turn to purple and then blue. This is real. I mean every kick, every punch.

I follow my Master, whose name is simply "Him." Master Him. His eyes are wise. This is not something you can do on a treadmill in Beverly Hills. Here, you have to focus, push yourself, and find your inner power. He is compassionate from the beginning. I expected that the Master would be like a drill sergeant, yelling, demanding, and putting us down, so we stretch beyond our limits. But his smile, his inner quiet, and his wise eyes touch me in a deep way. Like a mom who dresses her baby each morning, making sure that the shirt is tucked in, he first covers my hands with a long blue wrap. With much patience, he wraps first the fist, then fingers after finger, making sure it is tight up to the wrist. He smiles, he listens, he is perfectly focused on what he is doing. He is utterly in the present. I try to look within Him. *What is his real name? Does he ride a scooter to work? How come he loves this art so much? What does he think when he sees me standing there, looking clueless about what is going to happen next?*

Concentrate! It is not about the hit, the punch, the force exerted. It is about the balance, the energy created in motion, and the mind – fast moves that create more than a warrior's punch. I hear my mind and soul demanding my arms, my legs, even my toes—every curve and swing matter in this sinuous, all-encompassing dance.

I want to scream and let it all out. Three minutes of intensity, following Master, and then a one-minute rest. Repeat. After fifteen repetitions, the body is empty of all the knots, the thoughts, the manipulations. I am me again. I am reborn.

Him. Master Him. Pleasant, authentic, encouraging. He loves what he does and pays perfect attention. I fall in love with his teaching. He desires me to become perfect, but he is patient. He smiles, and I crave more. It is no longer about the punch but about the swivel of the exact muscle. I listen carefully to every word of his instructions.

Two police officers come to the arena. I am focused on Him, and now I need to focus even more. I try not to look at the officers; I know they are mental noise. Master Him is impeccably present. His devotion doesn't veer to the green uniforms who've come to disturb. They stare at us, and I wonder if the Universe just planted them here for me so I can practice with greater concentration. It's easy to be in the moment when there are no distractions, and another thing altogether when you're in a foreign country and grim-faced policemen are studying your every move.

In an hour, my being is changed. The tiny muscles that were in a deep sleep, the memory cells that were hidden all ignited together for me. I am well over 40, and I feel more alive than I did as a girl of 10.

Celebrate! I did it, and I am immensely proud. The sweat is dripping from my face, down my neck, all across my back, telling the story of touching what I longed to touch. My defenses are broken, at last.

January 8, 2015. 5:54 p.m.

I feel I am losing track of hours, days, places. "Ticking clock time" is a human invention. It can't capture where I am now, feeling each continuous moment, flowing forward.

It is my last sunset here in Phuket. I hold the moment close, and I don't let it vanish. It stays as a memory. Some of my memories are engraved, and some are forgotten. This will be the former, never to be lost.

A week in Thailand. *Was this a dream?* I left in two days and returned even faster. It was everything I wanted: a chance to take care of myself and not others. I was wearing bathing suits all day, walking on unpaved roads that led to powerful, endless sunsets. Stunning views that made me play with words. Stepping out onto the golden sand, seeing the waterfalls, and feasting on food that filled the soul more than the body. I slept in as I haven't slept in for years, nestled in the jungle.

I can tell you the raw truth about what life is all about, without the bullshit—riding a dirty moped in the gritty streets, watching clueless tourists, visiting loud bars, and hearing even louder beer drinkers. It's a blur, but I'm holding on to every moment, like watching a favorite music video over and over again.

Flight to Seoul, January 10, 2015

The future is knocking on my door: a career, a book, another book, our new place, my children, my authentic love.

I am tired of listening to all the gurus, palm readers, and psychics. I'm creating my life with You, Universe. Every time I lean on some stranger to tell me the future, they hurt the relationship between us. I focus on what another human tells me rather than listening to You directly and trusting that you will reveal everything in its own time.

I feel I am ready to date again.

The first date, the phone call, the excitement, is the journey of getting to know another soul that might mesh with your own. Why should I know everything before it starts?

318

I'm ready, Universe. I'm ready for a threesome with my love and you. I'm ready to take You on every date, ready to have you listen in during every phone call, save a chair for you at a romantic dinner.

This becomes the essence of my new life.

You took me to Thailand. There was an empty seat next to me. And now I realize that empty seat was Yours. I did nothing of myself. It was You, You next to me, taking me back, showing me what to do and how. I'm listening. I'll follow.

Please guide me. Who is this guy? I know he's not perfect, but allow me to be me without inhibitions. I even cuss, with words like shit and fuck. Authenticity is what I most crave. I need the real me, the real man, and the real You.

◉

Tel Aviv, August 1987

Uncle Ron takes me to the newest, trendiest restaurant on the Tel Aviv seashore. I am excited. I am only fourteen and already being treated to the most exclusive places in town: this time, no other adults, just him and me. Uncle Ron never simply spends his precious time. I am about to learn something.

I sit across from him, my big, confident, smart uncle. When he talks, I must listen.

Every woman who passes by our table stares at him flirtatiously with a sultry look in her eyes, flipping her hair to the other side. But he is focused on the menu. I can order anything I want on the menu, but I

319

don't. I wait for him. Uncle Ron orders the fanciest dishes for me, but for him, it is always the basic things in life.

"Cut the bullshit" is a favorite expression of his. Uncle Ron was always sharp and direct. Without adding any small talk, my Uncle starts what will be the most meaningful lesson of my life.

"Today, I want to teach you an important rule about dating," he starts.

"Dating?" I swallow the bite of the gourmet farfalle pasta in white sauce and almost choke.

I can feel how my cheeks flash red. I feel how my embarrassment is bigger than the plates on the table. I don't even have a boyfriend. Yes, there is a boy in school I really like, and we are more than just friends. But we are certainly not dating. I put my fork and knife down and look at my uncle. I am prepared for a lecture on how not to kiss a guy before he'd meet my parents and I meet his—instead, a question.

"What does a girl need to do when she goes out on a date?" he asks.

Was this a trick? Maybe I need to pretend I don't have a clue. Everything I know about dating or the S-word is from my bestie in school and from a secret book I found in my mom's bookshelf. I never talked about it with any adult. Definitely not with my mom. She is too busy complaining about men – my dad in particular.

"You see, when a girl prepares for a date," Uncle Ron starts to answer his own question, looking at me. He speaks with confident assurance "...she needs to buy a new dress, new shoes, do her hair, put on makeup, do her nails, shave, and carry a nice purse."

I am impressed by this list. Uncle Ron continued. "And what does a man need to do before a date?"

He knows I didn't have the answer.

"Jeans and a t-shirt."

I am still puzzled about the grooming tips my handsome uncle is giving me. He is known as the heartbreaker, even after he got divorced from my aunt, Emma. I trust he knows what he is talking about.

"Never pay for a man. That's the point: you prepare too hard before a date. Let your man be a man."

The waitress brings cheesecake with fresh strawberries, and it is the conclusion of my first dating lesson: always let yourself be treated by your man.

God is in the Pause.

What is reality? Seven billion people with seven billion experiences moment to moment. What is the reality to you? To her? To another? What is there for us, what is given, and what do we choose to focus on in a specific millisecond of time, even unintentionally, to take in and remember? How can we contain this enormity in our mind, our soul, our heart? It's a mind game.

Pause your reading right now and look around you, scan your surroundings – you may be reading these words in a room, airplane, or park. Glance around, choose an object you didn't notice before (I would say pick a person, but I would not want you to stare rudely at anyone). Describe it to yourself, seek out the details you didn't notice before, and now look again. Ask yourself who brought it here, where it was before, what its function is. Tell its story. Travel in time as needed. And bam – you just changed the perception of your reality in a few seconds. You took your mind from reading this paragraph to observing something else, something that only you could see in that particular way. You were present with something you hadn't even noticed five minutes ago.

Time is elastic – don't let it disappear with the noise of your life. Notice it. Appreciate it. It is the Now. Fill your lungs with air, your eyes with light, your ears with love, your mouth with sweetness. Hold it for a minute. That's awareness.

Breathe.

Breathe!

Breathing in life!

Chapter 21

~~No~~ Eye Contact Please

Aayin. Yud. Nun. ‏ע.י.נ.‏

Eye ‏עין‏ • Examine ‏מעין‏ • Inspect ‏מעיין‏ • Water Spring ‏מעיין‏

⊚

Los Angeles, August 2015

8/8, to be exact: double eights. Infinity. Friday evening.

I stare at the computer screen with pride, and my emotions gush forth. It is out for the world. Eight months after finalizing the divorce papers, I dared to expose something of me, my words of wisdom to parents in the world: Blue and yellow cover, only a few hours old.

Congratulations, baby-book. I finally published you.

After digging through words, paragraphs, and titles, and sleepless nights of writing, editing, erasing, rewriting, and rearranging, it is here. My newborn is out and ready to visit people's homes, studios, and libraries around the world. The adventure has begun, and it's past time to celebrate.

"It's OK, you can go," Karen insists on the phone firmly, "I will manage."

Karen and I have been back and forth on the phone for an hour now, each trying to convince the other not to give up. She has only two tickets to go to DJ Markus Schultz's house music event, a rare appearance in one of the biggest clubs in La La Land. Karen is one of my new friends after the divorce. Not only has my title changed, but so have the contacts on my phone. Karen bought the tickets months earlier, but she also knows I haven't danced in a club since I became a wife fifteen long years ago. It is a kiddo-free-weekend, a Saturday night, and I feel the butterflies in my belly as if I'm a kid riding a bicycle without training wheels or a teenager going to a real party for the first time.

This is childish. I return myself to reality. *I am a mom of two kids, long since a grown woman. What am I going to do in a club?* I talk myself out of it while Karen adamantly decides that I'm going. There is no arguing with Karen.

Why do I need to compete with skinny 21-year-olds with their tight mini-skirts?

I convince myself with all the resolve of a Ping Pong ball. *Yes. No.* I am going back and forth with this silly idea, afraid to dare, wanting to relive what I once used to be: free.

"No, I don't need to go. You've had these tickets for ages!"

I repeat myself to Karen. I don't want to admit that the more we talk about it, the more all I want to do is dance. I want to release my soul, let go, close my eyes, sense the bass through my feet, in my body, connect to the sounds, move each inch of myself, and dance to the powerful, liberating, and soul-sweeping music. I'm hungry to *feel* again.

324

Karen wins. She texts me the name of her girlfriend who will meet me at the club and will sell me my ticket. I am going to spend a night with a stranger, a new girlfriend, whom I know nothing about. But I don't care. All I want now is the legend, Markus Schultz. Call it House, Electronica, or Techno, it fuels me. It's what I need – to *Dance*.

The Universe is calling me. I feel like I am being driven in a driverless car, and it doesn't matter what I am going to do with the steering wheel. I am on autopilot with something pulling me inexorably towards the club. It is not Karen's insistence, or Markus Schultz, or the tickets. These are all props in what the Universe has in mind for me. I am simply *ordered* to go. I cannot explain it. I do not even remember how, but within two hours, after trying every little black dress that I have in my closet, seeing which ones match with tiny black spike heels, I find myself in an Uber on my way to the hottest, trendiest, hardest-to-get-in club in Hollywood, all by myself.

By myself?

Twenty minutes later, I step out of the Uber and right into a glitzy crime scene. There's a long, long line around the big, black, brick building. Tall girls, short girls, single guys, couples, whites, Asians, Latinos, blondes, brunettes. Everyone is busy – on their phones, heads down, not looking at each other, waiting to be spotted as the lucky ones to go in. Spotlights sweep the street, and I can feel the bass bouncing from the club. The air is thick with cigarettes and weed layered over the familiar mix of perfumes, aftershaves, and car fumes. I realize the line goes around the building twice; a few hundred trendy, mostly-much-younger people waiting for their turn to have their IDs checked and their barcodes scanned.

This line is too long. I've waited for fifteen years. That's plenty.

My autopilot is still on. I don't even have my ticket yet, but I keep walking straight like a secret agent listening to detailed directions through a tiny imaginary earpiece.

I walk straight towards the VIP entrance, which is also packed with couples and groups who are trying to get in first because they have a little more cash in their pocket, a bigger bra size, or a famous daddy. I don't see them. I approach, clicking my narrow high heels on the cement with a focused mission. The tall, muscular VIP bouncer stands like a concrete wall. He has all the time in the world. Like a judge in a reality dating show holding the magical flower, he has the power to decide my fate. Yes, no, loves me, loves me not.

In my black almost-leather dress, my flashy gold Kardashian necklace, an expensive matching purse, and full of confidence, I approach the bouncer. I very politely ask with my new faux English accent, my own strange voice catching even me by surprise:

"I'm staying at the W. May I go in?"

I point at the luxury W hotel on the other side of the street, across from the club. I look at the bouncer with piercing eyes, mentally removing any barred gate that might prevent me from freely entering.

"Are you alone?" He asks, world-weary, from the top of what must be a 6'6" inch frame.

Looking intently into his eyes, I elegantly smile. I think it's a British smile, too. He nods once.

And then, I am already inside.

The club is full of people. Three floors, a big stage with a DJ booth, sexy, almost naked dancers, and laser beams do their best to allure the night. I weave my way towards the dance floor. The rhythm calls me. The purple lights envelop me. I can hear my heart beating to the house music that makes me feel so utterly at home. *I am home.* I close my eyes for a few seconds. The music fills me. I am here. I am light. I hardly feel the floor. I am weightless, free from all the hurdles, the worry, the sadness of years past. The music resonates with colors, with textures, with feelings, and with waves. My hair flows through the notes, the sound electrifying each cell within me. The music sweeps me up and down in endless circles that ignite each sense in my body.

I want this moment captured for eternity. I hand my phone to a girl with an even shorter dress and even spikier heels to take my picture. Snap-flash. It is in my photo album to show my grandkids one day.

A little moment in life summed up in a big smile.

"Thank you, and I don't need the tickets after all," I text Karen, who texts the friend of the friend of the friend (exactly three links in the friend chain) and express my gratitude for her willingness to sell me the rare ticket. My English accent found another way to get in.

The third friend in that chain is at a VIP table. The main dance floor is surrounded by the Very Important People's booths guarded by velvet ropes and still more bouncers. Bottles of premium vodka are brought to the tables by stunning servers in little matching outfits that cover less than the minimum. Again, and even louder, the *do-it-now-*

and-exactly-as-I-tell-you-to-do-it voice guides me. I text that third friend and invite myself to their VIP table. After all, who wants to be crammed in a sweaty crowd?

Ding! I receive a text.

"There's no space here at the VIP table."

I reply, but not with words. I send the photo just taken of me. *If my words cannot do it, let my mini skirt and my witty eyes let me in.*

The reply is almost instant. "Come over! We are waiting for you. It is the first table across the DJ in the VIP area," she texts back.

I step towards their booth, trying not to trip in the dark. There are about fifteen people at the table. A mix of men and women holding drinks in their hands, laughing, talking, dancing. Here I am, just like my new book, ready to be opened. I, too, am fresh, ready for a grand adventure.

The music is flowing; I feel it in my body. I breathe it in, let each sound go in, and fill my heart with the beat. I raise my hands and close my eyes, letting the rhythm flow from the tip of my fingers, to my arms, to my head, to my shoulders, down my spine, all the way down as it meets my legs. I swirl like a little girl in the Holy City. I dance, flowing, twirling from the stage to the dance floor, back here. I am a Good Girl from Jerusalem, dancing, expressing my love without words, just with flowing music in my body. I feel the music and let go.

Dance, baby girl. Dance. Don't be afraid to feel. Let go.

And there he is. He's Leo, a captivating mix of a huge Costco teddy bear and a Russian gangster. Looking at him, you don't know whether to smile or to run for your life. He wears a plain black t-shirt and dark blue jeans; simple, yet sophisticated. With his bald head and cleanly shaven goatee, Leo looked like a bouncer, a private one. His look is piercing and sharp. Our eyes meet, and we gaze for a few seconds, and instantly I know.

Did you know that you can see the soul through the eyes?

◉

Los Angeles, November 2015

It has been three months since I set off on my new road at that famous Hollywood club. Since our eyes met in that spark of a moment to the beat of Markus Schultz, Leo has been trying to make his way into my heart. He is persistent and ignores any slow-down, stop, or yield signs. Leo is not embarrassed to keep showing me his interest and is following the speed limit signs I have posted. I sense he knows those signs come from my fear, not an absence of desire.

Like a farmer who prepares his soil for planting, he has been diligently calling me every day, texting me funny emojis, and talking with me for hours. Slowly, he makes me feel comfortable, relaxed, and all the more curious. Unlike any other man I have met after the divorce, Leo is different. There are no games, no waiting for his texts or phone calls, no playing hard to get. He is one of those confident, manly men who express what he wants, thinks, and needs at any given moment: no hesitations or second thoughts.

Leo is smart, intuitive, perceptive, and sophisticated. But most of all, Leo is curious. He is curious about people, curious about me.

He has questions – all sorts of questions. Like a kid in an airplane museum, he needs to know how engines look and how they operate. He remembers details, the smallest details of everything he is told. Inquisitive Leo triggers my cerebral cortex, my mind, both hemispheres of my brain.

Slowly, Leo exposes me to his world and introduces me to his friends and family without asking for a single official date. I am invited to gatherings, parties, and dinners. He never shies to compliment me on my looks, what I say, or my smile. It feels thrilling to be next to him but not yet with him.

Ella is waking up.

I dare to wear my hidden mini dresses and try on every high heel I own. My wardrobe grows to include more and more of what I want to wear, not just what I should be seen in. My compassion for myself is expanding. I see me – pure, desired, and loved – for the first time in fifteen years. The man beside me doesn't criticize the color and length of my clothes, the way I laugh, or the spices I put in my food; I slowly release myself again.

Leo learns to read my map. What type of coffee I like to drink (he likes chocolate milk), where I was born, my favorite Tic-Tac flavor, what particular scents do to my body, how I came to the States, what kind of flowers I like, what my kids like to eat, what makes me feel shy, and, of course, my favorite color: blue. Over these weeks, we also share deep, funny, crazy stories with each other, intimate truth, memories of pain and joy. And yet, we are never alone together.

The excitement phase and the pure rush from every ding on my phone are at their peak. The rings are from a stranger, yet someone who feels so familiar and close. Secretly, I am afraid. Afraid to be vulnerable, to give me to someone else who might take all of me again and who won't let me have my space to just be – the space that was taken by someone's addiction and my addiction to him. I don't have to explain any of this. Leo senses me. We slowly match rhythms and keep it all at a steady pace. I don't rush into his arms: no kisses, no touching, no holding hands. I learn to trust God and take it slowly because I know that if I ask quietly for answers, they will come.

It is my birthday, and he has asked me for a first date.

It took three months for our first date, alone. At exactly 8:00 p.m., Leo texts me from outside my place, "here." Like a princess on a walk outside of her palace, I walk gracefully outside. I wear one of my new black, sexy, form-fitting dresses with elegant pumps, matched jewelry, simple yet meticulously applied makeup, and my favorite sensual perfume. Leo is waiting for me next to his four-door sedan. He doesn't try hard to impress me with his Hummer or SUV. Unlike L.A.'s typical guys, Leo refrains from showing off and trying to impress by what he owns. As I draw closer, I see he has half a smile that hides his excitement, just as I hide mine. Leo opens the car door for me. He also smells good. His eyes are soft. He stares at me.

He wears dark blue jeans and a black t-shirt.

"You look stunning," Leo looks into my eyes. I blush in the dark.

Chill house music in the background, he drives us to an exclusive, chic Italian restaurant on the less crowded side of town. Big brown chandeliers hanging from the ceiling shine dimmed light onto each thick birch wood table. In the back of the restaurant, there is a big, open kitchen with a brick pizza oven, a pasta making machine with fresh dough, and an eclectic wine cellar. There are five chefs, but they cook in complete silence. There is a sense of serenity and peace – or maybe it is just within me. The beautiful young Italian hostess holds two menus and quietly signals us to follow her. Leo waits for me to walk first to the table and follows. He waits for me to choose a seat and only then sits.

I don't eat pasta, pizza, or drink wine. He remembers. Leo orders every seafood and vegetable dish on the menu. I trust every dish, every order, every morsel of shitake and enoki mushrooms, each East Coast – and West Coast – the oyster. Leo has a refined, exquisite taste for delicacies. He is a believer in the old axiom that when you eat, it is for the body, but when you dine, it is for the soul.

"Happy birthday, gorgeous Ella." We clink our drinks and look into each other's eyes.

Our eyes talk, our souls converse. He hears me, and I notice. Leo listens not only to what I say but how I say it, the way my posture expresses the smallest syllable, the way my eyes are dimmed or lit.

Leo pays the bill.

I let my man be a man.

We drive home in complete silence. I sink in the chair comfortably next to Leo; words are not necessary. We know what's happening between us. Letting the music guide the night, we arrive at my place. He parks the car, and he still says nothing. For the first time,

I notice a shy side of Leo. The man who always has an answer, who needs neither a literal nor a figurative GPS for anything, now needs to be guided. He listens to what my heart is saying, and he has the guidance he needs. Nothing needs to be said. He walks by my side to my entrance door.

I let him inside.

Our first kiss.

First touch.

First embrace.

We finally know each other.

Wrapped in Leo's arms, I feel loved, cherished, and protected. I smell us together. I feel the intense feelings flowing from one body to another. My face on his chest, I hear his heartbeat. I close my eyes and breathe at the moment. I pause. He hugs me closer.

Is there true love after a divorce? Before I met Leo, I wondered, where *do* you meet your true love? Do you meet them in the supermarket? Through friends? At the gym or at my kids' schoolyard?

Right after the divorce, my caring friends tried to convince me to go on one of those daunting dating apps. I told them I was afraid to be a number, and they told me my ego was too large. But I wondered, and still do, how could I feel myself genuinely on any of those social-dating-website-swiping-apps?

"Hello, I am number 89756," defined by the cyber-world algorithm. Summarize yourself in 140 words: earning power, social drinking preferences, favorite topping on pizza, unique hobbies, number of stamps in the passport, PC or Mac, baseball or soccer, pasta or tacos – all these silly binaries combined with filtered, ever-so-curated pictures from extraordinary photo-ops around the world.

The whole thing gets topped off with a simply implied disclaimer: *I am perfect. My baggage will be well hidden until I don't cover it up anymore. I might present my baggage to you after a few dates so you can try to sort it out. Take what I do not need to the scrapyard and admire the best of me. Can you do it for me? I can't.*

And the story continues. You meet the guy. He wants sex. Maybe you do, too. The ladies put out, if not on the first date, then surely on the second. For most people, all of this is worth it to net a partner who'll exchange rings with you and with whom you can ride off into the sunset for your "happily ever after" – at least for the first three months. It is a disposable culture, and flipping through profiles feeds the illusion.

It took me a divorce to know what men want. I used to think it was sex. I used to think the bigger the boobs, the blonder the girl, the more satisfied the man. Maybe it is a tall girl, with skinny legs exposed – always exposed. Or is it the wild laugh or the skillful maneuvers in bed? The culture is full of messages to women, offering advice on how best to seduce the one man who will add something precious to your life.

But look around you. Not all girls in red stilettos and tiny, flashy dresses are married. Bars are filled with lots of love-hungry women, the lines to the nightclubs are long and cold, especially to the half-naked girls freezing themselves to find the right knight. Men really fantasize about these women, just as women often fantasize about the hot muscular guy who will save us from our burning house. We're looking for the perfect combination of a firefighter and a Saudi oil billionaire. It is all fantasy.

Leo taught me what he – and what I think every man – truly wants. All they want is to have a woman who will simply love them and encourage them every step of the way. They want to hear that they are the best, no matter what. They want to hear that they are appreciated and loved and wanted. A lack of gratitude to your man is what wounds him more than anything. That is how complex guys are – or are not. That is the whole secret. Pretty simple, right? But there is a trick: for most women, it will feel like Mission Impossible, expressing our appreciation for our men. It is as if someone told us to stand on one foot on a high wire and balance for one hour straight. No moving, just singing three hundred times, "I appreciate you." It's so much harder than we realize.

Leo teaches me what real love is: real love has no rules. Real love is raw. Real love can hurt. Real love can heal. Real love looks you in the eyes. Real love is slow, steady. Real love feels dangerous. Yet, real love also feels safe. Real love is order. Real love is chaos. Real love is uncontrolled. Real love is deep inside, deep in the soul. Real love is one great big paradox.

Leo teaches me with his wide eyes and a full heart. He is clever, sharp, and quick. He has self-proclaimed quotes about life and relationships. Even if he doesn't know, he pretends, and he's almost always right. He has an instinct for truth.

"Man's power is in the feeling that his woman gives to him."

Leo teaches me to love life again, to love myself without being afraid. He teaches me to be proud of who I am, to laugh out loud and not be embarrassed, to take out my tiny little dresses from the back of the closet – and to add more dresses and high heels to the collection to show off my curves. Leo teaches me to stop cooking for five hours for people to just scarf it down in thirty-three minutes, leaving me to clean up for another two hours. He pushes me to listen to the music I love openly, not just with headphones. Perhaps most importantly, Leo pushes me to open my own studio, despite the doubts of everyone else.

With love, courage, and a safe space for me to just *be*, Leo teaches me how to stand up for myself.

It's a sunny, crisp California Tuesday morning. New beginnings manifest in my life. There's a new home for the kids and me, a new relationship – and the opening of my new studio. Leo and I are on our way to Ikea to purchase new furniture. I trust Leo's taste, but more than that, as a person who makes any decision slower than a sloth, I admire (and need) his quick yet practical decision-making.

My phone rings. I see Dan's name in upper case letters at the top of the screen. I let it ring a few times before answering hesitantly.

"You are an emotionally abusive person," Dan is yelling at me. "You are disturbed and dangerous to everyone around you. You are crazy! So crazy and dumb, you will never be able to find anyone."

I can feel Dan's fury. I am frozen. I can almost see the daggers in his eyes through the phone. He continues, "Seriously, everyone I know hates you, and that includes people you consider friends. You're an awful human being."

I feel like I'm choking. "You are pure garbage. You are crazy!"

I finally take in enough air to respond. "Me? I am crazy?" I answer with a pounding heart, half defending myself, half trying to convince Dan that I am not the insane one.

Leo, who is driving, looks at me with bewilderment. He gestures to mute the conversation on my end. Dan continues to yell loudly.

"Did he just call you crazy?" Leo asks, half-disturbed, half-perplexed. He pulls the car over to the side of the road and looks at me.

His gaze is sharp. He sits, waiting for an answer. I stall and look at Leo with glazed and teary eyes.

"I am used to it. It's fine," I whisper even though the call is on mute. I am still afraid.

Leo looks straight at me and says, "Now you tell him, 'Yes, I am crazy! Be careful!'"

He spots my hesitation and adds, "Now!" with one hand on the steering wheel and the other pointing at the phone with his finger. He starts to drive again.

I unmute the phone conversation, breathe in and gather all of my renewed strength.

"Yes, I am crazy! And you should be careful!" I tell Dan.

I feel like a little kid who, after too many awful recesses at school, finally stood up to the mean, tall, popular bully. *I am crazy.* Three short words. Ten pounds of heavyweight and fear drop from my shoulders.

I am crazy. Be careful! My heart sings.

I love Leo. He teaches me how to love myself. He restores my confidence and identity. He hands me a big eraser, and we both wipe away the negative cruel words which were engraved in my soul for more than a decade, one word at a time. We talk. We yell. We dance. We travel. We visit each other's work in the middle of the day. We fight. We make up. We take our lunch breaks together, we dine, we meet new people, we go away for the weekend spontaneously, we explore new places, we allow deep feelings, and we are proud of each other. We fall off the bed laughing.

And yet, despite how good it is, there are moments that I let my trepidations win. I let the committee in my head play the 'what if' game. What if it is only the beginning of the end? What if it is all an illusion? What if Leo turns into the proverbial frog one day? What if all of this is just a façade? What if it is all too good to be true? What if he's just another man pretending to be what he really isn't?

"What is happening with you?" Leo holds my chin, gently turning my head towards him. "Are you here? Are you with me?"

I sit on his lap, we hug tightly, forehead to forehead. We are close, but in my mind, a Greek tragedy is unfolding towards a dark climax. "Look into my eyes," he says, softly but firmly, and then takes my chin and turns my head towards him.

338

I look deeply into his eyes, into the part of the soul where the genuine feelings are held. Leo's eyes reflect mine. *No words,* just soft breathing. We do what we do so well and let everything else talk. A primal, essential part of my core speaks, but... *No words.* He sees me, and I see him, and I breathe easier than I've breathed in so very long. I am safe.

What you think about me is none of my business.

It was meant to be!

How many times were you in a certain place, at a precise moment in time, and encountered the right person? If you'd arrive an hour earlier, or two minutes later, you would have never known them. Your life would never have evolved the way it has. It seems like a radical, ridiculous coincidence, but the Universe makes no mistakes.

You start a job that you didn't even search for; you take the trip of your life without much planning, you find the home of your dreams, you meet the person who will forever be your best friend. When you are genuinely trusting and let the Universe lead you, when you let that *leading* happen without knowing all the details or outcomes in advance, the energy of creation in your life becomes immense.

How many times have you paused, pondered about the abundance in your life, and thought to yourself, "it's a miracle?" But it was not magic. Like rainbows after a storm, it only looks like magic. The Universe painted your life with light.

The moment you turn your own desires over, let go and trust a power greater than yourself. You must allow the Universe to lead you to something far better than you could have planned, something that will change you forever. A Higher Power always wants something greater and happier for you, but it waits for you to give it over, to turn fear into an almost blind trust. The true secret to letting the Universe take the lead is to follow that inner, strong, powerful voice and guide. You know it: it's called intuition. And it is loudest when we are quiet.

But we are never quiet. We have endless conversations in our heads. We ceaselessly mumble words of confusion, preconceptions, judgments, self-doubts, beliefs, and fears – some embedded in us since childhood.

We all plan to fall in love. We all want true love, especially after a heartbreak.

And then we look for signs. What are the signs of a real, profound, deep, intimate connection between two people? Is it only about the excitement of the last passionate date? About the anticipation of the next phone call or the text? Is it about the social media status he or she proudly posted? Is it about them introducing you to their family?

It's simpler. Much simpler. To be with him, or with her, is to flush out all the unnecessary garbage around you: the noise, the racing thoughts, the hypercritical judgments. Just sit with them and look into their soul. Meet in the tranquility of the moment, in front of each other, quiet any external sounds. Play soft music in the background and add dimension to the moment. Then, simply look into each other's eyes. Stare right into the pupils, into the soul, the deepest part that exposes who the person truly is.

Look at each other for one minute, two minutes, three. You're lifting the veil together. It is intimidating for the first few seconds but sticks with it as the soul is unmasked and revealed. Don't stop. Your thoughts will race, your judgment will try to interrupt you. Look deep inside as they do the same. You will start to see yourself in their eyes. It is profound and strong; the feelings will flow. Gradually, it will feel familiar, and it will feel deep, it will feel safe. Eyes to eyes. Heart to heart.

This is the first step to being with someone, exposing yourself, becoming vulnerable. In these few moments, you will feel how this connection is strong and intimate. This is how you know it is true love. This is how you give yourself to somebody else.

Trust yourself with your love, the unconditional love you have for yourself – the love that you can sometimes see reflected through another person's eyes.

The opposite of fear is not to love. The opposite of fear is trust.

You will learn to trust again.

הָעוֹלָם שֶׁלִּי

הָעוֹלָם שֶׁלִּי קָטָן וּפָשׁוּט,
בַּחֹם עוֹטֶפֶת אוֹתוֹ הַתְּמִימוּת.
עוֹלָם מָלֵא גֻמּוֹת חֵן וּצְחוֹקִים,
הַרְבֵּה פָּנִים מְאֻשָּׁרוֹת וְחִיּוּכִים.

בָּעוֹלָם שֶׁלִּי יֵשׁ מִין חָפְשִׁי,
אֵין רְכִילוּת הָאֶחָד עַל הַשֵּׁנִי.
בָּעוֹלָם שֶׁלִּי לֹא קַיָּמוֹת שְׁתֵּי מִלִּים,
"הוּא" וְהִיא" - גּוּף נִסְתָּרִים
הַכֹּל יָדוּעַ לְכֻלָּנוּ
יֵשׁ "אַתְּ", "אַתָּה" וַאֲנַחְנוּ".

כֻּלָּנוּ נוֹכְחִים וְאוֹהֲבִים אֶת הַחַיִּים,
אֵין מִשְׂחֲקֵי מַחְבּוֹאִים מְסֻכָּנִים.
בָּעוֹלָם הַזֶּה מַתִּירָנוּת כְּיָד הַדִּמְיוֹן
אֲבָל, יֵשׁ בּוֹ חִסָּרוֹן
בָּעוֹלָם הַזֶּה תּוֹשֶׁבֶת יְחִידָה,
זוֹ אֲנִי שֶׁלַּצְּפִיפוּת אֶכְלוּסִין מַמְתִּינָה!

אתל אסתר גיא
9.31.1990
בת 19 ירושלים

My world

My world is small and simple,

It is covered with pure naivete, ingenuousness, innocence.

Full of graceful grins and laughter,

Elated faces and smiles.

Free sex for all,

There is no gossip on one another.

Two words are absent, they don't exist,

"He" and "She" – the mysterious third persons.

Everything is known,

There is only "You" and "We."

We all exist together and love life,

There are no dangerous hide-and-seek games.

My world has unlimited permissiveness, lenience,

But, there's one shortcoming.

In this world, there is only one citizen,

It is me, who is patiently waiting for population density.

Ester, Etel Guy

9.31.1990

19 years old Jerusalem

Characters

Much respect, appreciation, and inspiration to those who touched my life with a bright, unique light. Each one of you has a special meaning which will forever shine with gratitude.

Ella = Terebinth Tree (Pistacia) Goddess
Dan = Judge
Lev = Heart
Liam = My nation
Imma = Mom, Mother
Abba = Dad, Father
Lee = To me (sister #2)
Sharon = A region in Israel, the root of sing (sister #3)
Libby = My heart (sister #4)
Sam Chai = Samuel Alive (brother #5)
Sasi = Sassy (brother #6)
Uncle Ron = Singing, joyous
Auntie Emma = Mother
Mrs. Goldberg = People from the "Town of Gold"
Lila = Night
Caleb = Dog
Michele = Proverb, fable, to reign
Grandma Esther = Esther the Queen, symbol of fertility
Sam = Samuel, named him God
Crashendo = Imaginary friend from a children's book
Freddie = Stubborn, mule, odd number
Rachel = Ewe, female symbol of purity
Hana = Mercy, grace
Ronnie = My joy
Vivi = Spring
Tony = My tone
Ethan = Strong
Adam = Man, human
Karen = Beam of light
Leo = Lion

AMEN

www.ingramcontent.com/pod-product-compliance
Lightning Source LLC
Chambersburg PA
CBHW051906090426
42811CB00003B/483